GENTLE
PIONEERS

Five Nineteenth-Century Canadians

by

AUDREY Y. MORRIS

PaperJacks

A division of General Publishing Co. Limited
Don Mills, Ontario

Published in Paperjacks 1973
by arrangement with Hodder and Stoughton
Limited

ISBN 0-7737-7034-8

Printed and bound in Canada

To
MY MOTHER AND FATHER

ACKNOWLEDGEMENTS

The author gratefully acknowledges permission to use excerpts from the following:

Authentic Letters from Upper Canada edited by T. Radcliff, *John A. Macdonald: the Young Politician* by Donald G. Creighton and *Life in the Clearings* by Susanna Moodie (edited by R. L. McDougall), all reprinted by permission of the author or editor and the Macmillan Company of Canada Limited; "Introduction to the Third Edition" of *Roughing it in the Bush* by Susanna Moodie and *Backwoods of Canada* by Catharine Parr Traill, reprinted by permission of McClelland and Stewart Limited; *The Valley of the Trent* edited by E. C. Guillet, published by the Champlain Society for the Government of Ontario, University of Toronto Press, reprinted by permission; and the Arthur Papers from Toronto Public Library.

The co-operation of the personnel of the Dominion Public Archives is gratefully acknowledged; the interest and assistance of many friends, particularly Reverend Canon W. L. Simmons and Mrs. Catherine Fahrig, is deeply appreciated.

Winnipeg, 1966

CONTENTS

INTRODUCTION

It takes many kinds of people with many different talents to build a nation – axemen, poets, civil servants, road-builders, soldiers, farmers, politicians, dreamers – all find a place in the great empty spaces of the frontier. So it was in Upper Canada in the early nineteenth century; into the young province thousands of emigrants tentatively made their way, each with his own hopes and his own motives for joining in the nation-building, each with his own special contribution to make. Whatever their backgrounds, whatever their personal talents, the emigrants were all faced with the inescapable *fact* of the frontier, unending miles of forest which had to be cleared to make room for farms, cities, commerce, and all the other components of any mature community.

Thus men who were better suited to be poets, blacksmiths, or soldiers were all choppers in the beginning. Similarly, the settlers' wives had to put aside their old ideas of homemaking and learn the new ways of the frontier, learn to live with poverty, fire, and illness in an isolated clearing, learn anew to cook, farm and sew, using only the very few materials they could bring with them, otherwise learning to substitute whatever they could find at hand in the bush itself.

Many were not suited to this kind of life, but they had to learn, for there was no other choice. Later, when their farms were cleared and if they had any energy left, they would turn to other things.

So it was with the Moodies, Traills and Stricklands, who came from the cultured and comfortable life of the British middle class to settle in the backwoods of Upper Canada.

Susanna Moodie and Catharine Parr Traill were sisters, both married to half-pay officers of the British Army. These women, with their brother Samuel Strickland and their husbands Lieutenants Moodie and Traill, were unlikely pioneers, given their refined and educated backgrounds; however, Catharine and Susanna not only coped with the trials of the frontier housewife but also managed to produce poetry, novels, and essays, writing in the evenings with home-made quills, home-made ink, by the light of home-made candles.

They had the imagination to see that a new society was being created in the backwoods which could be too engrossed with the simple problems of survival, thereby missing the main purpose – to create a better life. They were capable of modifying their political and social views, even their loyalties, to take account of the frontier, but their deeply ingrained respect for learning, art and good manners was not so easily compromised. As a result, these gentle settlers brought a special tone to early Canada, a contribution that in its own way managed to change the frontier, even perhaps to influence the development of the Canadian way of life.

As creative writers, neither of them was outstandingly gifted. In their poetry and fiction, they were often pretentious and stilted, too florid, a poor imitation of the Romantic style of the period. But when they turned to the subject of the backwoods, they necessarily cast off their attempts to reproduce the style of another world, allowing their strong personalities to shine through their works.

One might suppose that their lives and their literature would have gone unnoticed had they not emigrated. Their energetic but protected spirits needed the challenge of the bush to come to full fruition. Yet, as settlers and backwoodsmen, neither the Moodies nor the Traills can be called great successes. They readily admitted that they were not the right sort of people for such pioneering. In this they were not alone, for the challenge of the woods was too much for many of our forefathers. However, it is possible to learn as much from the experiences of those who failed as from those whose success makes it all seem easy in retrospect.

Their life stories tell a fascinating tale of personal development, of continuing emotional conflict in the adjustment to an unfamiliar and often hostile environment, the whole resolved through eventual compromise and adaptation. More than that, they form the very stuff of Canadian history. Their lives spanned the most important period of early growth in Upper Canada, including the stages of settlement and population growth, the building of railroads and canals, political growth from Colonial Office rule to responsible government to the creation of the new Dominion. These things they saw both as participants and as interested spectators, and their personal struggles are closely interwoven with the travail of their country's birth.

Like many so-called ordinary people, Catharine Traill and Susanna Moodie, with their families and friends, were anything but ordinary or typical. Their experiences were representative only in that they shared the same environment with everyone else. Their origins, personalities and attitudes were definitely extraordinary and as unique as any of the better known characters of Canadian history. The Moodies, Traills and Stricklands can become familiar to us because they wrote regularly and profusely about their personal problems and adventures. Through these writings it is possible to come to terms with them in much the same way as through frequent and long conversations with friends.

In most of the writing of Catharine and Susanna they use the approach of the "talented amateur". They are writing as if they were talking with a friend, sometimes casual, sometimes intensely serious, occasionally striking off with great enthusiasm on one of their favourite hobbyhorses, at other times re-telling a story they liked when they heard it at second- or third-hand. When talking about themselves, they tend to cover up a great deal, revealing only that which they think will put them in a good light. But, like most incessant talkers, they eventually reveal more than they intended. This is fortunate, for the image they wished to present is less attractive and less interesting than the personalities they failed to mask.

Canadian historians are well acquainted with the Stricklands; their writings are an important part of the source material for research into the period. And on occasion their literary efforts appear in Canadian anthologies. They have been virtually ignored as individuals; as a result, historians and literary critics often express judgements about them that are ill-founded. These people were not simple or direct: their observations on their environment were made through the great obscurity of their personal trials and prejudices, and should not always be taken at face value.

Though Susanna Moodie is credited with providing us with an invaluable objective commentary on pioneer life, her place of eminence in the literary world was won more on her entertaining and controversial presentation of material, rather than on any forthright accuracy. She made deliberate and successful attempts to amuse her readers, especially her British readers, by drawing exaggerated sketches of local characters, poking fun at them and winning laughs at their expense. These descriptions of her contemporaries have the incisiveness of caricatures. She saw no humour in herself or her husband, but if one sifts out and discards all the anecdotes and sketches of other people, her own story is revealed as an amazing tragi-comedy, more amusing and more preposterous than the subjects of her caricatures. Obviously, Susanna did not intend this, but she lacked the subtlety to hide the reality.

Susanna's sister, Catharine, on the other hand, tended to see everything through rose-coloured glasses; nevertheless, she was more astute and thorough in her observations, never playing for amusement at the expense of others nor at the expense of truth. When Catharine wished to obscure something, she went off on long and expert botanical discussions. As a chronicler of the backwoods, Catharine must be given first place, if only because she went there first and was able to cushion the shock of Susanna's initiation to the bush. Catharine knew more about the backwoods than Susanna, because she accepted it more readily and showed a more intelligent interest in it.

The Strickland who made the greatest tangible contribution to the development of the backwoods was neither Catharine nor Susanna, but their younger brother Samuel. Samuel devoted his whole life to settlement, and was successful. Yet his name has been virtually lost to Canadian history, except in local studies of the Peterborough vicinity.

The object here is to describe and re-evaluate their lives, not as literary figures nor as historical personages, but as real people whose stories are intrinsically interesting and heroic in a vital sense – heroic because of their weaknesses and prejudices. In this way we grant them the respect that they and the rest of our ancestors deserve – not as sterling characters from folk-lore or myth, but as ill-equipped fighters in a difficult battle, burdened by human failings, clumsily helping and hindering each other, but somehow surviving and out of it all, achieving a modicum of greatness.

CHAPTER ONE

The Stricklands of England

Thomas Strickland, a successful London businessman, was feeling old and tired. He had accumulated enough of a fortune to retire from his career in dock management in London to live as he had always wanted to live, the life of a country gentleman. His young wife had just presented him with their fifth daughter. He reasoned that when the time came that he could no longer look after his family they would be better living as country gentlefolk than as lower middle class Londoners. A son could have followed him in the business world, increased their fortune and provided for the family, but he had no son. None of his daughters could do this, for the year was 1802.

His fifth daughter, born just before the move from London, was named Catharine Parr, honouring Thomas Strickland's forebears, the Sizergh Castle Stricklands of northern England, the most illustrious of whom was one of the wives of Henry VIII.

It was in Suffolk in the following year, 1803, that Thomas Strickland's sixth daughter was born. This was Susanna, a golden-haired beautiful child, much prettier than all the rest, her fairness softening the disappointment of still another daughter.

As a typical businessman, Thomas had spent little time in the city with his family and still less time in leisure activities. With little to occupy his interest in the country, he began to organize his time with the same assiduity as he had in London. Business, his first interest, led him to teach his eldest daughter Elizabeth the secrets of handling money. He then turned his attention to the education of all his daughters.

He set aside a room in Reydon Hall, the new Strickland country home in Suffolk, and organized a schedule of study in literature, history, the classics, arithmetic, and some science – all the subjects that he knew about, because he was going to supervise the classes. When the older girls were able, he allowed them to take over more of the teaching of the younger ones, and he assumed the role of dean of studies in the little school.

At the same time, his wife ensured that the girls were not neglecting their training in the more usual arts of the gentlewoman, and they learned household management, deportment, needlework, sketching, and other skills befitting a lady of the times. The religion and morality of the Established Church were also serious subjects, intricately mixed with deportment, social behaviour and family tradition.

The girls responded well to the discipline and were appreciative of their unusual opportunity to have close contact with their parents. But they still had time to play. The two youngest girls, Catharine and Susanna, were very close; they built their own secret worlds of romance, ghosts, songs and verse, but they took with them to their play the same habit of organized, directed activity that they learned in the classroom.

Despite their closeness, there was competition between the two girls, and sharp differences developed in their attitudes to the world around them.

Catharine, "the Katie", was the favourite of everyone. Deep in her nature she carried unfailing cheerfulness, grace, and a love for the people, animals, birds and things around her. She seldom cried, for she had an innate talent for taking delight out of every occasion. She was also Thomas' favourite, his chosen companion for his fishing trips and walks through the woods. During these excursions, he continued to instruct Catharine in the science of botany and wildlife, but more important, he gave her his own love and understanding of the world of nature, a love that became an inseparable part of Catharine's personality.

In contrast, Susanna was a wilful, brooding and melancholy child, given to frequent tears, excessively sensitive to romantic tragedy, intense and responsive to every mood of a poem or a real situation. Had neither of the girls developed a close relationship with their father, the difference in personality might not have been so magnified, for they were both equally intelligent and imaginative. But Susanna was sombre and excessively fastidious, such a contrast with the laughing happy Katie that Thomas drew away in impatience, only to increase Susan's bid for attention and her tearfulness.

Thomas Strickland's wish for sons was fulfilled in the years following the birth of Susanna, but the boys' upbringing was more conventional. They were cared for by the elder girls and by servants until they were old enough to be enrolled in Dr. Volpy's School in nearby Norwich. Samuel was born a year after Susanna, then Thomas, and finally a third son who was the only one of the nine Strickland children who did not live to maturity.

There was trouble brewing in England, trouble that would disrupt Thomas Strickland's carefully planned idyllic existence for his family. The long Napoleonic Wars ended in 1815 and with the peace came a severe depression, an economic collapse that struck at the roots of the security of Reydon Hall. Thomas Strickland was aging and ill from gout, but he was forced back into an active interest in the business world. He had invested most of his capital with a partner, and had been forced to guarantee a loan to keep the business in operation. Despite his efforts, the business collapsed, wiping out most of Thomas' fortune. The worry, the intense pain from his illness, followed by the shock of business failure, were too much for the old man, and Thomas Strickland died in 1818.

Catharine and Susanna were still very young. They knew their father had been depressed and ill, but nothing could cushion the shock of his death – the man who had made a special place for himself in the hearts of each of them. Their grief was heightened by their knowledge of his disappointment over the failure of his plans and by fear for their own security. The way of life that he had created for them could no longer be sustained, and in their bewilderment the extent of their losses was exaggerated.

Elizabeth, the eldest daughter who had been her father's personal secretary and bookkeeper, was left with the task of salvaging something from the estate. In this she was helped by a businessman friend of her father who was appointed as guardian of the family. Reydon Hall was too expensive to keep up in the old style. The staff was reduced and part of the family moved in to the town house at Norwich.

Despite Elizabeth's competence and the self-reliance and discipline that all the girls had been taught, there was little they could do to help their situation. In 1818, young ladies had little opportunity to earn money. They were expected to marry or, if marriage eluded them, to live in gracious but uneconomic usefulness on their family estates. But marriage had not yet presented itself to any of the Strickland girls, and their chances would lessen as their lack of personal fortune became apparent. Work as such was out of the question, not befitting gentlewomen.

There followed then a period of gloom, worry, and strained nerves as they grimly determined to make the best of a bad situation. But such were not for the irrepressible Katie. She grieved for her father, but she was also excited by the new sights and sounds of the city of Norwich. The wealth of new impressions and strange people were grist to the mill of her imagination. Left to her own devices, she quickly resumed a habit that she had developed at Reydon, writing stories. She and Susanna had often entertained themselves writing poems and stories based on the inspiration of the books in their father's library at Reydon. Elizabeth, the martinet of the classroom, had disapproved of this; in her opinion it was a waste of time when they should have been studying. Indeed, Elizabeth had ordered Catharine to destroy her manuscripts, and the young girl had obeyed, willingly enough, except for one story which she surreptitiously hid from the keen eyes of Elizabeth. She tried to be cautious about her literary efforts in Norwich, but caution was not in her nature.

While Catharine was out for a walk one day in Norwich, Elizabeth was waiting for another visit from their guardian to discuss estate matters. He was shown into the study to await Elizabeth's appearance. There he found one of Catharine's manuscripts, carelessly left on the desk, and had time to read it before Elizabeth came in. To make matters worse, he assumed that Elizabeth was the author of it, and she was startled when he insisted on discussing it with her. She denied any knowledge of it, but as soon as Catharine returned from her walk, Elizabeth called her in.

Catharine was extremely embarrassed and then delighted when her guardian offered to correct it and send it to a publisher. He thought it showed real promise. A month later, he came again, bringing five gold guineas for Catharine.

In 1818 then, Catharine Parr Strickland became a professional writer with her book, *The Blind Highland Piper and Other Tales*.[1] This was the first money any of the girls had been able to earn; the method was socially acceptable, and since they had a good education in literature and composition, they are to be forgiven for their unwarranted optimism as they saw their future brightening on the strength of five guineas. One after the other, each of the sisters followed Catharine's lead.

The tradition of women writers in England had only just begun, with Jane Austen's work gaining some recognition and a few lesser lights among gentlewomen attempting belles-lettres, domestic novels and travel memoirs, despite a fairly general feeling that ladies were wasting their time writing. Yet it was an age of change and growing enlightenment. The increasing power of the middle classes with their respect for literacy created an increasing market for the burgeoning publishing industry. Thus it was not difficult for the Strickland girls to find outlets for their talents, though they often had to bargain for adequate payment and to fight bitterly against plagiarism.

After her success with *The Blind Highland Piper*, Catharine concentrated on stories for children. Susanna attempted poems and romantic stories. Two others of the sisters, Agnes and Jane, also wrote poetry and essays. Even Elizabeth entered the field, though her forte was in editing magazines.

The ten years after their father's death were spent quietly and diligently in Suffolk. Their guardian, with Elizabeth's help, was able to recover some of the family's financial security and Reydon Hall came back into its own, though never with the splendour of Thomas' time. The pleasant life was broken only occasionally by trips to London to visit city cousins, to talk with publishers, and to attend literary teas.

Young Samuel Strickland[2] finished his education in Norwich, and was in a quandary about his career. There was little at Reydon to occupy the strong and energetic young man, and he often made a nuisance of himself following workmen around the place, asking interminable questions and suggesting better ways for them to go about their trades. He might have been a soldier or a businessman, but both occupations held little promise and less adventure in the long period of peace and recession. He would have preferred to be a country gentleman, as his father had wanted to be, but he had no land.

Thus, when an offer came from an old family friend, an offer full of adventure and excitement, the young Samuel could not resist. Would he come to Upper Canada to learn frontier farming and to help build a new estate? Samuel most definitely would. He was barely twenty years old when in 1825 he sailed for the New World to seek his fortune. Samuel's younger brother Thomas soon was on his way too, but to pursue his adventures in India.

The Strickland household in Reydon Hall again consisted entirely of women. In such a situation, it was not difficult to become an old maid. Both Elizabeth and Agnes, the two eldest, were well along this road before their father had died. The only one to show any prospects of matrimony was Sara, who coincidentally was also the only one to fail in having any literary ambitions.

Nevertheless, the Strickland family had many connections, and a tradition of looking after its own. The London branch of the family persuaded the girls to make more frequent visits to the city and to take a more active part in the literary society of London.

The literary world was still in the firm possession of the gentry but was beginning to take on the more modern characteristics of philosophical reform. In fact, many of these "literary" groups were little more than outlets for the new liberalism of the day. A new social conscience was emerging, firmly based in romantic intellectualism and good manners, religion and belief in the rights of man, but strongly at odds with the obvious fact of brutality and hunger, the heritage of an earlier age and of the economic chaos that had lasted for too many years. The reform movement found its expression around the tea tables of the hypersensitive poets and essayists of the day.

There was little attraction in this for most of the Strickland girls. The exception was Susanna, moody and pessimistic by nature, yet highly conscious of the social regimen, capable of finding security only in a clearly-defined set of rules that could govern everyone's behaviour including her own. Susanna, the only one capable of finding personal hurt in the blissful life at Reydon Hall, the only one who rebelled against the sincerity of the Church of England and for a time experimented with Chapel, found more than literary discussion; she found an outlet for the anger in her and a new philosophy of social reform that was more than just a windmill to battle. She also found a substitute-father in Thomas Pringle,[3] one of the leaders of the reform movement and a frequent host of the literary teas.

Pringle was a protégé of Sir Walter Scott, and well-respected in his own right as a poet. He was an ardent leader of reform movements and was closely involved with Wilberforce and Clarkson in the campaign for abolition of slavery in the British Empire. In every respect, Pringle was typical of all aggressive, volatile and impractical reformers. He used his various editing and publishing jobs as a means to start intellectual fights with the established order which he always lost. He was thrown out of South Africa by an angry government; he was thrown out of *Blackwood's Magazine* by an angry publisher, although he was mainly responsible for founding it. His family often went hungry as he devoted his time to his new position as Secretary of the Anti-Slavery Society.

Among his many other pursuits, Pringle found time to help Susanna Strickland with her writing;[4] carefully reading and editing her efforts, he also managed to instil in her some of his crusading notions. Oddly, the Stricklands liked Pringle, but were not impressed by his more famous friend, Walter Scott, and apparently Sir Walter was equally unimpressed by the Stricklands.

More important as far as the Strickland household was concerned, at one of his teas Pringle introduced Susanna to an old friend from his South African days, John Wedderburn Dunbar Moodie.[5]

Moodie was a gentleman, originally from the Orkney Islands, north of Scotland; he had been wounded in the war and retired from the 21st Royal Fusiliers. When Susanna met him, he had just returned from ten years in South Africa where he had met Pringle earlier. Moodie had been seriously mauled by an elephant and was recuperating while writing about his experiences in the war and in South Africa. His quiet, gentlemanly bearing, his honourable wounds, and his exciting and heroic past appealed to Susanna. And the talented, pretty and ladylike Susanna appealed to Moodie, who was ready for marriage after all his escapades.

Despite the obvious contrast between the adventurous, scarred and well-travelled man and the sheltered and prim lady, John

Moodie* and Susanna Strickland had much in common. They were both interested in the arts and literature, in British history and in family tradition. Both had been directed into humanitarian interests by Thomas Pringle. And they had personal as well as philosophic experiences in common. Susanna was the last of a long line of daughters. John was the last of a long line of sons. Both had problems on this score. They were both well beyond the usual age for marriage. Neither could expect a spouse with much in the way of financial resources for they were both relatively poor for their class. Susanna regarded herself as a rather tragic, long-suffering soul. However unjustified Susanna was in this, John Moodie was entirely right in feeling this way about himself.

In many ways, Moodie seems the prototype of all unfortunate but well-intentioned men. Gentle, kind and sympathetic, he loved to compose verses and to play country tunes on his sweet-toned flute. Yet he held an image of himself as something of a rogue and adventurer with a military flair. He had been repeatedly frustrated in fulfilling this role because of his good manners and innate caution, and because circumstances so rarely lent themselves to adventurous opportunity. Besides, he was constantly being influenced, even dominated, by other people.

For the first half of his life, he had been known as "a brother of Donald Moodie"; the second half was to be spent as the husband of Susanna Moodie.

The romance in his soul had fed upon the glories of his family tradition.[6] His family was descended from the ancient Norwegian Earls of Orkney, the most intrepid of the Vikings. John's great-grandfather, Captain James Moodie of the Royal Navy, had won honours as a squadron commodore in the War of the Spanish Succession. But in 1725, at the age of eighty, Captain Moodie was murdered in the narrow streets of Kirkwall by Sir James Stewart, a follower of "The Pretender". For this senseless and

---

* Moodie always signed himself as "J. W. Dunbar Moodie"; however, we will be referring to him by the more simple "John Moodie".

violent attack on their most honoured member, the Moodie men vowed revenge but were foiled in carrying it out. Years later, Sir James was captured, but before he could be brought to trial for his dishonour, he committed suicide in the Tower of London.

This was a blot on the family honour that was never forgotten by the Moodie men. As a young boy, John had been instructed in all the gory details, and the story was deeply imbedded in the family's tradition of loyalty to the Crown and service in the Army and Navy. John's father had been an army major; two of his brothers held commissions in the Royal Navy. The eldest had been killed in a naval battle at Leghorn in 1814. The other, Donald, served with distinction in many theatres of war from 1808 to 1816.

John's own military career was short but honourable. In February 1813, at the age of sixteen, he was appointed Second Lieutenant in the Fusiliers. He went with the army to the Netherlands, and in an abortive attack on Bergen-op-Zoom, in which John showed great courage if little military sense, he was shot in the left wrist. That was in March 1814; the wounded young veteran was retired on half-pay in March 1816, having received only two years' disability compensation for wounds which would limit his physical activity for the rest of his life.

It is tempting to suggest that John's feelings of family pride and patriotism were more romantic than militaristic. As the fourth son of an all-male household, he more likely suffered from his brothers' aggressive high spirits rather than shared in them.

In any case, his duty paid to the military life expected of him, John turned to the other of his favourite roles, that of sportsman, with equally unhappy results.

In South Africa, where his successful brother Benjamin was supervising a settlement, John went big game hunting. During a brutally inept hunt, a wounded and enraged elephant cornered John and proceeded to stamp on him. He was lucky to escape with his life, but he was badly bruised in body and in pride.

His brother Donald Moodie, after a brilliant naval career,

followed Benjamin and John to South Africa, joined the colonial civil service in which he was equally brilliant, rising quickly to the exalted status of "resident magistrate". He managed to secure John a minor post with the government, but John's real interest in South Africa was neither employment nor sport.

He was fascinated by the ways of the people, and incensed by the relationships developing between the Boers and the negroes. His idealistic sense of justice and his profound human kindness brought him into friendship with men like Thomas Pringle whose social sensitivity made them more compatible to John than his more successful brothers.

Pringle and Moodie spent long hours roaming the veldt, discussing poetry and music and man's inhumanity to man. Their friendship must have been more than a little distressing to Donald Moodie, carving out his career as a successful civil servant, because Pringle had started a magazine in the colony that was so critical of policy that it had to be suppressed by the Governor. Pringle returned to England in 1826 to take up his post as Secretary of the Anti-Slavery Society. John Moodie returned in 1829 and immediately looked up his old friend, and met another friend in Susanna Strickland.

John had not given up his military and sportsmanlike pretensions by any means. First with Pringle's help, and then with Susanna's, he came to terms with his ambitions by writing about them. In 1831, he published a respectable treatise on The Campaign in Holland,[7] and in 1835 two volumes entitled Ten Years in South Africa, including a Particular Description of the Wild Sports.[8] ("Wild sports", incidentally, seemed to be the name given to big game hunting, and was considered a most appropriate pursuit for young gentlemen.)

Pringle and, soon, Susanna encouraged Moodie's efforts at creative writing and through this he was able to come to terms with his pet ambitions, but he wrote with authority only about the personal experiences of his life. He had a real facility with verse, but he had no pretensions toward being a poet, taking a

27

more light-hearted approach than either Pringle or Susanna.

Susanna Strickland and John W. D. Moodie were married in 1831; she was twenty-eight and he was thirty-four. They rented a home in Southwold, Suffolk, within easy distance of Reydon Hall and Norwich, and John Moodie became a welcome addition to the Strickland household. Thomas Pringle and his reform notions became little but a pleasant memory they had in common, for neither John nor Susanna wanted more than a pleasant and secure home and an end to adventures.

For John, marriage meant a kind of personal showdown with his dreams. His pretty, fastidious and genteel bride gave John a totally new role. He could no longer be the wandering dilettante searching for heroic adventures; he was a family man and he accepted his marital responsibilities with such gravity that they caused him an immense amount of indecision. The Orkney Moodies, being all male, had given him little experience with ladies; now, he had a wife and five sisters-in-law. He felt that he could no longer afford an error in judgement, because any further catastrophe would affect his wife and family as well as himself. The result was that he made more errors than he might have done had he been less tense about his affairs and responsibilities.

Shortly after the Strickland/Moodie wedding, the Reydon Hall household received word that the young Samuel had completed his probation in the Upper Canada style of farming, had found himself a wife, and was setting up his own pioneer estate in the backwoods of Canada. Samuel regularly wrote long and detailed letters about his plans and his experiences. Although his descriptions of life in the New World did include some harsh criticisms, they were for the most part full of confidence and enthusiasm. They induced Moodie to reconsider seriously the possibilities of colonial settlement, an idea he had formerly given up after his experiences in South Africa.

Soon, the Moodie house in Southwold became the meeting place for ex-Lieutenants of the 21st Fusiliers and other younger sons of old families, planning to take advantage of the government's special provisions for establishing them on the frontier. They read all the material available on the subject and attended meetings to hear speeches and discussions by colonial land salesmen.

Moodie's inclination was still towards South Africa because he had some knowledge and some connections. But the pressures towards Canada were growing and, despite Moodie's cautious nature, plans were made to migrate to the unknown land. Susanna's pregnancy held these in abeyance temporarily since they both feared the journey in her physical state.

While the Moodies hesitated, one of their frequent houseguests, a regimental brother of Moodie's and friend from the Orkneys, Thomas Traill, announced not only his own plans for an early departure in the spring to Canada, but also that he was taking Catharine Strickland with him as his wife.

The Stricklands and Moodies were shocked. Engrossed in their own affairs, they had been oblivious to the attraction building up between Catharine and Lieutenant Traill. They had no hint of Catharine getting married, let alone going off to the other side of the earth. Moreover, in their eyes, Thomas Traill was perhaps a little too sophisticated and experienced.

Traill was twelve years older than Catharine; he was definitely upper class, coming from one of the most distinguished families of the Orkneys. He was an Oxford graduate, an accomplished linguist, and had spent many years in the fashionable capitals of Europe. Moreover, he was a widower and had two sons who were being raised for him by his family. But whatever the Stricklands thought about all this, Catharine and Thomas were married at Reydon on 13 May 1832.

The Traills left on 20 May from London for a visit to Thomas' family and thence to Canada. Agnes and Jane Strickland tearfully saw them off at the London docks. Everyone knew there was little likelihood that Catharine would ever return.

Thomas proudly and enthusiastically showed his new wife

29

around Leith and Edinburgh, and then Kirkwall in the Orkneys where Catharine met her husband's relatives for the first and last time.

The Traill household was prepared to dislike her, for like the Stricklands they had rejected the idea of their favourite marrying and going off so precipitately to the colonies. But Catharine's happy spirit and her obviously genuine interest in all things Scottish soon won them over. When the couple left several weeks later, Catharine would be missed in the Islands almost as much as Thomas.

At Inverness they boarded a small passenger steamer bound for Greenock on the Clyde, one of the most active ports of the trans-Atlantic route. As usual, Catharine enjoyed herself tremendously, and made friends with everyone on the little vessel. But as they approached Greenock, her gregariousness was dampened by an illness severe enough to confine her to bed. There was some doubt whether she would be well enough to make the overseas trip. It was late in the season, however, and their passages were already booked. Though Catharine had to be carried aboard, they had no choice but to go, or lose their fare and wait for another year.

In the meantime, John and Susanna Moodie had already sailed for Quebec.

It is difficult to assess what the emigrants expected to find in Canada, for their own thoughts on the subject were none too clear. Even their reasons for choosing Canada were rather vague. John said it was his reckless pursuit of adventure. Susanna suggested that it was mostly a matter of fad; in the 1830s, all the half-pay officers were going to Canada.[9] Samuel obviously had some influence over their choice. Then too, there was vigorous promotion throughout England of the merits and beauties of Upper Canada, especially the excellence of its "wild sports".

The United States was not considered at all. For the Moodies and Traills, attachment to the Crown and British institutions was much too great to allow any thought of living in a republic.

They acknowledged that there would be hardship in the Upper Canadian bush, but neither Susanna nor Catharine had ever experienced any real physical discomfort, and their husbands had known it only on army manoeuvres or in sport. It was easy for them to anticipate some few troubles as an exciting challenge, an added spice to their adventure.

Because of their ignorance of the reality, their expectations were totally conditioned by their experiences of Britain. The colony was to solve for them the problems that were insoluble at home. These problems all related to the pre-Victorian class structure, a structure that was so rigid it was beginning to crack in the deep depression following the Napoleonic Wars. Yet there was no question that they accepted the dictates of this society; they were not protesting against it, for they knew no other possible system of standards; this in itself was a good part of their problem.

Real wealth and social status were still based on ownership of land, and land was very scarce in England. To preserve the status of the old families, land was passed on intact to the eldest son, which left the younger sons to fend for themselves. Both John Moodie and Thomas Traill were younger sons. Their lack of funds or prospects were an embarrassment to themselves and to their social equals. They expressed all the anger, hurt, and confusion of the person who through no fault of his own had been displaced

They had two choices: to accept a lower social status for themselves and their families, or to emigrate. Both choices meant being cut off completely from their friends and associates and from the manners and mores of a society which they had accepted as their own; but emigration at least had the advantage of escape from the embarrassment of casual contact with their former equals. Moreover, emigration carried the promise of landownership, the key to wealth in the old country, suggesting the possibility of establishing new dynasties of landed gentry.

In short, their reasons for leaving England were very clear, though their thoughts may have been fuzzy about their destination.

Their illusions were no more incorrect than were those of other classes of emigrants. The lower classes saw the new world as a way to resolve the inequities of the old, but not to change it. Susanna was to be surprised to hear a Scottish peasant gloating over his first step on Canadian soil, "We shall a' be lairds here!"[10]

Thus the steerage class and cabin class passengers all had their dreams for a great new world, dreams based on their particular experience with the old. Slowly, very slowly, these dreams would be destroyed by harsh experience, to be replaced by new and nobler dreams more capable of fulfilment.

CHAPTER TWO

Between Two Worlds

John and Susanna Moodie sailed from Leith on the brig *Anne*, on 1 July 1832, with their baby daughter and a maidservant, and seventy-two steerage class passengers.

Catharine and Thomas Traill sailed a week later from Greenock, on 7 July 1832, on the brig *Laurel*. The *Laurel* was a cargo ship and the Traills were the only paying passengers. The only other ship was "literally swarming with emigrants, chiefly of the lower class of Highlanders".[1] This comment of Catharine's arose not from social snobbery but from the reputation of the over-crowded, unsanitary emigrant ships for disease, starvation and death.

The Traills, who left Britain later than the Moodies, arrived at Quebec before them, mainly because the Moodies' ship, the *Anne*, was becalmed for three weeks on the Grand Banks.

Such wide variations in the time of crossing were not unusual in the days of wooden sailing ships. Most naval architects still considered that an iron ship would sink. Steamships, which would eventually bring order and schedules to trans-Atlantic travel, were then used only for short voyages and the coasting trade. As a result, with ships at the mercy of wind and weather, it could take anywhere from thirty to seventy-eight days[2] to make the ocean voyage. Delays often led to extreme hardship, especially for the steerage class passengers, many of whom purchased their passage only and brought their provisions with them.

The Moodies and Traills had their meals served to them by

c

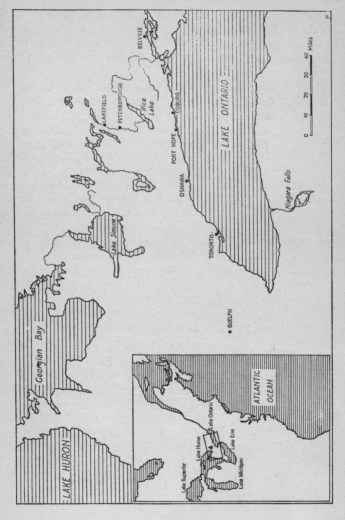

their shipping companies. Nevertheless, Susanna and John were deprived of a full menu on their excessively long voyage of sixty-two days, because the captain found it necessary to feed the steerage passengers out of the ship's stores for the latter part of the voyage.

By coincidence, the year 1832 marked a flood tide in British migration to Canada. Some 52,000[3] landed in Quebec that year, more than had ever been handled before in a shipping season. The season was very short, about two months, conditioned mainly by the freeze-up of the St. Lawrence. Because of the short season and the length of the crossing, facilities were stretched to the limit to handle the great wave of travellers. They were a motley bunch, of all social classes and trades, though most were very poor. The poor were usually assisted to emigrate by the government or by wealthy philanthropists trying to solve the problems of serious over-population and unemployment in England. Lip service was also paid to the need of the colony for immigrants.

Again by coincidence, this was the year that the Asiatic cholera, which had been spreading in epidemic proportions throughout Europe and the British Isles, crossed the Atlantic along with the emigrants. Early in the season rumours about the disease spread throughout the colonies and caused a major panic; the government had to plead with the frightened owners of travel accommodations to keep their establishments open.

These coincidences had an important impact on the comfort and ease with which the Moodies and Traills made their trips, although they did not recognize at the time that the conditions were unusual. Both Susanna and Catharine recorded their main impressions of the crossing itself to be deadly boredom, with nothing to do, no one to talk to, and nothing to look at. Their first sight of Canadian shores then was doubly exciting, the welcome end of a long monotonous voyage and the beginning of a new life. But the edge was taken off their enthusiasm by the length of the remainder of the trip.

Catharine and Thomas Traill on the *Laurel* reached the shores of Newfoundland about 1 August, and not until 11 August did they reach Grosse Isle, the quarantine station and the first official stopping place. Catharine wrote to her mother, "Though I cannot but dwell with feelings of wonder and admiration on the majesty and power of this mighty river, I begin to grow weary of its immensity . . ."[4]

Catharine had adopted her new country before she had even set foot on it. The more sophisticated Thomas annoyed her by not agreeing wholeheartedly with her rapturous statements that there was no place else in the world half so beautiful. She wanted desperately to go ashore and inspect the country immediately, but she was a captive on the ship.

At Grosse Isle, where the *Laurel* cast anchor to await inspection by medical and immigration officials, Catharine had to stay aboard because of the cholera regulations which were based on the size of the ship's passenger list. Those with few passengers were required to keep them aboard and the larger ships were required to send them ashore, a bureaucratic anomaly that Catharine did not fail to spoof. Despite all the official regulations and efforts to stem the spread of cholera, the disease was rampant in all the ports of the lower province.

Nevertheless, Catharine kept herself busy recording all her impressions in a diary and writing letters home to Reydon Hall. She found much to write about, with her usual breathless enthusiasm and excitement. Even at Quebec, she had to be satisfied with peering over the rail, but still found much to record.

She was entertained by the "horse ferry boats" that busily scurried back and forth between Quebec and Point Levis. These were flat, railed around except at the ends like conventional ferries, but in the centre were four horses in a cage-like affair who kept walking on a treadmill to work the paddlewheels on both sides of the vessel. The decks of the ferries were loaded on every trip with people, animals and produce. This bustling activity only made Catharine's enforced idleness more difficult to bear.

The suspense was ended at Montreal, where Catharine was finally released from the *Laurel*.

Her first impressions of Canada at close hand were anything but delighted. She set foot in Canada in one of the dirtiest harbours of the world, full of disease and pestilence. Public health facilities were non-existent in the colonial cities; open ditches of sewage and filth were common; public houses and hotels, overcrowded with immigrants, ignored hygiene precautions. The obvious destitution of many of the population, the litter and filth of the streets, combined with an oppressive sultry heat, made the Traills anxious to be on their way. They had not yet found their new world.

Unfortunately, the overworked customs officials delayed them for two days before their luggage could be cleared. After a few lethargic attempts at sightseeing, the Traills put in the time talking with other guests in their hotel. Most of these were new arrivals to Canada, and little could be learned from them.

Montreal had yet another blow for them. The night before the Traills were scheduled to leave for the Upper province, their baggage having been finally released, Catharine was struck down with the cholera. They had seen its effects in the city; they had experienced the government's anxious attempts to contain the spread of the scourge; but they were not prepared for it.

The violence of the attack so rattled Thomas that he was totally useless, until the landlady's sister heard of the trouble and sent him off to find a doctor. Then she began her personal nursing of Catharine. Though the disease was highly contagious, and everyone in the city was in a state of fear amounting to panic, Catharine was never left alone, nor in need of personal care and medical attention. The natural kindness and gentleness which she had shown earlier to the hotel employees were now rewarded by this demonstration by virtual strangers of the most basic form of respect and affection. This undoubtedly saved her life.

The worst stages of the disease were violent but short-lived, so that several days later, the Traills were able to board the stage for Lachine. Catharine was still very weak and depressed, the lingering after-effects of the disease, and was not able to give the trip her usual enthusiastic interest. But she commented on the Canadian stage-coach, which she liked, and on the Canadian roads, which she did not for they battered and bruised even the hardiest of travellers.

There were several different ways to make the rest of the journey. The Traills went by stage from Montreal to Lachine, by steamer from Lachine to Coteau-du-Lac, then again by stage to Cornwall, where they had their first unhappy experience with the tiny colonial inns (inadequate in size, furnishing, and cleanliness – the Traills could neither sleep nor eat the food), by stage again early the next morning on to Prescott where they boarded the big two-funnelled steamer *Great Britain* which would take them all the way to Cobourg.

Seven years earlier, Catharine's energetic young brother Samuel had chosen what was perhaps the most comfortable way to make the trip. He put his luggage on board a Durham boat and walked. This was obviously the fastest way, as well as the most comfortable, for he had to wait two or three days at Prescott for his luggage to catch up with him.[5]

When the Traills boarded the big comfortable steamer, Catharine was again taking an interest in her surroundings. Up-river at Brockville, she and Thomas watched and cheered with a festive crowd at a ship-launching. And in an American village in the Thousand Islands, she saw a curious arrangement of tiny model houses, replicas of the main houses, and was amused to learn they were houses for birds.

She liked the appearance of the Upper Canadian settlements along the river even better than those of Lower Canada, but not all her observations were uncritical. The Traills thought that the

The remainder of the Moodies' trip was similar to the Traills', except for two adventures, one at Grosse Isle and the other at Quebec.

On 31 August, the morning after the *Anne* dropped anchor at Grosse Isle, the sun drove away the fog and the travellers saw a beautiful and busy scene. Some twenty-five sailing ships lay at anchor, with smaller boats scurrying between the ships and the island.

While the *Anne* was being processed through the usual inspection routine, John received an invitation from the commanding officer of the island, who apparently thought he knew Lieutenant Moodie. John could not remember him, but he and Susanna decided to accept the invitation, on the strength of the familiar comradeship between officers and gentlemen. They went ashore the next morning and stood at the dock waiting for an escort. This was Susanna's first contact with Canada, though John had made some forays off the ship when they had stopped for water at various small islands down-river. Susanna had not been as anxious as Catharine to go ashore, and would not have done so at Grosse Isle had it not been for the personal invitation.

Unfortunately, their host belatedly withdrew his invitation, having corrected his error in recognition, and sent a message that the law must prevail – the Moodies would not be allowed beyond the quarantine area. John and Susanna then had to spend an uncomfortable day on the island, trying to keep a safe distance from the boisterous, sometimes angry, sometimes drunken crowds of immigrants. The experience confirmed Susanna's suspicions that the colony was more beautiful from a distance than at close hand. She was not eager to repeat the experience.

The *Anne* weighed anchor on the morning of the following day and the Moodies were soon at Quebec. Susanna was rapturous over the beauties of the historic old city, as seen from the decks of the *Anne*. But she stayed on board with her baby, for fear of the cholera.

Despite her precautions, she was not safe from danger of another sort. The St. Lawrence was jammed with ships of every description, and accidents were common. While the *Anne* was anchored below the cliffs of Quebec, a larger three-masted vessel, the *Horsley Hill*[1] from Waterford, with 300 Irish immigrants aboard, collided with the *Anne* in the dark. The *Horsley Hill*'s momentum on impact caused the larger ship's bows to ride out of the water, entangling the bowsprit and forward rigging of both ships in a great confusion of cordage and canvas.

The women passengers of the *Anne* swarmed up on deck, and crowded around the captain, screaming and praying. Susanna, who had come to know Captain Rogers fairly well during the long voyage, expressed her fear and indignation more directly. She demanded an explanation from the harassed officer. She failed to receive one.

Either her innate sense of responsibility, or a direct order from Captain Rogers, made her take charge of the women and lead them below out of the way. The women followed meekly, in the few moments of quiet following the initial impact. Then, as the great ship slid back, the wind filled her sails again causing her to ram the *Anne* amidships. The *Anne* heeled under the strain and the *Horsley Hill* moved off, her bowsprit, still intact, shearing the *Anne*'s upper deck fixtures. The resulting crashes were too much for the women to bear. The ships were free of each other and the real danger was passed by the time the women were again swarming up on the deck – all except Susanna, whose iron will and pride kept her below. Discipline, deportment befitting her class, or unwillingness to have another run-in with the Captain, were more compelling than physical fear.

Towed by a steamer, the *Anne* went on to Montreal, where the Moodies stayed on board until the last possible moment, the night before their stage was due to depart for Lachine. This reluctance to leave the ship was partly fear of cholera and partly money shortage. By government regulation, the shipping companies were required to provide for their passengers for several days at the end of the voyage. In any event, they escaped the cholera and had no further adventures until they reached Cobourg.

The Moodies' first encounter with Cobourg could have been very depressing for they arrived late on a rainy night, 9 September, the busiest part of the season. Strong's Steamboat Hotel was already packed and overflowing. Susanna waited in the busy foyer while John bustled off to bargain for space with the proprietor. Then Susanna saw in the crowd an old friend from Suffolk, and after many delighted words of recognition he learned of her plight and gave up his room for her and the child.

Tom Wilson was another of the class of younger sons of British gentry, with little money, wandering the world to make his fortune or just to find something to do. He had been a frequent guest in the Moodie and Strickland households in England, and a participant in the discussions and plans about their migration.

Though Susanna and her sisters had always regarded Tom Wilson as something of a clown, an irresponsible dreamer, his presence in the Cobourg hotel that night obviously did a great deal to soften the Moodies' arrival in Canada.

Catharine and Thomas Traill had been in Cobourg only a week earlier, but they had not stayed long. Susanna and Catharine had been out of touch for over three months. Neither knew the location of the other. Had there been any awareness that they were a mere week apart, Catharine would no doubt have awaited Susanna's arrival in Cobourg. But the season was late and the Traills were anxious to reach their intended destination, the home of Samuel Strickland in Douro Township, north of Peterborough.

On 1 September, with three other gentlemen and a lady, Catharine and Thomas had taken their places in a wagon going north to Rice Lake. Refreshed after their rest at Cobourg and becoming increasingly more excited as they neared their new home, they eagerly scanned the country, pointing out new and interesting things to each other, and chattering about the comfortable homesteads of this well-settled area. They made plans for their new home and talked about how they would decorate it, as Upper Canadians for some reason had failed to do with theirs.

One of their travelling companions who had been thirteen years in the backwoods could not refrain from entering into the conversation, but unlike some of their earlier contacts he was kind and helpful.

The veteran pioneer pointed out that they could not build a house without boards, and boards were not to be had unless there was a sawmill nearby – unlikely in a very new community. The only alternative was a log shanty. He told them their first few years would be entirely taken up with the enormous task of clearing the land and there would be no time for elegant decoration; this would have to be forgotten for at least ten to fifteen years.

Catharine and Thomas recognized that they were hearing from an experienced and successful settler. They believed him when he criticized as nonsense the generalizations of the books on settlement. He asked them to use their own reason and good sense in assessing the difficulties of completely removing the thick forest cover before crops could be planted, of building houses and even buying supplies when they might be cut off completely from any settled community.

The Traills listened and respectfully agreed, but they were not discouraged. They could see all around them the proof that the enormous task was possible, and they began to dream of the new communities that would rise in the prosperous areas through which they were passing. They were excited rather than depressed by the challenge, as participants in a great creative venture. Nor did they give up their own desire to make their future home as beautiful as possible, despite the insistence of the other colonists that this was impossible.

Besides, no one could be discouraged in the beautiful country of the Rice Lake Plains, in the most beautiful season of the Canadian year. Their wagon was comfortably upholstered with buffalo robes, the other passengers were congenial, and there were frequent clearings and settlements, even a tavern for a rest-stop halfway to Rice Lake. This tavern was in a clearing called Cold Springs, and Catharine speculated on its future as a great health spa a century or so hence.

It was night when they reached Sully (now Harwood) on Rice Lake, and they spent the night there in a two-room log house that also served as a tavern. The colonial inns were getting smaller all the time, but no less crowded. Catharine was getting used to them, and was happy to spend the night on a buffalo robe in the corner with only her "Scotch plaid cloak" as a covering.

The next morning, after an early breakfast of fried pork, potatoes and strong tea without milk, a breakfast enjoyed by everyone but the Traills at the crowded table, they boarded a small steamer which was to take them across the Lake and up the Otonabee River towards Peterborough. The unprepossessing appearance of this little vessel, the *Pem-o-Dash*, belied its importance to the commerce of the back country. Passengers and produce were loaded aboard at random. Though it was steam-powered it also carried a small sail, suggesting a lack of faith in the engine.

By noon they were seeing real forest at close hand for the first time – so close that they could almost reach out and touch the trees. The pines were thick and tall on the shores of the river and served as an effective windbreak for the passengers exposed on the deck of the little steamer. The forest also dampened some of the pioneers' enthusiasm – this was the bush that they had set out to conquer with their bare hands. The newly-weds' carefully nurtured courage was sorely strained.

But Catharine was never discouraged for long. She spotted some vines climbing among the boughs of the trees, with some good-sized grapes ripening on them; she settled on these as a more worthy subject for attention than the opaque forests; grape vines could be cultivated and improved for her own garden, perhaps.

Thomas, on his part, undertook to profit from the trip by entering into a technical discussion about steam engines with the engineer of the vessel. This young Scottish-Canadian, however, preferred to use the opportunity to give the British gentry a lesson in the equality of man. The crew of the *Pem-o-Dash* had met many gentry/settlers on their way to the Peterborough area, and perhaps it was a favourite sport to tease the naive upper classes, or perhaps there was something about the Traills that induced this young man to be personally recognized by them. In any case, he chose to be overly familiar with both Catharine and Thomas.

The ensuing confrontation wound up with this sally between Thomas and the engineer, as overheard and reported by Catharine : [8]

"There is comfort, I guess, in considering oneself equal to a gentleman," said the man.

"Particularly if you can induce the gentleman to think the same." This was a point that seemed to disconcert our candidate for equality . . .

"Now," said his tormentor, "you have explained your notions of Canadian independence; be so good as to explain the machinery of your engine, with which you seem very well acquainted."

The man eyed my husband for a minute, half sulking, half pleased at the implied compliment on his skill, and, walking off to the engine, discussed the management of it with considerable fluency, and from that time treated us with perfect respect.

Thus, while Thomas was a newcomer to the frontier, his self-confidence, education and experience with many different countries and cultures made him more than a match for any of his more youthful countrymen.

About half-way between Rice Lake and Peterborough the *Pem-o-Dash* stopped at a clearing to replenish its supply of firewood for the boiler. There was a tavern there, a rude structure built of logs, set alone at the edge of the clearing.

It looked like a typical log shanty to Catharine, the sort everyone was telling her she would have to live in, and she decided to find out what it was like inside. She had already seen the inside of log houses, but was aware of an important distinction between a log house and a log shanty. She was impatient to find out precisely what that distinction meant.

On the pretext of buying some milk, she ventured across the clearing and into the shanty/tavern. She was horrified at the sight: dirt floor, obvious chinks and holes in the walls and roof, rough-hewn furniture, and sick emigrants lying on pallets slightly raised from the floor by split cedar rails. Pigs, hens, and pigeons moved freely among the inhabitants, but a valuable calf was carefully penned in a corner.

In short, the environment was becoming a little less picturesque.

Further upstream, the steamer ran aground in the shallow Otonabee and could go no further. It then became apparent that the *Pem-o-Dash* had not really hoped to get as far as Peterborough anyway, and arrangements had been made for a large scow to come out and meet it.[9] But the steamer was still four miles from the usual rendezvous, Yankee Bonnet, marked by and named for a particularly tall pine tree.

The scow finally showed up, propelled by eight oarsmen who were disgruntled by their extra-long trip, and all thoroughly drunk from the whiskey they had consumed during their wait at Yankee Bonnet. It was dark by the time they were underway again, with all the passengers, parcels, furniture, luggage and miscellany moved from the stranded steamer to the scow.

Tired and hungry, but happy to be moving again, Catharine relaxed on her husband's shoulder, dozed and admired the stars

46

in the warm clear autumn night, lulled by the steady sound of the oars on the river.

Some two miles below Peterborough, the fractious crew crunched the boat in to shore and refused to go any further that night.

Before the Traills could rouse themselves to this new development, the other passengers who seemed to be accustomed to this sort of thing had piled out and set off on foot through the dark forest. Thomas snared the last man to leave and with some difficulty persuaded to him to guide them; equally tired and anxious to be home, the man agreed only on the condition that the Traills would keep up with his pace.

Catharine was still weak from illness and from hunger. She had to summon strength that she had never used before, to hurry through the dark woods after the rapidly disappearing stranger, back and forth by a canoe over the river, climbing over trees fallen across the path, through underbrush, falling headlong into a creek, and arriving at Peterborough at midnight, still soaking wet. One light showed in Peterborough, and they made for it, to learn that it was indeed an inn, but an inn whose rooms had long since been filled up.

Their guide had long since left them, and they stood in the yard of the inn, talking with the one person still awake in the little community. When he insisted there was no room for them there, they asked him to direct them to the home of Samuel Strickland. When he told them that Mr. Strickland lived many miles further on, through worse terrain than they had already passed, they were ready to bed down under the nearest tree.

They were saved from this foolhardy alternative. The innkeeper, Mrs. McFadden, had been listening to the conversation from her bedroom, and hearing the name of Samuel, she came down immediately. She led Catharine into the inn, gave her a chair by the fire, instructed a servant girl to bring some warm water and bathe the poor soaked traveller's feet, mixed a hot drink and insisted that Catharine drink it.

Mrs. McFadden then gave up her own bed, in the original of all air-conditioned rooms, through whose walls Catharine could admire the rapids of the Otonabee flashing in the moonlight. She woke refreshed and happy the next day, laughing about their adventures. She set off to tour the town.

Peterborough,[10] as opposed to Cobourg, was a very new community. Its first settler, Adam Scott, had arrived there only eleven years earlier to build a grist mill for the few English settlers in neighbouring townships. But the town had not been really established until the Honourable Peter Robinson made it his headquarters for the organization of a large settlement of Irish immigrants. In actual fact, the town was a mere seven years old when the Traills arrived.

There was a population of about 700, many of them well-educated professional and military people, for this was a favourite area for half-pay officer/settlers. There were several sawmills, grist mills and general stores, a distillery, a fulling mill, two inns, and a schoolhouse which also served as a church.

It even had the beginning of a slum, a shantytown outside the main part of town, where destitute emigrants lived – the "commuted pensioners" – people who had accepted free transportation and grants of land in return for their pension rights. These were the most unhappy sorts of immigrants. They were mainly from the city slums of Britain, ignorant of farming, and quite incapable of looking after themselves in the best of circumstances. The bush defeated them before they had even tried. They sold their land to get money for food, and were left worse off than before.

While Catharine was looking around the town, her new friend Mrs. McFadden had sent word up-river to Samuel, to tell them that his relatives had arrived.

Samuel came down immediately and, with his help, the Traills set about their arrangements for procuring a farm and settling in. Their long journey was at an end.

Thomas, as a military officer, was entitled to a grant of land for which his only payment was to be the performance of settlement duties, that is, improving the land by clearing a specified number of acres and taking up residence on it. But he also had in mind buying another lot which would connect his grant to a lake frontage and bring him closer to Samuel's settlement. Government land sales were held regularly and often in the major centres of new settlements and they did not have long to wait.

Meanwhile, at Cobourg, the Moodies had settled in and were engaged in much the same sort of activity, but with complications.

John Moodie's assets were his commission, some capital, and his rights to a grant of land as a military officer. Although he had considered himself poor in Britain, these assets made him a wealthy man in Upper Canada, and a target for colonials who immediately tried to separate him from his wealth. They were given some unexpected assistance in this endeavour from the government and from Moodie's own personality.

As a "half-pay officer", Moodie was retired from active service, but he still held his commission and was subject to recall at any time. The value was not the "half-pay", since even the full pay of an officer was only a nominal amount. The value was the commission itself, since military commissions were still bought and sold.

Shortly after Moodie's arrival in Canada, a general order from the army appeared in the local papers, calling on half-pay officers "to hold themselves in readiness to go on service or to sell their commissions".[11] Moodie took this announcement at face value, and it threw him into a quandary. He was loath to leave his family to their own devices in the colony. He therefore disposed of his commission. The government's need for officers immediately subsided and the general order was rescinded.

He might still have been all right, had it not been for the complex way he took to sell his commission. As he described it later, rather plaintively, in a letter to the Governor:[12]

49

D

... I was induced to accept an offer made me by a speculator in Cobourg of 25 shares in the *Cobourg* steam-boat, –
value £625 cur'cy., – for the sum I might receive from my
commission. The person with whom I made this unfortunate
bargain, and from which I might have receded in time, had I
not considered myself bound in honor to adhere to my verbal
agreement, promised to repay me whatever sum exceeding
£600 stg. I might possibly receive for my commission: which
promise on receiving the unexpected sum of £700 stg. he
forgot ...

It was obviously a very complex arrangement, involving two
sets of currency valuations and a swap of commission and speculative stock, in a transaction that lasted long enough for Moodie's
original need to avoid military service to be solved of its own
accord. As a matter of honour, however, he felt he had to
go through with the deal. On the face of it, the steam-boat stock
was not necessarily a poor proposition; the one thing the colony
needed most was better facilities for water transport. The particular venture that Moodie invested in, however, failed to develop.

Thus, Moodie was relieved of his commission as well as the
cash it was worth, and was left holding speculative stock which
never paid off and which a few years later he discovered he could
not sell at any price. The bitterness, the feeling that they had
been cheated, stayed with John and Susanna for the rest of
their lives.

Moodie still had some money and his right to a land grant. But
free land was always located in the backwoods, and Moodie did
not wish to take his family into the isolation and discomfort of
totally uncleared land with no access roads nor nearby settlements. At the same time, he was apparently unaware that he
would lose his rights to the land unless he actually took up residence on it.[13]

He chose, in any case, to buy land in a more mature community closer to the "Front", as the name was given to the lands bordering Lake Ontario. Since available Crown lands were scarce in this area, and he wanted a cleared farm anyway, he undertook to buy in a private sale.

This decision was not an easy one. Thomas Traill had gone through the same line of reasoning – was the free grant worth the effort? In the first place, the land was always hard to get to, harder still to identify once you got there, and there was no place to live once you found it. There was no guarantee that the land would be any good, and even if you took the trouble to inspect it, it was so covered with trees that it was hard to determine even which was high ground and which was low. Only the most experienced woodsman could look at a forest lot and evaluate its potential as arable land. There would be no income for the first few years, and all provisions had to be purchased at a high cost and brought in from great distances under the most difficult circumstances. Livestock for fresh milk and meat could not be kept until enough land had been cleared and fenced for crops and pastures.

Thomas Traill decided that the grant was worth all this trouble, particularly since he was able to purchase an adjoining lot with lake frontage. But his situation was rather different from John Moodie's.

Thomas had no children as yet to worry about, and no servants. His only care was Catharine, and she was eager and willing to go into the backwoods with him, especially since they would be so near her young brother.

John Moodie on the other hand had a baby daughter and a Scottish servant who was terrified of the bush. And he did not wish to subject his wife to more trials than were necessary, since she had not been too keen about migration in the first place. There may also have been a competitive urge, a desire to make it on his own without the help of his brother-in-law, in a more settled community where less time was needed to become successful.

Whatever his reasons, John Moodie set out to inspect farms in

Hamilton Township, in the vicinity of Cobourg. He was sold one in quick time, thereby disposing of the bulk of his remaining capital.

In most ways, John Moodie was personally unsuitable to the life of a settler. He was unaccustomed to manual labour and he was no longer physically strong. He knew nothing about farming and little about business, and he was far too honest and trusting to hold his own in the colonial struggle for survival. Other gentlemen-settlers were able to overcome similar difficulties if they were well supplied with cash. However, by swapping his commission for the steam-boat stock, Moodie had lost a good part of his assets within a few weeks of his arrival in the colony.

Thus, the outlook for the Moodie family's success in Upper Canada was none too promising. John was anything but the rugged and independent frontiersman. And Susanna was strait-laced, proud and intractable in her social attitudes, unaccustomed to softening or withholding her expressions of opinion. They would have many trials and conflicts before they would come to terms with their new environment.

While not the best of her poetry, these verses of Susanna, written shortly after they settled on their new farm, provide a clear statement of Susanna's views on her new situation. Oddly, they take the form of a young gentleman addressing his sweetheart: [14]

OH CAN YOU LEAVE YOUR NATIVE LAND

A Canadian Song

by Mrs. Moodie, Author of *Enthusiasm*

Oh can you leave your native land,
    An Exile's bride to be, –
Your Mother's home and cheerful hearth,
    To tempt the Main with me? –

Across the wide Atlantic,
    To trace our foaming track,
And know the wave that heaves us on,
    Will never bear us back?

And can you in Canadian woods
    With me the harvest bind,
Nor feel one ling'ring sad regret
    For all you leave behind?
Can lily hands unused to toil,
    The woodsman's wants supply —
Nor shrink beneath the chilly blast,
    When wintry storms are nigh?

Amid the shade of forest dark,
    Thy loved Isle will appear
An Eden, whose delicious bloom
    Will make the wild more drear.
And you in solitude may weep
    O'er scenes beloved in vain,
And pine away your soul to view
    Once more your native plain.

Then pause, dear Gul, ere those sweet lips
    Your Wand'rer's fate decide;
My spirit spurns the selfish wish: —
    Thou shalt not be my Bride!
But, oh! that smile — those tearful eyes
    My firmer purpose move;
Our hearts are one — and we will dare
    All perils, thus, to love!

Melsetter, near Cobourg, U.C.

53

CHAPTER THREE

The Moodies in Hamilton Township

Susanna, with her maid Hannah and her daughter Katie, stayed in the Steamboat Hotel in Cobourg from 9 to 22 September, while John bustled about, negotiating for a farm. She was bored, except when her friend from Suffolk, Tom Wilson, was around to entertain her, but most of the time she was lonely and unhappy. Dismayed at the roughness of the community and its inhabitants, she tried to read, but the local newspaper, the *Reformer*, was even rougher. Its violent partisan diatribes against the Tories and the simple straightforwardness of its choice of language deeply offended Susanna's literary and social senses. Homesickness, idleness and despair prevented her from seeing any good in her situation, and she admitted to frequent bouts of tears in her room in the dreary little inn.

Wilson was not the best possible companion for her wait. He was diverting, but he was also sick with "ague and fever" contracted during his thoroughly incompetent attempt to be a settler. He had lost all his money and intended to go home, defeated by a few months in the bush. His stories of settlement life were witty, but they were also highly critical and scornful, hardly the sort to cheer one about to stake everything on the same venture.

The only other available companions were the Cobourg locals. But these people were experienced and confident colonials, with little sympathy for Susanna's fine manners and tastes. Most of them seemed to be "Yankees" at least to Susanna's untrained eye, and indeed, many of them undoubtedly were, for the government in its many turnabouts in settlement policy had encouraged American settlers and Loyalist descendants to bring their experience to the colony. Many others came uninvited in the hunt for land during the time the U.S. middle west was closed by Indian wars. But Susanna tended to equate "Yankee" with anyone of rough manners, poor grammar and democratic tendencies. She saw in all of them the eagerness, vividly described by Tom Wilson, to take advantage of the inexperience of new settlers.

John Moodie hastened his preparations so that they could be under way in time to plough for fall wheat and to distract Susanna from her growing unhappiness.

For £300 cash he bought a farm from a Cobourg merchant and part-time land speculator who had taken it from the previous owner for debts. That the former owner had thus gone bankrupt on this farm did not disturb Moodie unduly, since the merchant made it clear that the debts were for whiskey. The Moodies' new farm was located on the western edge of Hamilton Township, closer to Port Hope than Cobourg. It seemed to meet their requirements exactly; most of the farm had been cleared and the house and barns were built; all the Moodies had to do was keep it going.

There was, however, one problem. The former owners were still living in the house, and the merchant convinced Moodie that according to the colonial custom, you never required anyone to move at any time other than winter. But there was an easy solution; there was an empty log house on a vacant neighbouring farm, which the merchant could easily make arrangements for the Moodies to rent at $4 a month, an amount that seemed reasonable enough at Cobourg.

In any case, they were anxious to get started. Susanna especially was eager to see her new home and equally eager to leave the Cobourg hotel. At the last moment, they decided to take Tom Wilson with them too, because his fever was worsening and they did not feel they could leave a friend alone, sick, and penniless.

The arrangements complete, they all set out from the hotel early one morning: John, Susanna, the maid Hannah, the baby daughter Catherine, Tom Wilson, a newly-acquired hired man James, and a Yankee driver who went with the extra carriage needed for the entourage. The women went ahead in the covered carriage with the driver; the men followed at a slower pace in two wagons with the luggage and household supplies.

The trip was short and easy; the road was good in contrast to real bush roads which had the trees but not the stumps removed. Such a road Susanna experienced only within sight of their new temporary quarters; the "driveway" was covered with stones, stumps and bumps. Towards the end of the trip, it had started to rain, making them all cold, wet and miserable.

It would have been wiser had Moodie led the procession, saving Susanna from the shock of being dumped off unceremoniously in a clearing which had been uninhabited long enough that the forest was again reclaiming it. With dismay amounting to disbelief, she gazed on a one-room log shanty, lacking window panes or a door, with gaping holes in the walls and roof, and tenanted only by stray animals. Susanna's driver, showing no surprise at the scene, took time only to chase the animals out of the hut before he turned his carriage around and headed back to Cobourg.

In perfect helplessness and dismay, Susanna sat down in the middle of the filth and watched the rain coming in through the walls, roof, door-opening and windows of her new home, while Hannah and the baby dissolved in tears.

Fortunately, the men were not far behind. They arrived within a few minutes, leaped from their wagons and vigorously set to work. James, the hired man, found wood for kindling and pulled up stumps from the yard, then set a fire in the hearth taking some of the chill and gloom away from the little cabin. He then built a rough ladder to the loft, which Tom Wilson used to stow the luggage away, thereby clearing some space in the middle of the floor. John, in the meantime, had located the door and fitted it in place. Hannah, getting in the spirit of things, grabbed a broom and raised such clouds of dust that she drove Susanna out into the rain.

By evening, the place was clean and, in contrast with its original state, quite snug and comfortable. Susanna was in the right frame of mind to receive her first caller.

Mrs. Moodie's description of this girl is a classic in pioneer literature, though it reveals almost as much about Susanna as it does about the subject:[1]

> Imagine a girl of seventeen or eighteen years of age, with sharp, knowing-looking features, a forward, impudent carriage, and a pert, flippant voice, standing upon one of the trunks, and surveying all our proceedings in the most impertinent manner. The creature was dressed in a ragged, dirty purple stuff gown, cut very low in the neck, with an old red cotton handkerchief tied over her head; her uncombed, tangled locks falling over her thin, inquisitive face, in a state of perfect nature. Her legs and feet were bare, and, in her coarse, dirty red hands, she swung to and fro an empty glass decanter.

Through the ensuing conversation, as the English lady became more mortified with embarrassment and the country girl more violent with anger, Susanna was finally able to determine that the girl wanted to borrow some whiskey for her father. Moodie thought the whole encounter was very amusing, and took advantage of the occasion to tease his bachelor friend Wilson as being an attraction for the local ladies.

This visitor, however, was the harbinger of the Moodies' long and involved problems with their scavenging neighbours. The girl came again, as did the rest of her family, and all the neighbours, on a series of "borrowing" visits, eventually expecting the Moodies to supply all their personal and household needs. They borrowed, but seldom returned anything, and when a borrowed article was returned it was no longer fit for the Moodies to use. But when the Moodies, convinced that borrowing was a custom of the country, tried out the system themselves, they discovered that the only way they could get anything out of the neighbours was by paying for it at the highest price that could be extorted.

In a series of complicated exchanges, the Moodies were cheated out of almost everything they had, including a good proportion of their self-respect. Susanna, in describing her first few months in the "bush", emphasized the loss of household and personal articles, such as food, cooking utensils, sewing materials, and clothing. Whatever form the transactions took, the Moodies were always the losers.

It was not so much the loss of the most essential of household items that troubled Susanna, though they were far enough away from Port Hope and Cobourg to make replacement difficult. More disturbing was the way these people wandered in and out whenever they felt like it, intruding on the privacy of even the little log shanty, and speaking a strange sort of English that Susanna rarely understood. Then after every visit, there was the vaguely unsettling feeling of being tricked again, by people who "did not know A from B and did not care to know".

Far more important than the household articles, however, was the extent to which they were tricked about the farm, its implements and produce, and the property itself. The first sign of this was the fate of Moodie's new plough, which was borrowed before he got a chance to use it, severely damaged in a rocky field, and cheerfully returned.

John and Susanna Moodie were not lacking in intelligence. They were not naive youngsters. And despite the neighbours' opinions, they were not wealthy. Why then did they so consistently allow themselves to be imposed upon to such extremes?

The rigidity of their values and manners was stiffened by each successive contact with their neighbours. They refused at all costs to sink to the same level or to play the same tricks, even in self-

rambling rail fences were ugly, in contrast to the neat hedgerows of England, and Catharine was puzzled by the lack of any apparent effort to decorate homes and properties on the Canadian side of the river. Catharine's love of natural beauty did not extend to admiring homesteads left in a state of nature.

The Traills landed at Cobourg at ten o'clock in the morning of 29 August, fifty-three days after they had left Scotland. They settled into the hotel for a short rest before continuing on the last lap of their journey into the bush.

Cobourg[6] was a place of rest for most immigrants, a place for planning the future, and for getting one's bearings before departure into the back townships of the Newcastle District. (Districts and townships were the main political subdivisions of the day; counties did not appear until much later.) Cobourg had been founded some twenty years earlier by United Empire Loyalists. It boasted an hotel – "Strong's Steamboat Hotel"; two weekly newspapers, the *Reformer* and the *Star*; several stores, mills, a bank, a church, and about a mile and a half away at the village of Amherst, there was a courthouse and gaol. The Cobourg community was thus a mature and settled center in Upper Canadian terms.

The comfortable prosperity of the town, as with all the older settlements the travellers had seen thus far along the St. Lawrence and Lake Ontario, did little to discourage the novice pioneers. Life looked easy, even though primitive in contrast with the antiquity of England.

Meanwhile, the brig *Anne* had finally found a wind in the Grand Banks, and Susanna and John Moodie were on their way up the St. Lawrence in a great fog. Unable to view the scenery as Catharine had done, and unwilling to be idle, Susanna occupied her time studying Voltaire's *History of Charles XII,* while quietly lamenting the absence of bread from the ship's dwindling supplies.

tranquil under the circumstances, they at least had a
their heads, and the reality of their own proper home wa
than just a hope.

But even the little cabin was not secure. One day, the merchant
found a buyer for Old Satan's farm, and decided to use the
opportunity to collect another set of debts. He brought the
newcomer around to see the place – a half-pay officer and
gentleman, but unlike Moodie, a man capable of demanding
immediate occupancy as a condition of sale.

Moodie agreed that they must vacate, but where could they
go? The resourceful merchant suggested that Uncle Joe must be
made to co-operate a bit more, and persuade his mother who
lived in the small cabin on Moodie's place to move into the main
house, despite her long-standing feud with Uncle Joe's wife. This
would leave the cabin available to the Moodies until such time as
Uncle Joe decided to leave. It was a pretty little log cabin, nestled
in the apple orchard, and much better maintained than the shanty
the Moodies had been in on Old Satan's place.

Moodie was agreeable, but Uncle Joe's mother was not. For
the first time, it became known to the Moodies that the old lady
still had a claim on the farm, a right of dower. Thus Moodie
learned that when he bought his farm he should have ensured not
only the immediate occupancy but also that he had a clear title.

The merchant was not in the least upset. He went with Moodie
to see the old lady, and helped him to persuade her to accept $20
as a bribe for moving in with her son, leaving the cabin free for
the Moodies. But Moodie was not to be caught on the same trick
twice; he refused to pay his ancient neighbour the tribute until
she had actually vacated the cabin. For the first time he won some
grudging respect from his colonial neighbours. An additional
$20, this time offered by the merchant, persuaded the old lady to
sign off her rights to Moodie's property.

In October the Moodies moved into the shack on their farm,
with Uncle Joe still occupying the farm and main house. He
uncharacteristically allowed Moodie to store hay in the barn.

Much later it was discovered by Moodie's hired man that Uncle Joe was using this hay for his own cattle. The produce of the orchard was lost by trickery of another neighbour who offered to make the apples up into "sarce" for Susanna in return for part of the produce, but the neighbour kept it all but the culls. Their flock of hens went in similar fashion. To make matters worse, the little cabin in the trees brought the Moodies in very close contact with Uncle Joe's brood who spent most of their time peering in the windows at Susanna when they could not work up enough courage to walk through the door. They thought it amusing to see Susanna crying so much.

In the spring, Uncle Joe finally left the farm that he would always think of as his homestead. His parting gift to the Moodies was a dead skunk hidden in a closet of the house the Moodies were so anxious to move into.

In the meantime, their non-paying and non-working guest, Tom Wilson, had also departed the Moodie household. He had been company for Susanna, but also had to be nursed through his frequent attacks of high fever. In despair, bitterness, and ill-health, he left the Moodies and the colony, having lost all but his passage money of the small fortune he had brought with him.

Now, John and Susanna were free of the worst of their scavenging neighbours, free of their house-guest, and in possession of their farm. It looked like clear sailing, until an English neighbour pointed out to Moodie that he might still be in difficulties with his farm because Canadian methods were peculiar and Moodie knew nothing about them. The neighbour told Moodie about the share-farming arrangements that were usually followed in such circumstances, and even recommended an experienced farm couple who might serve the Moodies in this way. The willing and gullible Moodie promptly finalized the arrangement, and installed the couple in the little cabin on his farm. Moodie was to provide the land, implements, livestock and seed, and his tenant was to do the work, with the produce shared. The share-farmer was permitted to keep his own livestock on

Moodie's farm; but the orchard was reserved for the Moodies' own use.

Later, Susanna described their experience with share-farming in these words:[3]

All the money we expended on the farm was entirely for these people's benefit, for by the joint contrivances very little of the crops fell to our share; and when any division was made, it was always when Moodie was absent from home and there was no person present to see fair play. They sold what apples and potatoes they pleased, and fed their hogs *ad libitum*. . . . I would gladly have given them all the proceeds of the farm to get rid of them, but the bargain was for twelve months, and, bad as it was, we could not break our engagement.

Evidently they lost their second orchard crop in the fall of 1833 as they had lost the previous year's apples, but this time the best of the remainder of the farm produce was also lost to them. The Moodies had exchanged Uncle Joe's trickery for the share-cropper's trickery, except that the latter seemed to have been even more adept at the art.

But they did not lose their honour. They stuck to the agreement anyway, even when they discovered that the helpful neighbour who had recommended the arrangement was simply trying to get rid of the couple himself.

The Moodies were having almost as much trouble with their domestic staff. Neither of them expected to have to do menial tasks, but because of the constant turnover among their servants, they were often forced to. James, the hired man Moodie had brought with him from Cobourg, was supposed to look after the livestock – a team of horses, a yoke of oxen, three cows and a litter of pigs, but when he walked off for a week without saying that he was going and leaving all these tasks, Moodie fired him. They had a Cornish lad named Dan for a while, and then John Monaghan attached himself to their service. Monaghan was a young Irish boy who had recently immigrated, and knew less about farming and Canadian ways than the Moodies. But he was hard up for a job, and very respectful of his betters, and was promptly hired.

Susanna had four different maid-servants. Hannah, who took on too many airs as soon as she got to "Meriky", was replaced by a Scots girl Bell, who left the day after John Monaghan was hired, being unwilling to stay in the same house with an Irishman. Another Bell was hired, this time Irish, who promptly got married and went off to set up her own household. She was followed by Mary Tate, who, like John Monaghan, had a rather longer tenure though she was very young and inexperienced. In addition, Susanna had a Cornish nursemaid named Dolly Rowe, hired to help with Susanna's new daughter Agnes who was born in the spring of 1833.

Thus in the space of less than a year, the Moodie household had at least eight different servants. Since these troubles had not been experienced in England, they naturally blamed them on the colony itself. On the other hand, neighbours like Uncle Joe did their best to help along the colonial spirit of equality by undermining the discipline of the Moodies' servants.

The household was often without any servants at all. Thus Susanna discovered something about pioneer cooking and household management, gardening and washing clothes, although she learned mostly by trial and error. When she did have servants, she never observed how they achieved these tasks with such effortless skill, and her neighbours refused to give her any advice without being paid for it. One neighbour, however, gave her a "free" lesson in poultry husbandry by killing her own rooster, after which Susanna's rooster went over to the neighbour's flock, taking the Moodies' hens with him.[4] Susanna was forced to learn how to milk a cow,[5] at the expense of many jeers from the other farm wives, but she never learned to like such menial tasks. Nor did she undertake them when there was anyone else around who might do them for her, such as Moodie himself or the hired man.

She had not learned the most important attribute of a pioneer wife, the ability to cheer, support and encourage her husband under the most trying conditions. She did not openly blame John for their troubles; rather, she developed a violent hatred for the colonials for persecuting and tricking him. But her attitudes and easy tears only added to John's burden.

Moreover, because of her unfortunate experiences with the scavenging borrowers, she was prejudiced against any form of mutual help, so essential to the survival of a frontier community. She could not distinguish between the "borrowing" of personal clothing, for example, and the practice of gathering up all the cutlery and dishes in the community for a "social" or large family gathering, still an accepted practice in modern rural communities.

Susanna's reports of their relations with the people of this settlement are at variance, not only with her sister's observations but also with those of many other chroniclers of pioneer life, and of rural life in any age. Yet Susanna was not making all these stories up out of whole cloth, though she did exaggerate for the sake of a good story, and though many of the stories could have a different interpretation than that given by Susanna. Obviously, the explanation both of Susanna's interpretations and of the events themselves lies in the characters and personalities of the Moodies, not in the sinful peculiarities of the neighbours.

The vengeful, rascally, drunken Uncle Joe became an itinerant preacher. Susanna claimed the only explanation for this was that anything was possible in this mixed-up colony. She may have been right, but a more plausible explanation in many ways could be that Uncle Joe was not quite the scoundrel that Susanna thought he was. After all, she liked him when she first met him; it was only after successive clashes between the two families that she began to take a different view of him, conflicts of two different cultures, two different ways of thought, the difference emphasized by the awkward situation created by the merchant *cum* land speculator.

The Moodies had not learned to adapt nor did they wish to

E

learn. The rigidity of their manners and habits was to a large extent responsible for their persecution by the locals. The resentment expressed by the "Yankee" neighbours was not entirely unfounded, nor was their scorn. It was ridiculous, for instance, in a one-room log cabin shared by the family and servants, to attempt to uphold English propriety by refusing to "sit down to table with the help", especially since the master and mistress of the house had to work side by side with the help all day long. Their attitude in this respect lost them valuable servants and antagonized the neighbours who could only assume that the Moodies needed to be instructed in the equality of man. They took odd ways of doing this; the dead skunk, for instance, or their habit of addressing the Moodies' servants as "Sir" or "Ma'am" while pointedly refusing any kind of courtesy to Susanna or John.[6] Upper class snobbery on one side was met with lower class snobbery on the other, and at no time was any attempt made at understanding.

An example of this lack of adaptation on both sides was expressed in the simple matter of visiting each other's houses. In the country, one neighbour visited another by simply walking through the door (the back door in preference to the front door, if the house was fortunate enough to have two); any other way of entering was considered unfriendly and excessively formal. To the Moodies, however, an Englishman's home was his castle; his privacy was his most important possession, and no one should enter another's home without express permission of the occupant. Thus, whenever a neighbour entered the Moodies' house in friendliness, they were confused by the cold anger of their reception. The Moodies were not inhospitable by nature, but their hospitality was seriously hampered by their shock at having their privacy invaded. And when the Moodies visited a neighbour, they knocked on the front door, an act interpreted by the occupants as being too formal. Neither side accepted the other's ways for what they were – an expression of courtesy. And neither would change nor attempt to understand. Why should the colonials change their habits just to accommodate one family that was different? How could the Moodies change a manner of living that they had been taught to practice since birth?

The social conflict seriously hampered the whole process of learning – including learning how to run the farm. Moodie was spending money like water, paying to get out of difficulties which should have been avoidable, paying simply in order to live. He had to pay a premium for cabins even though he already owned a house. He had to pay wages to a multiplicity of servants because neither he nor Susanna knew how to do anything for themselves. He had to buy all his tools and equipment and stock, as well as provisions for his family and servants. Since he lost or was tricked out of most of his crops, everything that went into the Moodie household had to be paid for. And, according to Susanna, much of what he bought ended up in the hands of the neighbours. Moodie knew this was not the way to run a farm, but he was seriously hampered in his attempts to learn the right way.

By the summer of 1833, he was faced with a crisis. His money was almost gone, and the farm still gave no indication that it would be able to supply him with either an income or a subsistence. He decided to give it all up before he lost everything. The future of his increasing family – he now had two daughters – was of deep concern to him, and equally worrying was his wife's obvious unhappiness with her environment.

He decided to take up his original land grant on Katchiwano Lake, a broadening of the Upper Otonabee River north of Peterborough. This was his last asset, and he had by now discovered that he would lose it unless he took up residence on it. It had the one advantage of bringing Susanna into close touch with her sister Catharine and her brother Samuel.

Whether or not John could succeed on a totally uncleared farm when he failed on a well-developed one was a gamble he was forced to take in order to remove Susanna from the hateful Yankee neighbours and give her and the children the more acceptable companionship of the Stricklands.

The Moodies' financial difficulties were relieved in the late summer of 1833 by a £700 legacy from Susanna's uncle. This good fortune, however, did not dissuade them from leaving Hamilton Township; rather, it helped make their resettlement easier. Moodie made a trip of inspection to his grant in the fall, and with Samuel's guidance, arranged to purchase an adjoining lot and to have the clearing and house-building commenced by a local farmer during the coming winter.

Moodie was also exploring other means of making an income. Putting together his recent connection with gentlemen in England and his even more recent experiences in land speculation in Canada, and with the help of his brother-in-law Samuel who had impressed Moodie with his knowledge, John tried to become a land speculator himself, as an agent for investors in England. His efforts, however, were abortive, possibly because he painted a picture for potential clients in England that seemed unrealistic even to them. Perhaps it was as well for John that his proposals were not accepted. It is difficult to imagine him making deals in the manner of the speculator who had swindled him a year before and yet without this capacity to make a deal, profits would have been minimal. John was not ready to become a part of the entreprenurial era in Canada.[7]

Yet John Moodie had recognized that the trade in land was the biggest activity of the colony, and that pioneer farming was deeply involved in this trade. Success or failure, happiness or unhappiness, especially for gentleman-settlers, depended as much on their ability to cope with economic problems as with social and agricultural problems. To put this in perspective, it is necessary to know something of the complexities of currency and of land values in this era of transition.

Buying anything in the 1830s in Canada was a complex operation.[8] The dollar was pushing the pound out of use, but this "dollar" bore little resemblance to the decimal-type dollar of later days. It was originally based on the old Spanish "piece-of-eight", and had come through the pre-Revolutionary American colonies to Quebec. It was then divided not into 100 cents but into eight parts called shillings. Because of the importance of trade between the British colonies and the United States, the dollar became well accepted in Canada.

But the Canadian dollar, in Halifax currency, was divided into five parts, also called shillings, on the principles of British sterling. Halifax currency was expressed in dollars and in pounds, with the pound (Halifax) worth less than the pound sterling. This caused a great deal of confusion. Moreover, the "York shilling" originating in Upper Canada rather than Quebec or Halifax was similar to the American currency in that it was the eighth part of a dollar. The York evaluation was officially frowned upon ("not worth a York shilling"), but it was still in common use when the Moodies were in Hamilton Township.

There were dozens of types of coins in circulation. Anything was acceptable, including buttons, because of the acute shortage of specie, a chronic situation caused by the colonies' adverse balance of trade; coinage was regularly being shipped out of the country to pay for imported produce and little was coming back in. The influx of emigrant money in the 1830's helped a good deal to right this situation, and indeed was one of the emigrants' most important contributions. This chronic shortage of money may have had something to do with the avidity with which the Moodies' neighbours tried to separate John from his cash.

During their stay in Hamilton Township, John and Susanna seemed to be using British sterling and "York" dollars/shillings, as often as Halifax currency. Susanna's writings were not as meticulous as they should have been in indicating which currency she meant. Her sister Catharine was more helpful on this point. Catharine included the official explanation as an appendix to her *Backwoods of Canada,* which said, in part:[9]

... 100 l. sterling is shown to be equal to 120 currency, or 480 dollars, the rule of conversion, in the absence of law, where no understanding to the contrary exists, should be, add one-fifth to sterling money, and carrying currency is obtained, or deduct one-sixth from currency, and sterling is found. . . .

Land was generally evaluated on the basis of Halifax currency, expressed in pounds, shillings and pence. This was evidently the medium Moodie had used when he purchased his first farm, because Uncle Joe's mother was quoted as objecting to the merchant's profit of $400. Calculating the price of £300, and Uncle Joe's debt of $800, this could be correct only if Halifax currency had been used.

Added to the difficulties of the currency, the purchase of land was complicated by a variety of land classifications, surveying problems, official grants of wide variety, and a compendium of amended and re-amended British and colonial legislation pertaining to the dispersion of land. This body of legislation showed the shifting policy in the use of land as a source of revenue and the use of free or cheap land as an incentive for settlement.

The colony needed people, pioneering people, to clear and work the land, to make the rest of the land valuable, and to form the basis for the growth of a viable economic community. But revenue was also needed from land sales; uncleared land in distant settlements could be made more productive of revenue if the population was spread through it. A settler who cleared his own land automatically made all the lots around him more attractive by making them look less deserted. These surrounding lands were kept by the government as Crown lands or clergy reserves, preventing the development of the close-knit communities that would have been so beneficial to the pioneer. In short, when land was used for revenue, it discouraged population growth, and vice versa.

Thus, before the big migration of 1832, there were only about one quarter million people in the whole of Upper Canada, scattered all the way from Cornwall to Lake Huron. Free granting of land and the sale of land had both failed, as evidenced by this small population and by the swarming land speculators who owned large tracts but did nothing to improve their holdings. In 1832, policy was more confused than ever. Free grants were frowned upon officially, except for U.E. Loyalists, and military, naval and militia claimants; grants for these were deeply entrenched in the public mind as a sort of reward for past national service. There were so many of such claimants that in spite of official policy, some 193,000 acres were *granted* in 1832, as compared to 10,000 acres of Crown land and 48,000 acres of clergy reserves *sold*.

John Moodie had received only sixty-six acres in his grant as a military officer, an unusually small amount, but it was on a lake front (a valuable point, since water was the primary means of transportation), and he was able to buy 200 acres of wild land at twenty shillings per acre to enlarge his holdings. This was a cheap price because "none of the neighbours who knew the land would oppose me".[10] Later, he bought another 100 acres for £150, considered a high price for uncleared land, but there was an expectation that the value would be enhanced by the construction of the Trent Canal, linking the Back Lakes (the Kawarthas) with the commerce of Lake Ontario. But it was fifty years before this dream would be fulfilled, too late for John to profit from it.

John and Susanna stayed on in Hamilton Township until February 1834, when they hired wagons and a guide to take them to Douro Township. Susanna described her feelings about the move in these words:[11]

> It was not without regret that I left Melsetter, for so my husband had called the place, after his father's estate in Orkney. It was a beautiful, picturesque spot; and, in spite of the evil neighbourhood, I had learned to love it; indeed, it was much against my wish that it was sold. I had a great dislike to removing, which involves a necessary loss, and is apt to give the emigrant roving and unsettled habits. But all regrets were now useless; and

happily unconscious of the life of toil and anxiety that awaited us in those dreadful woods, I tried my best to be cheerful, and to regard the future with a hopeful eye.

One can only speculate on John's reactions to Susanna's sudden change of heart about the old place, and to her noble suffering not too carefully hidden behind her forced cheerfulness.

The Moodies were forced to move in the wintertime because snow made a real improvement in the corduroy roads and at times avoided the necessity of travelling on roads at all. They went all the way by wagon, John, Susanna, their two daughters Katie and Addie, their latest maid-servant Mary Tate, John Monaghan, their driver, and their flock of hens. Only the cattle were left behind in Hamilton Township until such time as they could be accommodated in the bush.

For it was *real* bush they were going to this time, unlike their original settlement with its cleared land, orchards, fences, roads and nearby towns. Susanna, with fear and trepidation, was going to the bush that her sister Catharine had been coping with for over a year, to a part of the backwoods that her brother Samuel had been the first to settle, only two years earlier in the winter of 1831/32.

Samuel Strickland had been in Upper Canada for eight years, gathering experience in all types of settlement problems throughout the province. This experience and Samuel's position of leadership in the new community were to have a significant effect on the Moodies' future, and the presence of Thomas and Catharine Traill would help to soften the impact of the bush for the Moodies.

The coincidence of Thomas Traill and John Moodie drawing lots next door to each other and to their brother-in-law might well be wondered about. Add to this the fact that the local militia's commanding officer was Colonel Brown originally of the 21st Royal North British Fusiliers,[12] making him a regimental brother of John and Thomas, and the coincidence becomes too much. It appears that the random drawing of lots did not exist, at least for the gentry.

This is confirmed by the comments of some Irish gentlemen-emigrants, from an entirely different part of Upper Canada, who settled the same year the Moodies and Traills arrived. Thomas William Magrath, in comparing the relative advantages and disadvantages of settlement in the bush or on cleared land, cited in favour of the bush: "Cheaper land – a choice of district – a clear title – and the power of forming a neighbourhood of select friends."[13] Although Magrath was talking mainly about buying land, for which there would presumably be more choice than receiving a grant, nevertheless, the implication is clear that the settler already in the community had considerable influence over who joined him.

Incidentally, Moodie might have profited from Magrath's comments, had they been available to him:[14]

> . . . It is obviously of great importance, to derive land im-
> mediately from the government, or the Canada Company, as
> the case may be, rather than from individuals, who may have
> mortgages or other liens affecting their lots, which settlers may
> be unable to discover until too late . . .

Moodie had found this out the hard way. He had made at least two errors; buying land from an individual without securing a clear title, and settling on cleared land where he did not have "the power of forming a neighbourhood of select friends". These errors were to be rectified in Douro Township.

Before following the Moodies into Douro, however, it is necessary to review Samuel Strickland's career as a backwoods-man, for he was to become a key figure for the new settlers. Further, it would be well to know how the Traills had been faring in their year-old settlement in Douro.

73

CHAPTER FOUR

Samuel Strickland

After the long procession of baby daughters in Thomas Strickland's family, the birth of Samuel in 1804, one year after Susanna, was more of a welcome relief than a blessed event. Having spent so many years on the development of an educational arrangement suitable for girls, Thomas was able to give himself a freer rein with his son. Perhaps to offset the effect of the very feminine household, perhaps because Thomas felt more at home with the the boy, he ensured that the young Samuel should have a properly masculine education.

Samuel was encouraged in hunting, fishing, woodworking, sports, and any other sort of physical and manual activity that struck his fancy and was suitable for a gentleman. As a child, he was allowed the freedom of Reydon, to follow workmen around as he chose and help or hinder them in their work. And when he was old enough, he received a gentleman's education at a boys' private school in Norwich.

He grew into a strong, tall, healthy and confident young man, with immense energy and personal ambition. He had picked up a smattering of knowledge about many different trades, including carpentry, and "blood-letting" taught to him by the local physician. At the same time, he had a high respect for, and intimate knowledge of, literature, mathematics and other more academic subjects.

He was polished enough to toss off a poem of his own, or read a Shakespeare play, to while away his few sedentary hours. Yet, at the same time, he was totally confident, even naively sure, that the manners, morals, religion and habits of his family and his class were the only possible way of life; anything else was misguided aberration, the result of ignorance or social deprivation. For him there was no conflict between driving ambition and admiration for poetry, between fine manners in the drawing room and violent cruelty in blood-sports. In short, he was a model of a young English public-schoolboy gentleman, even though his family was not quite as upper class as it would like to be, even though he had very little cash, or prospects for making any, when he finished his education.

Samuel had just passed his twentieth birthday and was still at loose ends when, in 1825, he received an invitation to go to Upper Canada. A friend of the Stricklands, a Mr. Black, had been homesteading in a placed called Darlington, in the colony, and needed help. In return, he offered to teach Samuel the ways of the colonist and thus start the young man off on a settlement of his own. He was, in effect, suggesting that if Samuel had nothing better to do, he might think about taking a hand in the development of the Empire.

The idea appealed to Samuel. It was the opportunity to vent some of his physical energy, to be adventurous, to realize his training for leadership, and to make his fortune. He thought he knew something about farming, since Reydon Hall was in the country, but he was sensible enough to want to learn about the Canadian methods. He thought it would take him until the next spring to learn enough before he could start his own place.

Thus, on 28 March 1825, Samuel Strickland sailed for British North America, on the brig *William McGilevray*. He left behind him his six elder sisters, his mother, and one younger brother. He had a grand time on the voyage, continually getting in the way of the crew and thereby learning a good deal about sailing, and dropping his line over the side to catch fish as soon as the ship reached the Banks.

At Montreal, he was scheduled to take a Durham boat as far as

Prescott. But he found the oarsmen of the boat to be of such bad manners that he chose to walk rather than be packed in like a sardine with them for an extended period. During his trek, he met an Irish Canadian, and undertook to learn something about Canada from him and to be guided by him through the bush, in return for Samuel's efforts to correct the Irishman's misguided faith in the Catholic religion. Not until his companion threatened to knock him on the head and leave him to find his own way on the trail, did the young man understand and cease his first and last efforts to be a missionary in the colony.

Samuel felt more at home when he finally reached Darlington and the estate of his tutor, where the education, accent, class and manners were more familiar to him. This offset completely the shock of discovering that Mr. Black, with only a few months in the colony and a strictly urban background, knew even less about farming than Samuel.

The whole affair, however, worked out very well for both. The rather inept gentleman-farmer was appointed to the bench by the Government and made colonel of the local militia battalion, because, according to Samuel, he was "mild in manners, good natured, and very sensible".[1] He also succeeded in marrying off one of his daughters, Emma, to a most promising young colonist, Samuel Strickland.

Because of his tutor's lack of farming experience, Samuel took over much of the management of the farm. He made many mistakes and learned a great deal at his host's expense. His inexperience, for example, led directly to the death of one of the farm's oxen just at the time when the team was most needed. But it was nonetheless a good apprenticeship, for Samuel was intelligent, imaginative, and never had to learn the same lesson twice. In a very short time, he could use and care for oxen, cut hay, make ox-yokes and axe handles, build fences, destroy stumps, split logs, and perform most of the myriad other tasks necessary to early Canadian farming.

With every opportunity to practice, he trained his muscles to respond to the new arts until he became adept. But he did more than this. While he was learning he was conscious of the principles and theories behind the processes, constantly analyzing his activity and trying to work out faster, easier ways. He became an active member of the community, helping out at bees, attending church and socials, and enlisting as an ensign in the Durham Militia, all the time asking questions about farming and life at "The Front". In this way, he was able to prove that the time limit he had put on his apprenticeship had not been after all too optimistic.

Before the end of his first summer, Samuel had married Colonel Black's daughter, Emma. He stayed on in Darlington until the spring, in accordance with his plans. Then, having learned as much as he could at Darlington, and also having learned that he was going to be a father, he began in earnest to use the knowledge about farms and farming that he had gleaned from his many conversations on the subject.

One of the things he knew for certain was that locations (as farms were most often called) around Darlington were too expensive for him and anything except marginal land was very hard to find. But he had heard talk about a new settlement opening up north of Rice Lake, at Scott's Plains. One of his wife's relatives was already there, along with a few other English gentry. The fishing and hunting were reported to be excellent. And the prospects that the community would soon become a major developed area were ensured by a supervised settlement of some 2,000 Irish immigrants brought in that year by the Honourable Peter Robinson.

The original settlers of the area were T. A. Stewart and his brother-in-law Robert Reid, well-known gentlemen in the colony. They had emigrated four years earlier, and settled on adjacent lots in the then unsurveyed and unpopulated Douro Township. The size of their land-holdings was indicative of their importance in the colony; Reid had 2,000 acres and Stewart had 1,200.[2] Nevertheless, they had been ready to give it all up, because of the isolation, until the Robinson settlement came in.

When Samuel Strickland decided to investigate the area personally, he took with him letters of introduction to Peter Robinson, Robert Reid and T. A. Stewart. Samuel was impressed with the place, appreciative of the hospitality he received from the Reids especially, and the price of the land suited him. He bought 200 acres at fifteen shillings an acre in Otonabee Township, a mile north of the village and adjacent to the Reid settlement in Douro Township.

In May 1826, exactly one year after his arrival in Canada, Samuel started work on his new land. His wife Emma stayed in Darlington with her family, waiting the birth of their baby, while Samuel chopped trees, built himself the usual log shanty first, then started on the design and building of a log house. He made many mistakes both in technique and in timing, because his apprenticeship on the cleared farm at The Front had not given him much practice in the first stages of a bush settlement.

It was brutally hard and lonely labour, even for Samuel, but by the end of the summer he had the location well enough advanced that he could think of sending for his wife to join him. His personal incentive to have a farm of his own was intensified many times over by the thought of his wife and the child they would have.

He was thinking about this and working hard in his lonely clearing, when one of Emma's brothers appeared through the forest. He had walked up to tell Samuel that Emma was dangerously ill.

Leaving his brother-in-law to rest, Samuel left immediately, walked the fifty-five miles through the bush until, at Darlington Mills within five miles of his destination he was forced to stop for rest at at the inn. There he overheard a conversation that told him Emma was dead.

Samuel's wife had died in childbirth before her brother had even reached Samuel's clearing. She left him a son, but her death took away the heart he had put into his pioneering. He stayed around Darlington for a month, then, for want of something better to do, wandered back towards Otonabee, though it was now too late to plant a crop.

When he reached his location, however, his spirit was given a strong boost. A crop was growing vigorously; his neighbour Robert Reid had continued the work that Samuel had been forced to interrupt so precipitately. Samuel was astounded at such generosity; the Reids thought it was the only natural thing to do on the frontier where neighbours helped each other as a matter of course. In addition, it meant that Samuel had to set to work, whether or not he felt like it.

Robert Reid suggested that the young man should live with him, rather than alone in his shanty as he had done before. Samuel accepted, and worked on his farm during the day, returning each evening to the comfort and companionship of the Reid home and family. His infant son was also welcomed into the Reid home and one of the girls devoted most of her time to looking after the child. This extraordinary kindness and Samuel's own youthful resilience soon led to the young man's recovery. The hard labour that his farm required once again excited him and took the edge off his grief.

Thus Samuel spent the fall of 1826 and the long winter of '26/'27, a welcome guest first and then an accepted part of the Reid home, working beside and indulging in highjinks with the young Reid men, and all the time learning about bush settlement from the highly experienced Robert Reid. In fact, this was a more normal family than Samuel had ever experienced.

Before the end of 1827, Samuel was married again – to Robert Reid's eldest daughter, Mary.

It was essential for a bush settler to have a wife; indeed, children had almost reached the status of a negotiable commodity in the settlement, for they signified free labour. But this was not what Samuel was thinking about in his second marriage. He was an affectionate, gregarious and healthy young man, and Mary was an attractive and energetic girl, with as much experience in and enthusiasm for backwoods settlement as her bridegroom. Samuel had first noticed her, through the fog of his grief, because of her demonstration of courage and resourcefulness in setting off through the bush by herself to answer a call for help from a seriously injured settler. That a gentlewoman could also be a competent backwoodswoman excited Samuel's respect and admiration.

Samuel and Mary were an ideal pair, both from upper middle class families, both educated, both with a fearless love of the Canadian frontier. Their marriage was to be a happy and productive partnership for the next quarter of a century, during which thirteen children would be born to them.

In the year following Samuel's marriage into the prominent Reid-Stewart family, there was a great deal of enthusiastic talk going around about a new land development scheme in the western end of the province. The new Canada Company was about to open up lands of exceptionally high fertility at low cost, or so the rumours had it.

The Canada Company[3] was a privately-owned firm backed by British financiers, with headquarters in London. It had taken over large tracts of land throughout the province for the purpose of organizing settlements, selling farms, and thereby making large profits. The colonial government had turned over much of their Crown reserves to the company, expecting to secure enough revenue to meet most of the costs of colonial administration at the same time as they were relieved of the burden of day-to-day details of organizing migration and settlement.

The Company was similar in concept to the Hudson Bay Company, the East India Company, and other semi-public corporations which combined commercial profit-making with a large responsibility for civil administration.

The originator of the specific idea for the Canada Company was John Galt,[4] a British gentleman, better known as a novelist and man of letters than as a financier and colonizer. As Superintendent of the Canada Company, Galt was in charge of the operations in the colony, but responsible to the Board of Directors in England.

Samuel Strickland was always interested in any new development relating to land in the colony. His new and already growing family and his ambitions for it made him impatient with the usual colonial sources of information – the words of casual visitors – and he undertook to find out more about it personally.

In February 1828, he set off for York and an interview with John Galt. When the two men met in Galt's rooms at the Old Steamboat Hotel in York, they were strangers to each other, but there is a likelihood that Galt was familiar with Samuel's sisters who were beginning to make a name for themselves in the British literary world. Moreover, Galt's sons were in residence at Samuel's old school in Norwich, England. As a further coincidence, the Canada Company at the time was suffering from a dearth of skilled pioneers in its management, and Galt was trying to build up his staff in anticipation of the next summer's tide of emigrants from Britain.

Thus, when the young Samuel appeared, presenting a combination of social acceptability, education, and practical experience, Galt saw in him a prospective employee. Samuel's social background and connections both in the colony and in Britain must have been more important than his experience, for he was only twenty-three years old and had been in the colony less than three years. In any case, instead of Samuel questioning Galt about land in the Huron Tract, Galt quizzed Samuel about pioneering. The young man evidently managed to convey something of his own undaunted confidence in his abilities, for Galt offered him a job. With his usual enthusiasm, Samuel accepted immediately.

Samuel Strickland thus became the first "engineer" for the Canada Company, responsible for the practical aspects of settlement in the Guelph area, in charge of the Company labour-rolls, stores, and bridge-building. The matter of his salary was not

81

decided, but left for Galt to determine after a period of probation.

His decision meant that he would have to abandon his settlement in Otonabee, at least for a time. This was offset by the chance to accumulate more money to expand his own holdings, by the opportunity of being in on the beginnings of a new and exciting development, and by Samuel's immediate affinity with and admiration for John Galt. Moreover, if Canada Company lands were as good as they were said to be, Samuel's new official position would give him an ideal opportunity to secure some of this land for himself.

Since work would not begin until spring, Samuel returned to his farm, discussed his new career with Mary and his in-laws, and made arrangements for his family to stay with the Reids until he could prepare a home in the new community.

At York again in April, Samuel met the rest of the Canada Company team. Dr. William Dunlop,[5] the Company's Warden of the Forests, better known as the "Tiger" after his exploits in the War of 1812, was assigned to build a road across the Tract from Guelph to Goderich. Charles Pryor, who had been overseer of the Guelph settlement the year before, was to set up the new settlement in Goderich. Samuel was to be in charge of continuing the development of Guelph.

These three men, Strickland, Dunlop and Pryor, who set off through the woods together to the site of the town of Guelph, were soon to become close friends, drawn together by their common interests in bush life and "wild sports" and by their common devotion to John Galt.

Galt, the creative writer, had a belief in the value of symbols and ceremony, and he saw a special need for such things in the isolation and dreariness of the woods. He had a feeling for history, an awareness of the permanent significance of his pioneers' efforts, and a desire to celebrate appropriately the establishment of what he knew would be an important and prosperous community. Samuel Strickland was among the few colonials who appreciated what Galt felt about this. The average Upper Canadian jeered at this quirk in an otherwise sensible personality. For instance, less than a year earlier, Galt had insisted on a public ceremony when the first tree was cut to mark the site of Guelph; his tiny audience was mystified, and participated only to humour their artist/leader. It was left to Samuel to complete the ceremony; one of the first things he did when he arrived in Guelph was to build a fence to mark the spot as a kind of memorial to Galt and to the beginnings of the settlement.[6]

The only building available for the new engineer was Galt's "coach-house", which Samuel commandeered and converted into an office and store room. Then he was ready for business, undertaking any task that needed to be done, whether or not he knew how to do it. His jobs ranged all the way from designing and supervising the construction of two log bridges, to acting as first aid man to the community, bleeding patients and pulling teeth with the approval of his friend the physician Dr. Dunlop.

His work took him on long trips through the forest. Though he was lost on many occasions, he eventually became highly adept at survival in the bush, and well-known throughout the western end of the province. He made friends with people like Colonel Anthony Van Egmond, a Dutch veteran of the Napoleonic Wars and the first settler in the Huron Tract; and John Brant, the politically astute Indian leader, son of Joseph Brant.

The men of the Canada Company worked hard and played hard. Samuel and his colleagues were rugged, fun-loving men, with much joy of living, a love of the outdoors, carousing and joking, within the limits of gentlemanly propriety. Their amusements were necessarily simple, derived from the environment itself, mainly hunting and fishing excursions and concocting the practical jokes to which Dunlop was especially addicted. Some of the jokes Samuel thought up to amuse Dunlop seem rather cruel in retrospect (like putting a captured porcupine in a barrel of nails and asking everyone who came along to bring out a handful of nails), but the environment and the way of life were cruel.

This combination of hard work and hard play, coupled with their ambitions and their sense of responsibility, made these men leaders in the settlement of the Huron Tract. The uncertain, inexperienced emigrants of different social origins looked to them for guidance.

Their work and their fun became more and more advantageous to themselves and their community and less to the Canada Company. Galt was under attack for paying his favourites too much and the Company too little, squandering funds on charitable support of poor emigrants and ignoring the wishes of the provincial nabobs at York. Thus, when the headquarters in England sent out an accountant to put a rein on Galt, Messrs. Dunlop and Strickland could not resist showing the accountant his place by a series of practical jokes, terrifying the poor clerk in his first foray through the woods. They attacked their leader's enemies and indulged themselves all at the same time in a pyrotechnic display of their woodsman's skills. Their antics did nothing to advance Galt's now uncertain position with the Company.

Samuel had brought his wife and new daughter Maria to Guelph. "My dear little boy had remained at Douro with my wife's sister Eliza, of whom he was so fond that my wife did not like to separate such friends."⁷ This first-born son, from Samuel's brief and tragic first marriage, had been weak from birth, and died at the age of three.

Samuel worked in and around the town of Guelph until 1829, when he was sent on a tour of the Newcastle District, selling land and collecting money for the Company. While there he received word that Galt was resigning. Galt asked Samuel to return to York and to bring with him the money he had collected. At York, Samuel found Dunlop already there and as disturbed about the resignation of the Superintendent.

Galt had seen the Company as something more than land speculation for profit; rather, he saw it as a necessary public service, relieving over-population in Britain and assisting poor emigrants over the first hard stages of bush settlement. In the new lands, by undertaking organized public works such as road and bridge building, he provided employment for new settlers as well as a better community for them to live in. Galt's approach was very paternal, but he felt that the emigrants needed all the help he could give them. He saw the profits to the Company coming not so much from the pockets of the first settlers as from the immediate increase in land values that resulted from his public works and his settlers' efforts.

Galt was not popular with the Upper Canadian government, the Family Compact and the Lieutenant Governor. His visions were not theirs. He looked to the future of the province; they looked to immediate returns, for the revenue from the Company paid their salaries. Further, Galt chose to live in the settlements, not in York, and he spurned the drawing rooms and dining tables of those in power. When these people made representations to the directors of the Canada Company in England, they received a favourable hearing. The directors listened to suggestions that Galt was squandering money and was building some sort of empire for his own aggrandizement without proper deference to the colonial authorities.

By and large, the Commissioners who replaced Galt continued the same methods, though the new administration was far less humane in its dealing with settlers. Further, they became intricately involved in provincial politics to the point where the Company was an active supporter of the Family Compact and protagonist in the Rebellion eight years later.

Samuel Strickland was a loyal admirer of Galt. He was convinced of the validity of Galt's reasoning that inexperienced settlers scattered at random through the bush had less chance of survival than in an organized settlement where roads, supplies and markets were assured.

Only the most loyal supporters of Galt – Dunlop, and Strickland – went to the wharf with him in April 1829, when he left for

England. Sadness, pathos, regret, and above all, confusion were the feelings of the young Samuel; he believed in Galt, but he was also concerned about his own future. His appreciation of the corporate and colonial politics that led to Galt's departure was rather vague, because his information came mainly from Galt himself and because of his own inexperience with such intricacies.

Thus, on the same day he said good-bye to Galt, he could accept with an open mind Dunlop's offer to introduce him to one of the new commissioners who were Galt's replacements. Thomas Mercer Jones and William Allen had been appointed to take over direction of the Company's affairs in Canada.

Samuel thought Mercer Jones was "A fine gentlemanly-looking person";[8] he gave Samuel the impression that he had the same visions as Galt. The young man was prepared to give the same loyalty to the new administration.

Samuel was not a turncoat. Somewhere in the relationship with Galt he had acquired ideals about the development of Canada and it never occurred to the naive young man that the newcomer might not also hold them. It was less a question of loyalty to a man, perhaps, than of loyalty to ideas. Galt was an idealist, a literary man with few practical talents; it was men like Samuel Strickland who took the vague ideas and turned them into reality and having done this, became committed. But Thomas Mercer Jones evidently did not feel so friendly to Strickland, Dunlop and Pryor, who were identified as supporters of the old regime that he had come to reform. In Mercer Jones' intentions, the end was in sight for all of them.

The unsuspecting Samuel returned to Guelph to learn that his services were no longer needed there; he was transferred to Goderich and his pay was reduced. Willingly enough, he set off again, as usual leaving Mary and the family behind until he could make suitable arrangements for housing them. He bought a lot in the new settlement, but it had only a tiny log shanty on it, so that he had to start building another house. He expected it would take until winter before the roads would be fit for Mary to bring up their household belongings and before he would have their new house ready.

But Mary Strickland was not prepared to wait that long. Unwilling to be left behind any longer, she packed up and set off by herself through the woods, without telling Samuel she was coming. It was a difficult trip for her, made more so by the occasional travellers she met who wanted to be helpful. But it was worth it to see the startled delight on Samuel's face when he came home from work one day to find his baby daughter Maria playing on his front steps. Samuel was proud but a little frightened at his wife's initiative; yet in fact Mary Strickland had lived longer in the bush than her husband and was almost as experienced.

The Strickland family stayed on in Goderich, happily enough despite company politics, until a son was born to them.

The increase in his family and the reduction in his salary, along with a general rising discontent over the penurious policies of the Company, led Samuel and Mary to the decision that they would be better off on their own farm. In contrast with the general unhappiness in the Huron Tract population, they were hearing very glowing reports about the new prosperity of their former home of Peterborough.

Samuel cashed in on his small speculations in land in Goderich, and they were on their way. He had bought two town lots for $25 each, improved them at a cost of about $200, and sold them for $500, doubling his investment within two years. Thus, Samuel's original faith in the Tract was confirmed, and his original motive for joining the Canada Company was realized – to accumulate capital. There was little bitterness then in their leave-taking.

On 13 February 1831, Samuel and Mary, with their daughter and son, left Goderich and headed for their old location in Otonabee Township. He was a wiser and more experienced man in every way, but particularly in his broadened knowledge of

Upper Canada, its settlement problems, its politics and its geography. In his own way, he would continue to apply what he had learned for the rest of his life.

Once again as a settler with money in his pocket and faith in his country, Samuel decided to take advantage of the growth of the Peterborough area and re-invest in an unsettled area. He was offered a trade, his 200 acres in Otonabee, close to Peterborough for an equal number of acres further north in Douro, plus $600 in cash. The most compelling reason for his acceptance of this offer was the availability of other lands around the Douro location. In spite of his profit in the Huron Tract, land values had changed so rapidly around Peterborough that he could no longer afford to increase his holdings there. Yet eight miles further north, in Douro, he could buy large amounts of uncleared land with the money he had made out of his Goderich and Otanabee transactions.

Besides, "the situation of my new purchase was more beautiful, the land better, and the fishing and shooting second to none in the Province – a great temptation for a young man, and especially to one fond of wild sports."[9]

Samuel had been writing letters about his plans to his family in Reydon Hall, and in return was informed about his sister Susanna's marriage to Lieutenant John Moodie and their thoughts about migration. He also heard from his sister Jane Margaret in a more direct way; she sent him a tradesman from Suffolk who because of lack of work was being forced to migrate. As was the custom with his class, Samuel had often used the letter of introduction to gain admittance or help wherever he went. The shoe was on the other foot when Jane sent a letter of introduction requesting Samuel to help out Copping; she had no way of knowing just how much trouble this was going to cause Samuel.

Copping knew nothing about farming and less about the bush. Nevertheless, Samuel was agreeable, even delighted. He helped Copping find employment in Peterborough for the summer, unwilling to let him go into the bush by himself, and Samuel would not be ready to go until fall. Then he helped Copping secure 120 acres of land, at fifteen shillings an acre (to be paid over five years with the usual proviso of actual settlement on the land). Copping's location was about two miles beyond Samuel's, in Douro, but further back in the woods.

Copping, Samuel, and a man called Rowlandson who was a friend of Samuel's and was going along to help and learn, left Peterborough for the bush on 20 September. Each carried an axe and eighty pounds of supplies. They had to walk, following the course of the Otonabee River. The first four miles were fairly easy, because a road clearance had been cut out that far. But the remaining trek, only about another eight miles, was so rugged that the novice Copping became hopelessly fatigued and frightened, ready to give up the whole idea. The two younger men encouraged him, and took over his pack for him, until they reached their first stopping point.

This was Samuel's new location, where the Otonabee expands into Lake Katchiwano, the first of the Back Lakes (Kawarthas). The men cleared a bit of land, enough to make room for a shanty. Copping was learning all the while and slowly toughening to the woods environment.

Then, with the aid of a pocket compass and a rough map, they struck off straight into the woods in the general direction of Copping's land. After a good deal of searching, they found a surveyor's marker and from this, with the use of the compass, calculated the direction of the concession lines to identify the limits of Copping's location in the middle of the bush. Again, they cleared a few acres, helped Copping build his shanty, and ensured that he was well started on his new settlement before they left him to return to Samuel's place.

Few settlers had such practical and experienced help to start them off, and Copping made the most of it. Later, Samuel was gratified at his quick success. Copping started blacksmithing on his farm, and within three years he had found enough business in the expanding community to pay for his land, make improvements on it, and sell part of it at a good profit.

Samuel and Rowlandson returned to the Lake and started the hard work of underbrushing twenty-five acres and completing the walls of the house within the two months before the snow would make such operations too difficult.

It was to be a proper house that Samuel intended to build, not an earthen floored shanty. With the nearest sawmill twelve miles away at Peterborough, and no way to bring boards up from there, Samuel had to split logs with an axe and wedges to make the planking which would form the inside walls and flooring of the log structure. Again, he was experimenting; though he had never worked with stone before, he wanted his house to have a fireplace and chimney. Not knowing any other designs, he designed one himself, all the time acutely aware of the problems he might fall into. When he removed the arched plank over which had formed the stonework, the fireplace stood as intended and his satisfaction was complete when he set the fire and found that the chimney drew perfectly.

The fireplace was simply a pleasant interlude in the enormous work that still had to be done. In the meantime, the house was not advanced enough even for Samuel, and he lived in the traditional woodsman's dwelling, an open-ended slab hut that looked like little more than a windbreak and was heated by a campfire placed in front of the open side. Since he was not able to move into his house until New Year's Day, 1832, this hut became very uncomfortable and cold. But Samuel was accustomed to this sort of thing, and was enjoying himself tremendously.

He hired another man, and recruited some neighbours further down the Otonabee to cut out a sleigh road to Peterborough. Before snowfall, he had underbrushed twenty-five acres. When the snow came, he hired two Irishmen from Peterborough to help him log the twenty-five acres.

By spring, he had a house that was livable and a crop planted in his twenty-five cleared acres. But the house, only twenty feet by fourteen, was not big enough, he thought, so he built another room on it. Then, in preparation for the arrival of his wife and family, he made a provisioning trip to Peterborough; to do this, he had to design and build a special type of wagon that could traverse the bush road that was still high with stumps. Even with the help of Rowlandson and one of the Reid men, it still took him more than a day to make the upward trip from Peterborough with his load of supplies.

Mary Strickland had stayed with her family during the winter. She would have been up earlier to join Samuel, but she was delayed by her confinement with her third child, after which Samuel insisted she wait until she was able to walk up, because the trip by wagon was so difficult and dangerous. In the meantime, Samuel made several trips to visit her and tell her enthusiastically about how their new farm was progressing. As the time approached for his family to join him, however, Samuel began to worry that they would not like it:[10]

> My dear Mary had never yet seen my location. All she knew of it had been derived from my description, which I daresay I had drawn in very glowing colours ... My location this time had little attraction to the ardent admirer of natural beauties; for as yet I had not opened my clearing to the lake ... the recently burnt fallow with its blackened stumps and charred rampikes did not contribute much ... Whatever might have been her thoughts, she wisely kept them to herself; she praised everything I had done, and prepared at once to assist me in making the inside of our house as comfortable as possible.

Samuel's diffidence was natural; he wanted the equivalent of a palace for his family, and despite all the special little touches he had put into it with such loving care, the grimness of the early settlement was still only too obvious. But Mary Strickland was knowledgeable enough to realize the tremendous amount that Samuel had achieved since the previous fall. She had shown many times that she was not a novice to the bush. Besides, Samuel had left something for her to do.

While Mary went to work on the inside of the house, Samuel went on with underbrushing, chopping, burning, adding to and improving the house, and planting twenty acres of fall wheat. It was gruelling work, undertaken with the driving energy inspired by their companionship and by the rewards associated with creating a self-sufficient home out of the wilderness.

This was the scene when Mary's brother William Reid came in to the Strickland clearing, relaying a message from Mrs. McFadden of the Peterborough inn, telling Samuel that his sister and her husband had arrived. It had been the evening before that Catharine and Thomas Traill appeared at the inn, wet, cold and hungry, and were given accommodation in the crowded inn only because Catharine was Samuel's sister. As early as possible the next morning, Mrs. McFadden had sent a messenger as far as the Reids, and William Reid carried it the rest of the way, reaching the Strickland location late in the evening.

Samuel was surprised; he had not known that Catharine had married nor that she and her husband were coming to join him.

His excitement and anxiety to see her were so keen that he risked his life and that of his brother-in-law by launching a canoe into the rapids of the Otonabee and paddling ten miles in the dark, a feat that had never been attempted before by anyone. With the help of the rushing Otonabee, he and William made the trip in record time, reaching Peterborough the same night. Catharine of course was in bed by the time they got there, but she heard the men clumping about downstairs and recognized her brother's voice in the confusion. Equally excited, she hurriedly dressed, roused Thomas, and went down to greet her young brother whom she had not seen in seven years.

Though Catharine could not yet appreciate Samuel's achievement in successfully navigating the Otonabee after dark, she did appreciate the extent that he had matured in the years filled with personal tragedy, adventure, and pioneering labour. They talked about personal and family things that night, Samuel telling about his children, and Catharine giving all the news from Reydon Hall.

The next day, the conversation turned to plans for the Traill's future. Samuel of course made most of the decisions and all of the arrangements, and the Traills were entirely willing to leave things in his capable hands. The first problem was to get Catharine comfortably settled; she was too weak yet from cholera to walk up to his place through the bush. He made arrangements for her to say at Auburn, just north of Peterborough, with his friends the T. A. Stewarts.

T. A. Stewart was perhaps the most prominent member of Peterborough society, as Justice of the Peace, Member of the Legislative Council of Upper Canada, and, with his brother-in-law Robert Reid, the first settler in the district. His wife, Frances Stewart, was a successful lady of letters, and she and Catharine formed a life-long friendship during Catharine's brief visit.

In the meantime, Samuel took Thomas Traill off with him to inspect available land near Samuel's location and to finalize the legalities of the new Traill farm, returning to Peterborough for the next Government land sale.

The imminent prospect of having his sister Catharine visit his place was giving Samuel some qualms. He had matured both physically and mentally into a strong man, fearless, confident, competent, well-respected by his colleagues, and successful in coping with the most difficult problems his chosen environment could set for him. But this environment was entirely different from that of his home, and his success was about to be tested in the most difficult of all tests, the scrutiny of his elder sister. He thought back to the old days of Reydon Hall and wondered if his achievements would appear very real in contrast. His wife Mary had been able to appreciate Samuel's efforts because she understood what was involved, but Catharine was arriving directly from the comfort of England, albeit with many adventures and a taste of hardship on the way. And there were all those letters Samuel had written home, describing the charms of the wilderness and his own great success, in perhaps too favourable terms.

The community around the spot where the Upper Otonabee joins the Back Lakes was variously known as Nelson's, Herriott's Falls, Selby, North Douro, and finally Lakefield. It was Herriott's Falls when Catharine and Thomas Traill arrived in 1832, and the Strickland settlement was the only one in the immediate neighbourhood.

The population of the whole Douro Township at the time was 126 people, 3 horses, 82 oxen, 105 cows, and 44 "other horned cattle".[11]

On the other side of the river, the Smith Township side, there was apparently more settlement, and the road ran up that way from Peterborough, requiring people to ford the river to reach Douro. Samuel, with the help of his neighbours, would build a bridge a year or so later, but in 1832 the crossing was by canoe.

Late in September, Catharine and Thomas Traill set off on the Smithtown road, in a wagon drawn by two horses and driven by a man from Peterborough who, as it turned out was not too clear about the route. The wagon carried not only the Traills' possessions but also bags of flour, salt pork and other parcels destined for the clearings of the scattered settlers along the way.

The trip was marked by mud holes, fallen trees and stumps, which had to be avoided or crossed over by the horses and wagon, not always successfully. The sides and floorboards kept falling off, along with many of the provisions. Once, the driver himself was jolted out as they bump-bumped over the stones, stumps and corduroy.

Catharine and Thomas managed to keep their seats through all this but not their equanimity. The reasoning behind Samuel's preference for walking the distance became clear. Each successive stage of Catharine's journey from England seemed worse than the one before. On this last stretch, the travellers were much too busy just hanging on to the wagon and to their courage to continue their happy speculations about their new home.

Catharine was bone-weary and hungry as the dark forest turned darker to tell her it was evening, and they had still not reached their destination. The embarrassed driver then admitted that he did not know where they were, and must have missed the road . . . a difficult thing to do since there was only one road. He stopped the team and walked on ahead, looking for the lake, but came back none the wiser. With great difficulty in the middle of the forest, he turned the wagon around and headed back, unwilling to go any further through what looked like nothing but untracked swamp.

They were relieved when they met a young boy on the trail, but he told them they had been right all the time and had been within a short distance of their destination. The driver, impatient and more than a little flustered, turned around again, drove them straight through the swamp to the edge of the lake, threw off their belongings, and disappeared, anxious to be home since it was well after dark by this time.

Samuel was supposed to meet them there and take them across the river, but there was no sign of him. Catharine sat down on a moss-covered rock, with her household possessions scattered around her, while Thomas tramped along the shore shouting. The only reply was the sound of the rapids.

They could not go back the way they had come, for they knew they would be lost before they covered the two miles back to the last settlement. So, leaving Catharine seated upon her rock, Thomas went off again through the woods by the lakeshore. He had been to Samuel's place earlier, and though it was dark, he had a fairly good idea of its general direction. Eventually, he was rewarded by the sight of a dim light showing, on the other side of the water. This time, the strength of his shouts in the quiet night raised a response. Samuel, it seems, had waited for them for hours before deciding that they were not coming that day and had gone to bed.

Meanwhile, Catharine was strangely not frightened. The calm, starlit night, the hypnotic sound of the water, and the certainty that her journey was near an end, made her vigil calm and rather pleasant, if a little melancholy. "At last my reverie was broken by the light plash of a paddle, and a bright line of light showed a canoe dancing over the lake: in a few minutes a well-known and friendly voice greeted me as the little bark was moored among the cedars at my feet."[12]

Quickly, Catharine was taken across the water to Samuel's home and introduced to Mary Strickland. Then, though it was late at night, the excitement was keen, and Samuel's three children were taken out of their cribs to be shown off to their aunt.

> A bright fire blazed on the hearth of the loghouse ... Our welcome was given with that unaffected cordiality that is so grateful to the heart: it was as sincere as it was kind. All means were adopted to soften the roughness of our accommodation, which, if it lacked that elegance and convenience to which we had been accustomed in England, was not devoid of rustic comfort; at all events, it was such as many settlers of the first respectability have been glad to content themselves with, and many have not been half so well lodged as we now are.[13]

Thus wrote Catharine to her mother. And thus were Samuel's efforts over the past year, the culmination of his seven years' experience in Upper Canada, rewarded in an unexpected way, by the approval of his sister who had known no other home than their stately mansion in England.

Catharine and Samuel were probably the most cheerful and warmhearted of the Strickland family. They were delighted with each other, with their new-found in-laws, and with the idea of pioneering the Douro woods together. Neither of them could ever dwell long on troubles or hardship, and they were impatient with those who did. The important thing for them was to get on with it, hopefully, energetically, and with a will.

CHAPTER FIVE

Settlement in Douro

Thomas Traill had drawn his military grant in upper Douro Township, near Samuel Strickland's location, and had purchased another lot which joined his property to Samuel's. Three acres were cleared and a rough workmen's shanty built on the part he bought. According to Catharine, the five and a half dollars an acre which he paid was a high price for remote land; however, it was a good location with water frontage. Official reports on land values show the average paid for clergy reserves was thirteen shillings, three-and-three quarter pence, Halifax currency. Converting the dollars to shillings, Thomas paid twenty-seven shillings, sixpence per acre, more than double the average for clergy reserves and three times the average for Crown lands. But averages had little significance because of the extreme variation in conditions which affected values throughout the Province. A better comparison is Samuel's friend Copping who, a year earlier, had paid fifteen shillings per acre in Douro Township for uncleared, inaccessible land with no waterfront. In this context, the Traills' purchase was not unreasonable.

House-building, underbrushing, chopping and burning started immediately on the Traill location. A few workmen were hired from time to time to speed the development.

In the meantime, Catharine and Thomas lived with the Stricklands, where they were gently introduced to the difficulties and privations of an isolated settlement.

Supplies had to be brought up from Peterborough by wagon

over the poor roads. Sometimes only half the order arrived intact:
"... behold rice, sugar, currants, pepper, mustard all jumbled
into one mess. What think you of a rice-pudding seasoned
plentifully with pepper, mustard, and maybe, a little rappee
(snuff) or princes's mixture (tobacco) added by way of sauce?"
Provisions were often scarce, but Samuel and his family had lived
through greater privation long before this.

Catharine described one good-humoured family dinner
scene:[1]

Once our supply of tea was exhausted ... In this dilemma
milk would have been an excellent substitute, or coffee, if we
had possessed it; but we agreed to try a Yankee tea – hemlock
sprigs boiled. This proved, to my taste, a vile decoction ...
Samuel laughed at our wry faces, declaring the potation was
excellent; and he set us all an example by drinking six cups of
this truly sylvan beverage. His eloquence failed in gaining a
single convert ... To his assurance that to its other good quali-
ties it united medicinal virtues, we replied that, like all other
physic, it was very unpalatable.

But Samuel won the exchange by this didactic argument:[2]

"After all," said Samuel, with a thoughtful air, "the blessings
and the evils of this life owe their chief effect to the force of
contrast ... We should not appreciate the comforts we enjoy
half so much did we not occasionally feel the want of
them ..."

Catharine and Thomas had expected some sort of hardship,
and these few inconveniences were cheerfully accepted. They had
been over the bog that was called the road to Peterborough and
could understand the reasons for occasional shortages of supplies.
And they could see that the Strickland family were well
accustomed to it all.

Catharine was more interested in the rewards of the back-woods than in its privations. She loved the autumn, and quickly adopted "fall" as the Canadian name for it. With Samuel's children, she roamed the woods near the clearing, looking for and finding varieties of flowers that she had never seen before, identifying them and collecting specimens. This was her favourite hobby, and one that she could indulge to her heart's content, at the same time as it brought her closer in understanding to her new home. She was cautious at first, however, taking specimens of strange berries, herbs and mushrooms back to Samuel for identification before she would venture to experiment in cooking with them.[3]

At the end of October they held a bee for raising the walls of the Traill's new house. This would have been done sooner, but the yoke of oxen they had purchased to pull the logs up to the site had wandered off into the bush for several weeks. This was a fairly common occurrence before settlers had cleared enough land to justify building fences, before there were any pastures so that animals had to be allowed to graze in the woods near the clearing.

The Traill's first bee was a great success, both socially and productively. Sixteen neighbours had been invited and all accepted. A "picnic" was laid out for them in the loggers' shanty: whiskey, huge joints of salt pork, a peck of potatoes, bread, and rice pudding. Thomas reported to Catharine that evening that though there was a great difference in origin among those at the bee they all worked well together, and perhaps more important, the feast laid on for them was more than adequate.

The next day, Catharine eagerly walked over from Samuel's place to inspect her new dwelling:[4]

> ... But I was sorely puzzled, as it presented little appearance of a house. It was merely an oblong square of logs raised one above the other, with open spaces between every row of logs. The spaces for the door and windows were not then sawn out,

and the rafters were not up . . . I returned home a little disappointed, and wondering that my husband should be so well pleased with the progress that had been made.

Evidently Catharine still had some lingering belief in the rumours circulated in England to the effect that a house could be built in a day in Canada. Their house progressed fairly quickly despite many difficulties: a man had to be hired to saw logs by hand to make the floor boards because there was still no sawmill in the little community; the plaster intended to fill the chinks between the logs of the walls froze solid during an early frost; and Thomas had to learn to be a glazier to install glass in the windows. But with Samuel's ever-willing help, the Traills were able to move into their new home on 11 December, three months in all since they arrived in the bush. In the tradition of English settlers, they named the place "Lake House".

The house was not entirely finished, but a good portion of the ground floor was habitable; a small sitting room with closet, a kitchen, pantry, and a bedroom. There was space on the second floor for three more bedrooms. Eventually, when boards became easier to get, they would add a frame front and a verandah, another parlour, hall and bedroom.

Their sitting room had windows and a glass door overlooking the lake. It was furnished with a Franklin stove with brass gallery and fender, a sofa, Canadian painted chairs and a stained pine table, green and white muslin curtains, and an Indian mat. One side of the room was filled with their books, and large maps and prints hung on the rough walls.

This was an unusual level of comfort for the first home of new settlers, and the Traills were justifiably proud of it. Catharine's detailed, even loving description in her letters home belie the modesty of her concluding statement; 'We do not, however, lack comfort in our humble home, and though it is not exactly such as we could wish, it is as good as, under existing circumstances, we could expect to obtain."[5] Perhaps she was concerned that the inhabitants of Reydon Hall expected her to be living in a mansion four months after her arrival in the colony.

They had achieved a great deal in a very short time. Thomas must have spent much more money hiring help than Catharine admits. He was not skilled in pioneer housebuilding, and it is doubtful that Samuel could have had much time to spare in helping them on the actual work of the house since he was developing his own farm.

They spent the winter of 1832/33 exploring the lakes and woods, planning for the spring, experimenting with recipes for cooking cranberries, and working on the inside of the house.

Catharine was charmed with all new experiences, such as the time Samuel took her for an unexpected ride on a sleigh. She and Thomas had walked out on the ice of the lake for about three-quarters of a mile:[6]

> We were overtaken on our return by Samuel with a hand-sleigh, which is a sort of barrow, such as porters use, without sides, and instead of a wheel, is fixed on wooden runners, which you can drag over the ice and snow with the greatest ease, if ever so heavily laden. Samuel insisted that he would draw me home over the ice like a Lapland lady on a sledge. I was soon seated in state, and in another minute felt myself impelled forward with a velocity that nearly took away my breath. By the time we had reached the shore I was in a glow from head to foot.

Except for three days in the early part of March when there was a particularly severe cold snap and the temperature inside their house dropped to twenty-five degrees, it was a good season and a happy one. Because there was little work that could yet be done on the farm, they occupied themselves with exploration of the forest and the border of the Lake. Catharine wrote long letters home, documenting the progress of their house, the trees, flowers and animals she found, and her own feelings about her new home.

She was obviously loving the place, but already was finding it difficult to explain why, and her letters often sounded argumentative and apologetic, assuming that the people in Reydon would have a difficult time to understand it all. She dwelt on the comforts and rewards of the bush, to offset the notion of privation and hardship that the bush was expected to represent. But like many other pioneer observers of Upper Canada, she had to apologize for the lack of history. Her elder sisters were now preoccupied with the study of British history, but the assumption was widely held that there simply was not enough history of that sort to study in Upper Canada.

In the early spring, Catharine and Thomas again consulted Samuel, this time for details on how to make maple syrup and maple sugar. Thomas and his hired man tapped the trees, and built a fire out in the open, suspending an iron kettle over it to boil the sap down to syrup. Catharine stood by in the kitchen to receive the syrup and boil it still further to sugar. They could not make very much because they did not have enough kettles, but the results were high in quality, and they were pleased with their achievement.

(Down in Hamilton Township, Susanna was also trying her hand at sugar-making with dismal results. Her adviser on the art was the hired man, John Monaghan, who had little idea of how to go about it. After much labour, the stuff was all thrown out.)

The summer of 1833 was a very busy time in Douro. A timber bridge was built across the Otonabee, for easier access to Peterborough on the Smithtown road. Several new settlers arrived, mostly half-pay army and navy officers from Britain, and they too held bees. A band of Indian hunters pitched camp in the neighbourhood and a brisk trade developed between them and the English settlers. In short, though the population was still very small and thinly scattered, people moved around a good deal, trading and helping each other, and making the bush seem less deserted.

Samuel Strickland was in the centre of all this activity. Not content with developing his own farm and helping his sister and brother-in-law, he was also developing the community around him, building a much-needed sawmill in partnership with Robert Reid, and laying out a townsite on his property for the new village of Lakefield.

Douro was no longer the frontier of that part of the bush; there were several settlements of English gentry scattered all along the Back Lakes, and these people regularly stopped by at Lakefield on their way to and from Peterborough. One of these, Thomas Need from Pigeon Lake in Verulam Township, came past in July 1833 and reported his impressions with respect and obvious envy:[7]

> On my return, I visited some recent settlers in Douro township, and also an enterprising young man who was building an extensive sawmill, and laying out the ground plan of a village, which he hoped soon to see erected and peopled on his property. The site was well chosen, and very beautiful, but not more so than my own; and I could not help dreaming, that in a few years my own lonely hut might be surrounded with a thriving village, and the now idle waters of the cascade be diverted to turn a mill. It was a dream perhaps, but Canada is the land of dreams, and what seems a "baseless vision" one day, is a reality the next.

This was the time of dreams in the Peterborough area, the Otonabee and the Back Lakes. Different areas had different times of popularity, based on the general expectation of their prospects. The first group of settlers into a district usually attracted a few more, and then a flood, partly based on the degree to which land values could fluctuate wildly in a few months (ideally, the settler wanted an area that was just beginning to develop, where the price was still cheap but expected to rise immediately), partly on the need to have at least a few neighbours to help at bees and to encourage the development of sawmills and grist mills. The

Stewarts and Reids had waited a long time for their hopes of a community in the upper part of the Newcastle District. Their dreams had been realized by the time Samuel Strickland arrived; it was time now to dream about the development of North Douro and the Back Lakes. Settlement was increasing all the time, land values were rising, prospects were good – but all was dependent on the expectation that the Government would make the Trent/Otonabee/Back Lakes water system navigable by steamers. While that hope held firm, the future was bright for those who wanted to build homes and communities and for those who simply wanted to make a profit by cashing in on rising land values.

On the Traill farm, the chopping continued and a logging bee was held. The neighbours came with their oxen and piled up the logs from the chopping for Thomas and his hired man to burn. Oats, corn, pumpkins, potatoes and turnips were then planted in the cleared space among the stumps. The Traill location was beginning to look more like a proper farm.

Their farm implements were simple and few: two reaping hooks, several axes, a spade, a couple of hoes, and "a queer sort of harrow that is made in the shape of a triangle for the better passing between the stumps." Ploughs were not used at this stage of clearing and would not be needed until the stumps decayed enough to be removed and the soil required more intensive cultivation. The soil was so fertile from its recent forest cover and natural mulch that the settler needed only to scratch the earth lightly and scatter the seed.

The Traills' original livestock, which consisted only of two oxen, could now be increased by "two cows, two calves, three small pigs, ten hens, and three ducks." This was a small flock yet, but a precious one, symbolizing progress and making the little clearing seem less deserted.

Their property was also increased. Catharine received a legacy that summer from an uncle in England (as Susanna also had done), and the Traills with their firm faith in the future of their community reinvested it in an adjoining lot of land, though they had not yet been able to clear all their original holdings.

The Traills were justifiably satisfied with the progress of their farm, but this was nothing compared to the great excitement that came with the birth of their first child in the early summer.

They called their son James, or "Jamie", and in Catharine's words, he was "the pride and delight of his foolish mother's heart. His father, who loves him as much as I do myself, often laughs at my fondness, and asks if I do not think him the ninth wonder of the world."[8] Catharine had always loved children and been fascinated by them, in that special way that only a few "born mothers" have; in England she had devoted most of her time to writing stories for their special benefit. And her love for children spilled over into affection and concern for all forms of weak and wild creatures. For all settlers, including the Traills, the Stricklands, and the Moodies, the birth of a child made clear the real reason why they were there and gave a driving force to their labours.

Despite her doting on her first-born, Catharine was still a farmer's wife and had much to do. She cultivated a garden, studied and developed her skill in making "hop-rising" (a form of yeast), bread, butter, porridge from Indian corn, and preserves. She salted away meat and fish; she spun wool, dyed yarn, knitted, and sewed. And she looked after their small flock of poultry. It was very hard work, especially at first while she was still learning the best way to do these things, with Mary Strickland's help.

And somehow, between looking after her baby and attending to the household chores, she found time to continue her study of wildlife, observing and attempting to identify new species of flowers, butterflies, birds and small animals, and collecting specimens where possible to send back to her sisters in England and to a professor at Edinburgh University (a connection of Thomas'). She was especially concerned now that these things should not go unnoticed in the woods; they were the natural inheritance of her own new Canadian, Jamie. And also for

Jamie's sake, she was concerned that the gruelling work of the settlement should not be allowed to push aside their heritage of culture and education.

On at least one occasion, however, her love of nature came into conflict with her duties as a housewife. As she was gathering ripe sunflower seeds to use as chicken-feed in the coming winter, she discovered two red squirrels with similar notions. Catharine's presence around the bed of wild sunflowers did not frighten nor discourage them from their business. The squirrels left only when they had a full load. Catharine quickly cut all the other flowers and took them back to her garden where she left them in a basket in the sun. Sitting on her front step, Catharine had turned to shelling beans when she was interrupted by the squirrels who had followed her back and were scolding her about the basket of sunflowers.

In all honesty, Catharine knew they had a right to scold; they had been willing to share their favourite harvest with the interloper, but Catharine had taken it all. Catharine did not help them, but on the other hand, she did not hinder them, as they laboured until they had carried off the total contents of the basket. Catharine had to find something else for her chickens to eat. Her only consolation came in the spring when she saw them again – a healthy family of fat squirrels.

In short, Catharine was enjoying herself tremendously in the backwoods, calm, content, and gentle. Her kind of gentleness was uncommon in the colony where brutal hardship often created brutality in the settlers. But oddly, the other settlers respected her for it, when they well might have laughed. Yet Catharine was not too sentimental to have any compunction about catching and stuffing specimens of squirrels and birds for the edification of the nature-study enthusiasts among her old friends in England.

In addition to her housewifely duties and biology studies, Catharine took an active interest in affairs of the farm, eagerly discussing with Thomas all his plans and the technicalities that he was working hard to learn. She sent home detailed descriptions and evaluations of various techniques for raising cattle in the colony, planting and cultivating corn, wheat, pumpkins, etc., methods of transporting and marketing farm produce, the diseases of cattle and corn and all the other peculiarities of a backwoods settlement that could not possibly be lonely because it was too busy.

Besides, the Traills were not all by themselves in their clearing. During the summer, Thomas had at least two hired men, and Catharine, after trying a young Irish girl, hired an older girl, the daughter of a Wiltshire immigrant, who was "neat and clever, and respectful and industrious". After Jamie arrived, she also had a nursemaid for a short while.

The Traills did not seem to have as much difficulty with their servants as did other upper class immigrants, especially the Moodies. Perhaps they paid them more, or gave them better accommodation. On the other hand, it may have been simply that the worker-immigrants who came directly into the Back Townships were less tainted with the Yankee ways of egalitarianism – less, certainly, than those at the "Front" where the Moodies were having such trouble. Douro Township in fact had experienced something like a complete transplant of the social structure of the old country which frontier conditions were not yet breaking down.

But complaints from others were so general that Catharine found it necessary to report: [9]

> Our servants are as respectable, or nearly so, as those at home; nor are they admitted to our tables, or placed on an equality with us, excepting at "bees", and such kinds of public meetings; when they usually conduct themselves with a propriety that would afford an example to some that call themselves gentlemen, viz., young men who voluntarily throw aside those restraints that society expects from persons filling a respectable situation.

The social attitudes and class structure of England were still clearly there in the Douro woods, felt no less strongly by the Traills and Stricklands than by the Moodies. The difference seemed to be that the Moodies in Hamilton township were the only ones there who still worried about such things.

There was also another difference which may have had as much or more to do with it. The Traills had no compunctions about doing manual tasks which in England would have been done only by servants. Nor did they feel any loss of status by so doing.[10]

> ... as a British officer must needs be a gentleman and his wife a lady, perhaps we repose quietly in that incontestable proof of our gentility, and can afford to be useful without injuring it.

Regardless of origin, everyone in Douro worked at whatever he could do; if the settler was able to hire help, the enormous task went more quickly. But the function of the servant was to help, not to take over all the labour, nor to enhance the prestige of the master. The Traills understood this, and their settlement developed steadily, with their own labour and with the help of their servants.

When winter came, there was more time for friendships and social activities. For all pioneers, including the Traills, winter was the time for travelling and meeting neighbours on a more relaxed basis than the summertime bee, when the work was less pressing and the snow-covered roads made moving about so much easier.

Catharine continued her friendship with Mary Strickland's aunt, Mrs. T. A. Stewart, through their mutual interest in writing and botany. Mrs. Stewart had the only botanical textbook in the backwoods, Frederick Pursh's *North American Flora*. Catharine borrowed it to satisfy her growing desire to know more about the forests around her, but she had to call upon Thomas as the classical scholar to translate it for her since it was mostly in Latin.[11]

Thomas Traill, on his part, became active in Peterborough community activities; he helped with the church building fund, and saw the cornerstone of St. John's Church laid, two years later.[12]

Similarly, visits were exchanged with the Mississauga Indian family encamped nearby. The Stricklands and Traills had become acquainted with the Indians during the summer, mainly through trading. Catharine had equipped her house with decorative and useful Indian-made baskets and trays, and had traded with them for moccasins, fish, duck and meat.

Samuel Strickland was a special favourite with the Indians. He respected their skills and had learned much from them about hunting and fishing. Samuel could use the techniques of the Indian hunter or the British hunter with equal ease. In the Huron Tract he had been interested in the Indian tribal structure and, through John Brant and other Indian leaders there, had learned something about it. It was this that earned him his nickname in Douro. When Samuel discussed the relationship of the Mississaugas of Douro with the Chippewas of The Tract, the Indians were pleased and re-named Samuel "Chippewa", a name which almost everyone in Douro then started to call him.

The wars between Indians and settlers had long since gone, if they had ever existed in this part of the country. They lived together amicably and with mutual respect in Douro Township. The little band near Lakefield was Christian, and the younger Indians were fluent in English and had learned to read and write. Yet their education and close contact with settlers had not changed their traditional way of life; they still hunted with bows and arrows, gathered wild rice, fished with spears, and lived in camps of birchbark wigwams.

The chief of the local band was Peter Nogun; he, his wife and eldest son were well known to the Traills and Stricklands. Catharine had asked Mrs. Nogun to tea, and been charmed by the Indian woman's decorum. That winter, Catharine asked Samuel if he would arrange a return visit. The Indians were more than willing, and the invitation was extended not only to the Traills and Stricklands but also to several of the Reid family who were visiting Samuel at the time.

It was, therefore, a large and happy party in the Noguns' cosy birch wigwam. Peter Nogun gave Samuel the seat of honour beside him and Catharine shared Mrs. Nogun's blanket. At Catharine's request, the chief led his family in singing hymns in their own language. Then the guests were instructed in Indian games and were laughed at good-humouredly for their lack of adroitness.

Catharine was particularly interested in the housekeeping arrangements, and Mrs. Nogun gave her a tour of her home. Among other things, the Indian hostess demonstrated her "cupboard" arrangements, pouches formed by the double walls of the wigwam in which were kept, in orderly fashion, all their food supplies, clothing, sewing and other equipment. The mutual respect and interest established in this and similar meetings was a foundation for lasting friendship.

Thus, in a little over a year, Catharine and Thomas Traill were well established and acclimatized. Their farm, though not very productive yet, was making them more self-sufficient. Their house was almost complete and was comfortably furnished. The community around them was growing rapidly and a small village was starting – with a sawmill, grist mill and general store. The logging industry around the Back Lakes was developing and providing much-needed employment for the poorer settlers who required a source of ready cash to develop their lands. The Traills and Stricklands were an important part of this new community; they gave to it every bit as much as they gained from it.

In the late autumn of 1833, John Moodie visited the Douro settlement, and the Traills and Stricklands learned that all was not well with the family in Hamilton Township. His difficulties with the farm property, with the neighbours, and with the share-farming arrangement contrasted sadly with the peace and promise of the Lakefield community.

When John made his intentions clear, Samuel and Thomas helped him buy a lot next to the Traills and to hire men to start the clearing and housebuilding operations immediately. For the early part of the winter, the Traills and Stricklands watched over these operations, and in February 1834 the Moodie family arrived.

They stayed with Catharine and Thomas Traill for a week. Because of a temporary shortage of boards the Moodie house was not yet ready for them. It must have been rather crowded in the Traills' log house, with John and Susanna, their daughters Katie and Addie, their servant Mary Tate, along with Catharine, Thomas and Jamie Traill, the Traill servants, and Moodie's man John Monaghan.

Though the welcome was warm, Susanna's spirits were not immediately cheered by the challenge of carving out a new life in the backwoods. She had hated much about her life at the Front, but she had last-minute regrets about leaving it. There had been some pleasant moments there, and perhaps after all they might have been able to make a good life if they had stuck it out a little longer. Her journey into the forest did little to change her mind. She had been knocked unconscious by a blow from a horse's head; she had been terrified by the crossing of a log bridge over the Otonabee rapids (the bridge that Samuel had worked so hard to build); and most of her crockery had been broken when the wagon was pulled over a tree fallen across the road just outside Samuel's place.

Yet the trip might have been a great deal worse. The day after the Moodies' arrival there was a sudden thaw, soaking everything and turning the ground to slush and mud. Their wagons would have been hopelessly mired in the bush had the thaw begun a day earlier. As it was, the thaw only served to discourage Susanna from trekking through the bush to see her new house. Nor was she was very impressed by the Traill home:[13]

The prospect from the windows of my sister's log hut was not very prepossessing . . . The clearing round the house was very small, and only just reclaimed from the wilderness, and the greater part of it was covered with piles of brushwood to be burnt the first dry days of spring. The charred and blackened stumps on the few acres that had been cleared during the preceding year were everything but picturesque; and I concluded, as I turned, disgusted, from the prospect before me, that there was very little beauty to be found in the backwoods.

One can hope that Susanna had the sensitivity not to express such thoughts to Catharine. The Traills did not live in a "hut"; their log house was a substantial one in contrast with the usual first home of settlers. And Catharine had been able to find a great deal of beauty in the woods, though in fairness even she would have to admit that the black stumps and piles of wet logs held little attraction.

During the next few days, the men went out early to work on their lots and Catharine and Susanna remained inside with the children. They had much to talk about, and undoubtedly Susanna expressed all her unhappiness and disappointment over her dismal experiences in Hamilton Township, the miserable shanty which had been their first home, the unscrupulous merchant who had taken advantage of them in their land purchases, the loss of Moodie's commission and capital in the steam-boat stock, and their desperate need to establish some sort of income as quickly as possible – all this along with her unwillingness to move to the backwoods.

Catharine, on her part, must have tried to convey something of her hope and affection for her new land, by telling Susanna about the developments in Douro, about their respectable naval and military community, about their friends the Indians and the Indian handicraft that decorated her home, and about the rewards of nature study in the wilderness.

But their conversation must also have dropped into nostalgic reminiscences of their home and family in England, talk about their childhood escapades at Reydon, and talk about the news of Agnes and Elizabeth and their sisters' new interest in social and literary pursuits in England.

Eventually, the drizzling thaw cleared up, and Catharine decided to dispel the gloom by insisting on taking Susanna through the woods to see her new home. Susanna was frightened at the idea of walking through "the vast forest" between the two locations, with only a woman as a guide. But, as she said, she kept her fears to herself, lest she be laughed at. Yet her fears were natural; she could not see and did not know, that the opaque forest at the edge of the clearing hid the shortness of the distance between the two clearings.

The walk was long enough, however, for Catharine to make it into something of a guided tour of the forest. Unintentionally, Catharine was being superior both in pioneering and in adaptability. She wore moccasins, specially made and decorated for her with dyed porcupine quills and ribbon by Mrs. Peter Nogun.[14] It was icy underfoot after the thaw and quick freeze, and the moccasins proved their worth, as Susanna with conventional footwear "stumbled at every step".

But Catharine's confidence and kindness worked their intended therapy. In Susanna's words:[15]

> . . . I greatly enjoyed my first walk in the woods. Naturally of a cheerful, hopeful disposition, my sister was enthusiastic in her admiration of the woods. She drew such a lively picture of the charms of a summer residence in the forest, that I began to feel greatly interested in her descriptions, and to rejoice that we, too, were to be her near neighbours and dwellers in the woods; and this circumstance not a little reconciled me to the change.

When she was a child, Susanna had been easily led by her sister's optimism and enthusiasm, and it was natural for her to fall back into this habit. Susanna had as much, or more, imagination

H

as Catharine, perhaps too much – so that she too often visualized the horrible things that might happen. But she was still capable of responding to Catharine's dreams of how things might be. Moreover, she wanted to believe.[16]

When we reached the top of the ridge that overlooked our cot, my sister stopped, and pointed out a log-house among the trees. "There, Susan," she said, "is your house. When that black cedar swamp is cleared away, that now hides the lake from us, you will have a very pretty view." My conversation with her had quite altered the aspect of the country, and pre-disposed me to view things in the most favourable light.

In the clearing, the women could see the men at work piling underbrush – Moodie and Monaghan, a neighbour named Morgan, and one of the ubiquitous Reid men. Smoke was coming from the chimney of the little house, because Susanna's servant, Mary Tate, had come over with the men that morning and built a cheerful fire in the kitchen stove. When Catharine and Susanna arrived, she was busily scrubbing the parlour.

Susanna was pleased. The Moodie house was much smaller than either Catharine's or Samuel's, which Susanna had not been impressed by, but thanks to Catharine's interpretation, her fear of the woods was gone; her composure was recovered:[17]

The house was made of cedar logs, and presented a superior air of comfort to most dwellings of the same kind. The dimensions were thirty-six feet in length by thirty-two feet in breadth, which gave us a nice parlour, a kitchen, and two small bedrooms, which were divided by plank partitions ... Such as it was, it was a palace when compared to Old Satan's log hut, or the miserable cabin we had wintered in during the severe winter of 1833, and I regarded it with complacency as my future home.

A few days later, the Moodies moved into their new home. John and Monaghan went on with the chopping, of course, but this was a period of calm. Because their farm was so little advanced, the hardest toil had not yet started, and Susanna, as Catharine before her had done, took advantage of the respite to get acquainted with the setting.

John bought a canoe from the Indians, fixed a keel and sail for it, and as soon as the ice went out, he and Susanna explored the lakes.

The very isolation of the place spoke in its favour for John and Susanna, a welcome change from their former neighbours. They settled in and quickly learned to enjoy "the august grandeur of the vast forest that hemmed us in on every side and shut us out from the rest of the world."[18]

Thus, the Strickland family was reunited, at least a good part of it, Catharine, Susanna and Samuel, with their families, side by side on the shores of Lake Katchiwano, helping each other in their struggle against the forest, entertaining each other at family dinners and bees, their children playing together, and all combining their efforts to make something out of their new community. Each little clearing was a world of its own, because each branch of the family had to work out its own survival, and each was at a different stage of development. But the nearness of the others brought hope and security to all.

CHAPTER SIX

Scenes and Adventures
in the Backwoods

For the next four years, the Stricklands, Traills and Moodies were totally immersed in their rather one-sided battle with the bush. It was indeed a battle, one which would test the mettle of each of them; their aims and ambitions would be simplified and concentrated into a struggle for plain survival; as their physical stamina was exercised and through exercise was strengthened, so their moral stamina and courage were tested and developed. With poetic justice, the least suited to the battle, John and Susanna Moodie, were to face the most severe tests and to gain the most in personal development if not in material wealth.

The trip through the bush was not enough to change Susanna's intractable, prudish ways, nor John's eternal bad luck. The problem of the "hateful Yankee neighbours" was gone, leaving them all their energies to devote to the problem of survival. At least it should have, but for the Moodies things were never that simple.

John made friends immediately with their neighbours, the Indians; he invited them into his home, played his flute for them. When one of Peter Nogun's sons showed a particular interest, John taught him how to play the instrument.

Susanna accepted all this, but not with very good grace. She considered "the noble savages" to be highly over-rated. The best she could say of them was that they were honest. On the other hand, the Indians loved Susanna. They had a child-like curiosity about all the white man's ways and possessions, but Susanna particularly fascinated them, for two reasons. One of her most prized possessions was a finely-tooled Japanese ceremonial sword; its workmanship was studied and appreciated by the Indians much more perhaps than by Susanna herself. The second attraction Susanna had was her talent for sketching; she had learned to draw as one of the gentle arts of the lady, and had shown a particular gift for quick, deft sketches of people, sketches that were true to life though not always flattering. Over the years, she had developed a habit, when she was bored or angry, of drawing sketches of any curious face around her.

Having once demonstrated these – the sword and the sketching – to selected Indians, Susanna found herself faced with queues of others who were intensely interested, each wanting to see and examine the sword, each with a childish desire to have his picture drawn. With remarkable ill-grace, Susanna refused. Yet Susanna's fame spread, and the Indians' admiration for her was not reduced.

The Moodies' ineptitude for the social life of the backwoods was again demonstrated in their logging bees. In late July 1834, thirty-two men were invited to their first bee. Samuel Strickland supervised the work, and Thomas Traill acted as Grog Boss. To supply the proper food, Susanna and Mary Tate cooked for two days before the bee, to provide "the best fare that could be procured in the bush, pea-soup, legs of pork, venison, eel, and raspberry pies, garnished with plenty of potatoes, and whiskey to wash them down, besides a large iron kettle of tea."[1] This was a much larger affair than the Traills' first bee, with more men invited, and much greater quantity and variety of food. The Moodies were anxious to do it properly, but also with flair.

They knew that a bee was more than just an essential and traditional way of getting work done in the bush. They knew that it was also an important social occasion, that they were playing host for the first time to their neighbours. They must do it right, even though they had to buy most of the provisions and liquor; though the hospitality of the normal bee came solely from the produce of the farm itself, the Moodie farm as yet, of course, had no produce. Yet the fare they laid on had to be the best, for they were hosts.

The work was completed, somehow, under Samuel's supervision, despite the selection of Thomas Traill as Grog Boss. John Moodie would probably not have done any better in this most important function of the bee, but his friend Thomas was not much more experienced than John. Thomas had not learned that the best way to be Grog Boss was to ration the refreshments closely during the early part of the proceedings, using the liquor to ensure that every worker was properly enthusiastic about labouring for his neighbour without pay, while carefully measuring each man's portion to ensure that it did not interfere with his efficiency.

Whatever went on in the clearing, by the time the workmen came in to supper they were all drunk, except for a few like Samuel, Thomas, and John. The whiskey with the meal did little to improve matters, and Susanna and Mary Tate escaped to cower in the bedroom listening to the profanity and the crashes as the uproarious guests broke up the place. The few that were sober left immediately after supper, and John retired in disgust to the parlour, leaving the party in the kitchen to go on for the rest of the night.

Susanna was furious. She interpreted the whole bee system as simply an excuse for carousing and taking advantage of a neighbour's hospitality. In the light of the expense and trouble they had gone to, she could not help but conclude that they should simply have hired men to do the work and dispensed entirely with the bee arrangement. In short, Susanna's opinion was that bees, like the noble savages, were highly over-rated. Despite Susanna's opinion, the Moodies had three more bees before their sixteen acres could be ready for fall wheat.

Moreover, John Moodie had to attend other people's bees in return, as a matter of honour. But Moodie, being Moodie, was seriously hurt at both the first two bees he attended. Unwilling or unable to try it again, but still owing work to the many men who came to his bees, he sent his team of oxen and his hired man to take his place. This easy way out ended when his precious team was so abused under the hands of a stranger that one of his oxen had to be shot, at a time when Moodie had no money either to purchase or to hire another.[2]

The one thing that Susanna most detested about bees and for that matter about the colony in general was drunkenness. While not so vehement about it, both Samuel and Catharine agreed with her.

From very much wider experience, Samuel documented the horrors that went on at bees (much worse in fact than at the Moodies' bees), fights started from drunkenness, often ending in death. Samuel recognized that bees were essential to the early life of any settlement. But he also saw that they started a habit and people had bees when they were not entirely necessary – for the sake of a party or for the sake of simply returning hospitality that was due.

xication was not confined to bees. Whiskey was almost as ntiful and ubiquitous in the bush as trees. Distilleries in almost every town as soon as the first grist mills and wheat, the major cash crop, found its way into often as into bread. For many settlers, the only market eat was at the distilleries, especially when their wheat w quality or when there was no form of transport to take it to any other market. Matching the growth in es was the growth in temperance societies – and the that still characterizes the province to this day was

To the disgust of both Susanna and Catharine, many of the drunks in the colony were originally officers and gentlemen, men who should have known better and who should have lived up to the standards of behaviour expected of their class, but also men who were most unsuited to the hard life of the bush settler.

Earlier in Hamilton Township, Uncle Joe's old and experienced mother had warned John Moodie that just such a fate was in store for him:[3]

> I never saw a gentleman from the old country make a good Canadian farmer. The work is rough and hard and they get out of humour with it, and leave it to their hired helps, and then all goes wrong. They are cheated on all sides, and in despair take to the whiskey bottle, and that fixes them ... I give you just three years to spend your money and ruin yourself; and then you will become a confirmed drunkard like the rest.

In general, this comment was based on truth, for this was the fate of many gentleman-settlers. But it must also be remembered that Uncle Joe's mother was extremely resentful of the Moodies, for their airs and for taking away her son's farm; the implication is that she wished nothing but the worst for Moodie.

Susanna, however, was confident of Moodie's ability to avoid the pitfalls of liquor. Oddly, she seemed to feel that both Moodie and her brother Samuel were entirely pure in this respect claimed unequivocally that Samuel and his friends temperance men.[4]

But John Moodie had certainly not been a teetotaller marriage; Dutch gin was a part of his *Campaign* Moreover, by Susanna's own words, the Moodie hou all other frontier farms was never without its barrel whiskey even when they had to dine off boiled squ dandelion coffee, though the spirits were intended workmen.

Samuel Strickland disapproved of excesses in drinking, but he extolled the virtues of whiskey for medicinal purposes or as a preventive against the cold, or just as good cheer. He heartily disapproved of, and sometimes ridiculed, the temperance societies for carrying absolute prohibition to "unchristian lengths".[5]

The difficulties with bees and booze were minor annoyances,

however, in contrast with the real troubles in the little settlement which were just beginning.

In August and September 1834, both the Traill and Moodie homes were stricken with "ague and lake fever", a malaria that attacked almost all new emigrants and many of the old ones, particularly those near lakes and rivers. Thomas, Catharine and Jamie Traill, and their servant, all caught the ailment at once. Because of the epidemic proportions of the disease it was impossible to hire anyone to look after the Traills. Mary Strickland and Susanna had to take over the Traill household for the fortnight that Catharine was ill.

Then the Moodies were struck – John, their baby daughter Agnes, John Monaghan and the choppers, and eventually everyone.

To add to the difficulty, Mary Tate had left them, and just the commencement of the outbreak Susanna gave birth to her third child, John A. Dunbar Moodie. Susanna had hired a nurse to help during her confinement, but the nurse caught the fever and had to be taken home. No other help was to be had, for the Traills and Stricklands were all still sick. Ultimately, friends heard of the trouble and sent what help they could; in the meantime, the Moodies' hired man Jacob took over the nursing, cooking, churning, milking, and all the other household tasks in addition to his work in the fields.

Susanna was grateful to Jacob, yet she later referred to her faithful servant this way:[6]

> Jacob's attachment to us, in its simplicity and fidelity, greatly resembled that of a dog; and sometimes, like the dog, he would push himself in where he was not wanted, and gratuitously give his advice, and make remarks which were not required.

The ague was a frightful experience for everyone, especially when the Moodies' new baby developed a fever. With no medical help available, and pitiably few of the settlers still able to walk and attend the sick, backwoods isolation lost some of its adventure. But their survival depended on the crops, and long before they were well enough, Thomas Traill and John Moodie were back out in the fields. The result was that the men took many more months before they were completely free of the after-effects of the disease – a lingering nervous depression that took away much of their heart for the toil of developing their farms.

The Traill farm did develop, rather slowly they thought, but steadily. By the spring of 1835, they had a frame-barn with granary, stable and chicken house, a root house and dairy, a dug well, and they had made further additions to their house, including an extra room and a verandah. The chopping and land clearing continued, and despite the discouraging comments of more experienced settlers, Catharine had made some progress in developing the kind of well-planned and orderly garden she had always dreamed about.

Thus, she could confidently report:

> . . . our chief difficulties are now over, at least we hope so, and we trust soon to enjoy the comforts of a cleared farm. My husband is becoming more reconciled to the country, and I daily feel my attachment to it strengthening.

This was the first indication in any of Catharine's reports that Thomas Traill had not responded to the bush with quite as much enthusiasm as his wife. Yet Catharine was premature in her own optimism that their difficulties were over. Thomas' dwindling supply of cash had to act as a buffer, often inadequate, between them and the difficulties of the next few years.

The first edition of Catharine Parr Traill's *Backwoods of Canada* appeared in London in 1836, a collection of her letters home and notes from her journal. It brought the Traill story up to May 1835, describing their personal adventures, the plants and wildlife Catharine had found, and many technical notes to assist prospective immigrants. Though it was by no means the whitewash of colonial conditions that many other such works were, it did contain all of Catharine's hope and optimistic faith. It was very well received in Britain, so well that Catharine had to add two more chapters later.

Those part of *Backwoods* written after 1835 have quite a different tone; for example: [8]

> Many circumstances have combined to keep us back and depress the energies of the settlers of this township. The want of emigrants during the last three years has been one great cause, and we attribute this to the dread of cholera, which visited us in '32 and again in '34; then the dread of civil commotions, which we consider to have been quite unfounded in our Province. The high price of crown lands has also been a bar to emigration ... also the want of good roads, or navigable steamers for conveyance of commodities to market ...

This was an excellent statement on the economic and political problems, as the Traills, Stricklands and Moodies saw them; its tone suggests that Catharine was summarizing family conversations reflecting disappointments over the failure of their community to grow.

Their farms were not developing as well as they had expected, and Catharine's early pride was exchanged for greater caution in her letters home:

> You see matters go but slowly with us; we creep up the hill a few paces, and then slip back nearly to the point from which we set out – but still we *do* contrive to get forward a little bit, and are always upheld by the hope of Colonial prosperity.[9]
>
> We go but slowly clearing from eight to ten acres a year; this gives us a crop of wheat and potatoes, and oats, and sometimes turnips and Indian corn ...[10]

This was extraordinary pessimism from the usually sparkling and sanguine Catharine, and probably reflects an even greater impatience in the others. But Catharine had deep consolation in her growing family. Jamie had been joined in 1836 by Katharine and in 1837 by Harry. The month of June 1837, marked not only Harry Traill's birth, but also the ascent to the throne of the young Queen Victoria. The latter occasion, however, seems to have gone almost unnoticed amid the troubles of the backwoods.

If the Traills were not doing quite as well as they had hoped, the Moodie establishment was in a shambles. John had very little cash when he came to Douro, and even this was gone by the summer of 1835.

It was force of circumstance that required the pioneer to use the barter system more often than money. He paid for having his grain ground by leaving some of it with the miller, for having his logs sawed by giving some of his lumber to the sawmill operator, and in the bee system, he paid for labour by giving his own labour in return. But for the first few years on any farm, the settler had no crops or produce with which to barter, nor did he manage to raise enough food even to meet his own needs. Therefore he required money, whatever his social origin.

The upper class settlers brought money with them; the middle class craftsman sought employment to raise the necessary cash to develop his settlement; the pauper, with no money and no trade, simply starved on his free land, unless he could work as a servant or unskilled labourer at rates of pay that were ordinarily far too low for him to save enough to have a farm. Thus, Upper Canada was never a haven for the downtrodden, nor for a man with nothing to offer but willingness.

John Moodie had brought cash with him, but it had been lost in Hamilton Township; most of Susanna's legacy went into purchasing land in Douro. By 1835 they had no money and only sixteen acres cleared – a pitifully small farm to raise food for the family as well as a cash crop of wheat.

Farming on a shoestring is a dangerous proposition at any time, but even more so on a pioneer farm with small acreage where one crop failure or market depression could mean disaster. Moodie's wheat crop was severely damaged by excessive rain in 1835. It was a tiny crop, of very low quality; they were barely able to salvage enough to make their bread; the rest was fit only for the distillery where the payment for it had to be in whiskey.

The crop failure was general throughout the colony, although the Traills were able to take off a bit more from their larger acreage and to capitalize in a small way on the inflated price of wheat – but not enough to be able to give any real help to the Moodies.

It was obviously essential for John Moodie to increase his acreage. The survival of a pioneer farm depended upon clearing new acres every year because of the particular cultivating techniques that had to be used. Besides, too small a farm made him vulnerable to all possible losses and calamities. Unable to work his farm and keep up with the tree-chopping at the same time, because of lack of time and because of his poor physical condition resulting from his war wounds, Moodie contracted with a neighbouring farmer for the clearing of another ten acres.

In so doing, he went into debt for the first time, a debt which weighed on his sense of honour because he had no prospects of repaying it. Then he had to go still further in debt to pay his hired help and to buy food for his family.

In these most difficult circumstances, Susanna's aggressive intractability became an asset for the first time. She swallowed her pride, or at least exchanged it for a new kind of pride, and went to work in the fields. Moreover, she had spunk enough to keep John going too. Susanna could rationalize any situation in her own favour and convince herself and her husband that poverty was no disgrace since it was not of their own doing! Rather, it had been sent by God to try their strength and under no circumstances should they be found wanting:[11]

The independent in soul can rise above the seeming disgrace of poverty, and hold fast to their integrity, in defiance of the world and its selfish and unwise maxims. To them, no labour is too great, no trial too severe; they will unflinchingly exert every faculty of mind and body before they will submit to become a burden to others.

Here was Susanna at her most pompous, but in this case it was useful.

The capacity to rationalize every situation and turn it to their own advantage was a characteristic common to the whole Strickland family, except perhaps that it had failed their father in his later years. Agnes, the historian, even rationalized the actions of those royal personages with whom she claimed kinship; indeed, she was severely criticized for being biased and unprofessional in these parts of her work.

Catharine too was not immune; her eternal optimism was simply another form of rationalization, and her interest in flora and fauna was at least in part escapist, although she conducted her research with such diligence that she too won a very high reputation from it.

Of all the Stricklands, however, Susanna was the champion of this, perhaps because she had more chance to exercise the capacity. Having rationalized her situation, she discovered she actually enjoyed it:[12]

> We found that manual toil, however distasteful to those unaccustomed to it, was not after all such a dreadful hardship . . . I have contemplated a well-hoed ridge of potatoes on that bush farm with as much delight as in years long past I had experienced in examining a fine painting in some well-appointed drawing-room.

Susanna had come a very long way. Many of her notions about her role on the farm had changed completely, but she was still in character – if she had to hoe potatoes, it would be a neat and tidy row.

Hunting and fishing now were something more than gentlemanly "wild sports"; they provided the necessities of life. And when John was too busy, Susanna and her eldest daughter took out the canoe and went fishing. While Catharine had made a hobby out of devising recipes for anything she found in the bush, Susanna was forced into it and became every bit as skilled. She learned to trap and cook squirrels and chipmunks and to concoct wonderful things from dandelions, including salads and ersatz coffee. The occasional deer or bear that wandered near their clearing was manna, a great event and a greater contribution to their larder.

But most of the time they subsisted on potatoes and bread. This was all they had when at the end of a hard winter, in May 1836, their fourth child Donald was born. Susanna was weak and undernourished, a condition adding critically to the dangers of childbirth in the isolated bush. John went begging and came back with baskets of food from the neighbours, although their neighbours, including Catharine and Samuel, were not much better off. Crop failure and money shortage were affecting everyone.

Oddly, the Moodies still had servants, the "faithful Jacob" to help John, and Mary Pine from Dummer Township who helped both in the house and in the fields. But these people were evidently working for nothing except promises and their keep, such as it was. For Susanna, one of the most trying aspects of poverty was having servants witness their master's degradation. There is no reason to suppose that Susanna was exaggerating the seriousness of their situation.

John and Jacob had managed to clear another eight acres in the winter of 1835/36. Since Moodie had still not been able to pay the men who had chopped for him the previous year, he had to be satisfied with only what he and Jacob could do. This still gave them only thirty-four acres, and to add to their difficulties, Jacob decided to leave. This was a double calamity; they needed his help, and, as a matter of honour, his wages had now to be paid. To do this, they sold their best cow and most of Moodie's wardrobe. Susanna's best clothing had already been sold. They kept only her wedding dress and the baby things her mother had sent from England.

Susanna commented, in what was an understatement for her, "Nothing is more distressing than being obliged to part with articles of dress which you know you cannot replace."[13]

While Susanna was buckling down to do battle with poverty, the ill-fated John was still contributing his share of misfortune in his characteristic way. Susanna told the story of a squatter from one of the Back Lakes who stole a young bull from Moodie's barn. With great resolve, Moodie went after it and got it back. Not to be outdone by a gentleman, the squatter came back a few days later and drove six of Moodie's hogs into the lake where they drowned. This was one of the reaons why the house was so destitute in the winter of 1835/36. (A "squatter" was not necessarily someone living on land that did not belong to him; he may have been just someone you did not like. Also, Susanna does not say specifically that anyone saw the hogs go into the lake; it may have been only suspicion that the squatter drove them in.)

Then, in the spring of 1836, a penurious gentleman who had been a failure at pioneering and was being chased by the sheriff walked into the Moodie house and stayed for nine months because John could not think of a nice way to ask him to leave. The Moodies had fallen into this trap before, with Tom Wilson. But the situation was not so favourable with their new gentleman-visitor.

Apparently John had met this man before and had casually suggested that if the gentleman ever happened to be in the Moodies' neighbourhood he should drop in. When he did so, Moodie put forward his best effort at being blunt, but he was not blunt enough:[14]

> "To tell you the truth, Malcolm," said Moodie, "we are so badly off that we can scarcely find food for ourselves and the children. It is out of our power to make you comfortable, or to keep an additional hand . . ."

Moodie should have stopped there, but no, he had to soften his display of inhospitality:

"... without he is willing to render some little help on the farm. If you can do this, I will endeavour to get a few necessaries on credit, to make your stay more agreeable."

And Malcolm stayed of course, but he did very little work, preferring to lie in bed reading Moodie's books and drinking Moodie's whiskey.

Malcolm enjoyed baiting Susanna, suggesting that she was a domineering dictatorial type of woman – which of course she was – but it was hardly the place of a guest to say so. Nor did he often bait Susanna in Moodie's presence, so that John thought Malcolm was not too bad a fellow, though a bit lazy and, after all, he had in a way been invited. All in all, Moodie enjoyed Malcolm's witty and learned conversation, and Susanna enjoyed having someone to fight with and take her mind off bush poverty.

Months later, however, Malcolm forgot himself, as too old and too familiar friends are apt to do. He complained about the bill of fare, which insulted not only Moodie's ability to provide but also Susanna's competence as a cook:[15]

"What an infernal dish!" he cried, pushing away his plate with an air of great disgust. "These eels taste as if they had been stewed in oil. Moodie, you should teach your wife to be a better cook."

The hot blood burnt upon Moodie's cheeks. I saw indignation blazing in his eye.

"If you don't like what is prepared for you, sir, you may leave the table and my house, if you please. I will put up with your ungentlemanly and ungrateful conduct to Mrs. Moodie no longer."

Out stalked the offending party.

But of course Malcolm came back and stayed until it suited

him to leave, although he worked a little harder than he had before. When he departed finally he simply walked out and never troubled to satisfy the Moodies' natural curiosity as to where he went or what happened to him.

Thus, while John and Susanna were finding new strength to fight physical privations more severe than any they had known before, they were still helplessly permissive with people, especially any parasite who chose to call himself a gentleman.

On New Year's Day 1837, John Moodie felt compelled to do something to improve their situation. He wrote down a description of all his troubles to date and sent it off in appeal to the Governor to rescue him.[16]

He told about the loss of his commission, the steam-boat stock speculation, the loss of his first farm in Hamilton Township, the poverty that his wife and four infant children had to put up with, and his physical inability to cope with the labours of a pioneer farm. Nor did he fail to mention his successful brother in the Cape Colony public service, when he beseeched the Governor for an appointment.

He received the politely standard reply, for the Governor's Office regularly received such plaintive appeals from gentlemen all over the colony who had discovered too late that they were hopelessly unsuited physically and mentally to life on a backwoods farm. Moodie's appeal might have come to something in time, for men of education were needed in the growing public service, but larger events intervened to distract the Governor's attention.

In the meantime, the Moodies missed scarcely one disaster of the many the bush could offer. The year 1837 dealt them the final two – fire and physical injury. But their earlier trials had so tempered their spirits that these latest difficulties were faced with courage and self-reliance.

On one of the coldest days in the very cold winter of '37, when Moodie was away at the Traills' place, a chimney-fire set the roof of their log house ablaze. Susanna quickly sent her servant girl to fetch Moodie, filled the offending stove with wet blankets which stopped the chimney fire though not the fire on the roof, and commenced carrying and dragging things out of the house into the snow.

Moodie came a-running, with Thomas Traill and Samuel Strickland not far behind. Thomas shouted: [17]

"Moodie, the house is gone; save what you can of your winter stores and furniture."

Moodie thought differently. Prompt and energetic in danger, and possessing admirable presence of mind and coolness when others yield to agitation and despair, he sprang upon the burning loft and called for water.

These words of Susanna were very complimentary to Moodie, less so to Thomas. But it was Moodie's house, his last real possession, that was going up in flames. His brave gesture from the roof top had a temporary setback when it was explained that Susanna had already used all the water to put out the fire in the chimney. There was a ready substitute near at hand; she and Thomas started handing up pails of snow to Moodie who packed it all over the roof. It worked, and with the help of other neighbours who eventually came, the house was saved from being a total loss.

Samuel showed he had as much presence of mind as Moodie. His first concern was for his sister and the children who were already suffering from exposure in the bitter cold. He had brought a team and sleigh and took Susanna and Katie home with him.

It took Moodie several weeks to make their house habitable again. In the meantime, John, Susanna and the baby lived with the Traills, while Samuel and Mary Strickland looked after the other three children.

In the following spring and summer of 1837, the Moodie affairs seemed to be improving. Samuel had found Moodie a reliable man to help him. The crops were coming along very well, and the fishing and hunting were good. They had enough food again, good prospects, and new hope.

Then Moodie lost one of his oxen, through ill-treatment at a bee, right in the middle of harvesting. He had to sink further in debt to get another, but not before a good deal of his crop was damaged, despite the active assistance of Susanna and her latest maid, Jenny Buchanan.

The ultimate disaster struck when Moodie broke his leg. He was alone working in the fields sowing fall wheat with his new team of oxen. The oxen were pulling the pioneer harrow – a triangular shaped drag with iron teeth – a very heavy implement that was used both to prepare the soil for planting and to bury the scattered seed. Its peculiar shape allowed the oxen to swing it around and between the stumps that were still dotted throughout the cleared fields. Moodie's harrow was working in just this way when it caught against a stump, was pulled off by the oxen, and swung against Moodie's left leg.

Somehow he managed to unhitch the team and to crawl back to the house. With Susanna's help, he bandaged his leg. They sent to Peterborough for a doctor but as usual none came.

Moodie was now forty years old. The resilience and strength of youth, needed for the continuous heavy labour, were gone. Their great hopes for success in the new land could stand very few more setbacks.

Susanna's courage left her for a short while on the evening of the accident: [18]

> Fortune seemed never tired of playing us some ugly trick. The hope which had so long sustained me seemed about to desert me altogether; when I saw him on whom we all depended for subsistence, and whose kindly voice ever cheered us under the pressure of calamity, smitten down helpless, all my courage and faith in the goodness of the Divine Father seemed to forsake me, and I wept long and bitterly.

Susanna was very much in love with John Moodie; it was for his sake that she came to Upper Canada, and it was for his sake that she learned to hate the colony for each successive disappointment that it dealt him. Her righteous indignation over the rude manners of the people turned to bitterness whenever John suffered.

But John Moodie had not given up by any means. His real worth always showed itself during the greatest calamities. While he was still too crippled to move around, he occupied himself whittling a set of crutches, new paddles for the canoe, axe-handles, and yokes for the oxen.

Then, with the help of his paddles and crutches, he determined to take his grain to the grist mill at the other end of Lake Katchiwano. Susanna did not discourage him from trying it; instead, she went along with him to help, for she was now highly skilled with the canoe. It was well she did, for the season was late and they were caught in an ice storm on the way back. It took both of them to bring the heavily laden canoe back down the lake.

Good news surprised them on their return. At least, it was ultimately to be good news both for them and for the colony. The Rebellion of 1837 and the call-up of militia brought a rejuvenation to the backwoods when it was most needed. War stirs the spirit and makes a nice change from the dull problems of day-to-day existence. John Moodie heard the call to arms and, broken leg or no broken leg, he mounted a borrowed horse and reported for duty, not too far behind Thomas Traill, Samuel Strickland, and all the other half-pay and militia officers and men of the community.

But not one of them had the faintest idea what the fight was about.

CHAPTER SEVEN

Rebellion

Most of the troubles of the little Lakefield settlement in Douro were also being experienced throughout the colony: crop failures, shortage of money, a slow-down in immigration, struggles with inadequate transportation facilities, epidemics of cholera and ague, all adding up to disappointment and smashed dreams. Upper Douro was vaguely aware of this, but there was little consolation in the knowledge that they were not alone in their difficulties. They did not see any connection between the hardships they were suffering and the rumours of civil unrest in the colony.

The Moodies, Stricklands and Traills had been touched only slightly by colonial politics during their first years in the backwoods. Like other recent British immigrants, if they thought about it all all, they tended to regard government as a British institution, located in London with a branch in York. The colonial administration was simply an offshoot of the fountain-head of all government at Westminister.

In the same way, their social and political philosophy was an expression of pre-Victorian England, with first premises based on the realities of the Old Country, as yet unmodified by the realities of the colony. These views were also held by the colonial officials themselves: the divine right of the British privileged classes to rule according to their own judgement. This was the concept that lay behind the Stricklands' views of class as well as politics, for the two were closely interwoven; a gentleman must necessarily be "responsible" at all times, no matter where he was nor how bad his personal situation. To be a gentleman was not only a privilege; it was a burden, with rigid standards of personal and social behaviour, with a heavy responsibility for service to the less privileged. It was a burden that the gentleman was born to. He was not "better" than others because of any personal, intrinsic superiority; he was better because the standards he was required to live by were superior. Any failure to live up to them was severely castigated, while success in living up to them was not rewarded because it was so obviously expected.

This philosophy for the Stricklands meant horror when a gentleman-pioneer got drunk (but not when anyone else did), and it meant John Moodie's fulfilment of agreements as a matter of honour even when others did not uphold their part of the bargain. It meant that their poverty was a greater burden, for it did not release them from their responsibilities for maintaining the required standards of behaviour. And it meant their unquestioning acceptance of a government run by gentlemen.

Nevertheless, the success of their farms was deeply affected by the activities of the government of the day. Their continued survival in the bush depended on their ability to create a thriving community, and this depended on attracting many more immigrants, markets for their produce, reasonable roads and communication systems to reach those markets. These things were under the control of the colonial government. There was little the settlers by themselves could do to create the conditions necessary for development.

The colonial government consisted of a Lieutenant Governor appointed by the Colonial Office of Britain, an Executive Council and a Legislative Council appointed by the Governor on the nomination of the local aristocracy (the Family Compact), and a gadfly of an elected Assembly which had power only to criticize the system publicly and to vote for or against a small part of the provincial budget.

The system was grossly inefficient and was hindering as often as helping the development of settlements. Clergy Reserves –

public lands set aside for the support of the Church – were desperately needed by the colonists, yet the price of such lands when they were available at all was artificially inflated to support the court of Bishop Strachan, the senior member of the Family Compact in York (Toronto). These Reserves, spread throughout the colony, prevented the development of cohesive settlements and expansion of population. Despite the sacrifice implied in the Clergy Reserves, there was rarely a clergyman of the Established Church to be seen anywhere in the backwoods, a lack deeply felt by the English of the Douro settlement.

A good deal of "roughing it" was forced upon the Douro settlers by the bad roads. Their courageous efforts to remain cheerful would have been greatly strengthened if they had been able to keep their table supplied with the ordinary delicacies of tea and spices. Tea could be brought all the way around the world from the Orient to Peterborough, but even when the settlers could afford to buy it, it was seldom able to make the last ten miles to Douro without being dumped in a bog.

Next to land and roads or canals, the settlers most needed markets for their produce. Wheat and timber were their main cash crops. The colonial economy was not growing fast enough to use all that could be produced and markets had to be found in the United States or Britain. The development of such markets required vigorous trade policies from the colonial government, but vigour was not an outstanding attribute of the Family Compact. Colonial trade policies were confused and lacking in direction, and in conflict with the new theories in Britain where free trade was the slogan of the burgeoning industrial economy, resistant to the colonists' need for a protected market in the Mother Country.

The weakness of the system was manifest in 1837, after a series of crop failures throughout the colony and a commercial crisis which left the government of Upper Canada almost bankrupt, halted all public works on roads and canals, and put hundreds of labourers out of work.

Yet there was little understanding in the colony about what was happening to them. The emigrants of British Tory origin and most of the Family Compact still believed that the all-wise, all-loving Mother Country would come to their aid – a feeling that their close relatives in Britain would never let them down.

Britain itself, however, was changing drastically; it was not the same place the Moodies and Traills had known five years earlier. The persistent depression following the Napoleonic Wars was causing economic and political re-thinking that amounted to revolution. Britain was turning its back on the colonies in an effort to solve its own problems.

Most of the colonial government and all of the army were paid for by Britain. After the Boston Tea Party, no further attempts were made to tax a colony, and the increasing drain on Britain's resources seemed to many to be a futile and endless waste. The rising commercial middle class of the industrial revolution, given political force through the Reform Bills, did not have the same feelings about the Empire and would not tolerate their taxes being drained out of the country to support the colonies.

In contrast to Britain, the colonial needs were those of a primitive, weak, agricultural community, lacking the resources to undertake the rapid development of social capital which would take it out of its primitive state. It needed and expected the help of Britain, but Britain's needs were no longer complementary to those of the colony. With the wisdom of hindsight, it appears now obvious that decisions made to benefit the Mother Country would not benefit the colony. If the colony was to survive, it would have to work out its own destiny, but it did not have the constitutional means to do so.

Some of the Reformers in Upper Canada saw this, but their spokesmen confused the whole issue with philosophical dogma that smacked of American democracy. For those who still hoped for help from the Mother Country, and these were in the majority, the Reformers' attacks on the Colonial Office and the

Family Compact, their demands for responsible government and colonial self-rule, all sounded like treason.

After all, the majority of the people in Upper Canada were there because they preferred to live under the Crown on British soil. Had they felt otherwise they would have migrated to the United States where life and prospects were much better. Even the "Yankees" of Upper Canada were mainly Loyalists, people who had deliberately renounced life under the republic, often at great cost to themselves. Moreover, many of the Irish colonials were Ulstermen – Orangemen whose trademark was loyalty.

Few settlers had developed any feelings of colonial nationalism since most of them had arrived only a few years before. People were still identified more often by the county they came from in the British Isles than by district they settled in. There was therefore little emotional appeal for them in cries of freedom from their native land; they feared being cast loose from the protection of England, left to fend for themselves in a hostile environment.

Had William Lyon Mackenzie[1] and his followers concentrated their appeal for reform on specific economic issues, they might have gained more converts. Instead, they attacked the political system. As Professor Creighton described it:[2]

> In the opinion of the radicals, the whole system of privilege and abuse was held together in its own interest by a little oligarchy of appointed executive and legislative councillors at Toronto called the "Family Compact", and by a network of little local family compacts, composed of appointed justices of the peace who governed the countryside.

Upper Douro Township, a full day of hard travel away from Peterborough, had not been involved or very well informed about the progress of the argument as it developed along the Front and in Toronto. Their mental isolation was even greater than their geographic isolation. The noises of a few rabble-rousing radicals, most of whom were not even grammatical, could never touch their refined Tory souls in any real sense, even though the fortunes of their personal community were directly involved in the noise. They were aware that something was going on, but they discounted its importance. Catharine, for instance, felt that the "dread of civil commotion" was "quite unfounded" and should not be allowed to discourage prospective emigrants.[3]

Susanna had come into contact with the reform movement as soon as she arrived in Upper Canada, through exposure to the Cobourg *Reformer*, a newspaper that had even more troubles than Mackenzie's own *Colonial Advocate*. But Susanna would not read it. She flung it from her because of "the vulgar abuse that defiled every page." As she saw it, "Men, in Canada, may call each other rogues and miscreants, in the most approved Billingsgate, through the medium of the newspapers, which are a sort of safety valve to let off all the bad feelings and malignant passions floating through the country, without any dread of the horsewhip."[4] And the horsewhip, by implication, is what they should have received. Susanna was terribly wrong in her assessment of the newspapers as a safety-valve; on the contrary, they were the implements for stirring up revolt.

Douro Township had its own "little local family compact". Samuel Strickland, Thomas Traill, Robert Reid, and a few other neighbourhood gentlemen (but not John Moodie), were appointed justices of the peace. As such, they exercised judicial, police and administrative functions, sometimes performing marriages, certifying bounty payments on wolves, and carrying out the other little official duties necessary to the operation of the community. T. A. Stewart, who was related to the Stricklands and Reids by marriage and whose wife was an intimate friend of Catharine Traill, held a life appointment to the Legislative Council, the upper house of the colonial legislature. This then, was a family compact in the literal as well as the figurative sense. Its members held their offices more because of their social origins and their connections with the notables of the colonial government than because of their superior wisdom or experience.

Yet the system worked very well for Douro, where the people were accustomed to accepting leadership from "gentlemen", where energies were so absorbed in fighting the bush that there was little left over for reform. A more sophisticated political system would have been inappropriate. In any case, there was not a great deal for the J.P.s to do. Their authority was anything but onerous, and when they did exercise it, it was always in the interests of the community because the J.P.s were very much a part of the community. For that matter, there were so many J.P.s in the little community that they were practically in the majority.

Samuel Strickland, in describing his little "Court of Requests", admitted that it was all very informal, dealing only with cases involving less than £10. No records were kept, nor were they hampered by much knowledge of the law. They simply passed out judgements that observed common sense and local needs:[5]

> ... The Commissioners were generally appointed from the magistracy [the J.P.s] or from the most influential persons in the division ... Messrs. Traill, Thompson and myself used to hold a court once a month for our division. The average number of cases did not exceed fifteen, and the amount sued for seldom exceeded two pounds upon each summons. The Commissioners were entitled to one shilling each for every case decided by them ...

Obviously, the people of Douro did not object too strenuously to this system or they would not have taken so many of their small disputes to court. For a thinly populated, underdeveloped, isolated community, it would be hard to conceive of a better system. On the other hand, when the same approach was applied to the government of the whole province, it did not work so well, and the reform movement was gathering strength.

Mackenzie, as newspaperman, Member of the Legislative Assembly and Chairman of the Grievance Committee, attacked the system and demanded among other things responsible government, that is, that the Assembly should be able to control all the expenditures of the Executive. The power of the purse lay with the Family Compact rather than the Assembly because most of the costs of government and defence were paid for out of Canada Company funds or by the Colonial Office.

The viciousness of Mackenzie's attacks and the radical dogma expressed in his speeches and newspaper led people into the mistaken belief that responsible government meant severing the British connection. Instead, most of the Reformers wanted the Executive to be responsible to the elected Assembly, so that Upper Canada could be run in the best interests of the colony rather than in the interests of Britain and the Family Compact. There should not have been anything revolutionary in the idea; it was basically the same form of government as existed at Westminster. It had simply never been practised before in a colony. Despite the American Revolution, political thought in Britain still could not conceive of any delegation or division of the central authority of the Crown.

Yet Mackenzie and the Reformers were able to catalogue so many specific and real grievances against the colonial administration that they managed to win a widespread following and to take control of the Assembly. Through their efforts, the British government was forced to withdraw the central target of the Reformers' criticism, Lieutenant Governor Sir John Colborne. Unfortunately, Colborne's successor was anything but an improvement.

Sir Francis Bond Head, a pompous little man with no experience whatever in politics or in Upper Canada, was probably the most inept official ever to be foisted on an unsuspecting colony. With an enthusiasm that could only come from total ignorance, Head determined that his sacred duty in the name of the Crown was to rid the colony of all rebels, reformers and democrats. His first attempts were amazingly successful; by personally campaigning throughout the colony in an Assembly election, he managed to have Mackenzie and most of the Reformers ousted from their seats.

Toryism was victorious – too much so. Mackenzie was backed into a corner. His vocal extremism, which might yet have died a natural death before the taciturnity of the farmer-settlers, was now met by the equally frantic extremism of the victorious Bond Head. The grievances were still very real and in the face of the general depression of 1837, brought about partly by the extraordinarily inefficient financial management of the government, the reform movement recovered some of its strength and all of its hunger. With an armed uprising already under way in Lower Canada, Mackenzie threatened more forceful action for Upper Canada.

The sequence of events which followed are now indelibly inscribed in Canada's history – a preposterous series of blunders which brought about the armed revolt that no one really wanted. The pitiful sword-rattling of the rebels, as the Reformers were now called, was only meant to intimidate the government and force at least some measure of reform. But the government from its olympian heights refused to pay any attention.

While Mackenzie was making inflammatory speeches throughout the Home District (around Toronto), while the rebels were openly casting bullets, and while little groups of farmers were imitating military drill with their shotguns and pitch forks, Bond Head sent all the regular troops out of Upper Canada to help put down the rebels in Lower Canada. Toronto was completely unguarded. This was interpreted by the Upper Canadian rebels both as an insult and as a golden opportunity.

It is hardly surprising that the people in the Douro backwoods were totally ignorant of the situation when Bond Head himself refused to be concerned even as the rebels were forming just outside the capital.

The only Tory in Toronto to express any concern was Colonel Fitzgibbon,[6] who tried to rally the local gentlemen to defend themselves. He succeeded only in making everyone think him as mad as Mackenzie (though Fitzgibbon was an honoured hero of the War of 1812, the officer whom Laura Secord went to warn in her famous walk through the woods). Incidentally, Fitzgibbon was a personal friend of Agnes Strickland and visited her every time he went to London; his son would eventually marry John and Susanna Moodie's daughter Agnes.

The designated military leader of the rebels was another ancient hero, Anthony Van Egmond, the first settler of the Huron Tract, well known to Samuel Strickland. Samuel's old friend, Tiger Dunlop, and Dunlop's brother Robert, who had retired from the Royal Navy and was the first member of the Assembly from Huron, were also much involved. The founder of Peterborough, Peter Robinson, and his brother, John Beverley Robinson, were central figures in the Family Compact. In short, while the Douro people were not well informed about the dispute, many of the contenders on both sides were well known to them.

Not until the first shots were fired and the first man died, in an accidental skirmish on 4 December 1837, did Sir Francis Bond Head begin to take alarm. As it happened, the first martyr was a Tory from Richmond Hill, north of Toronto, who was named Colonel Moodie, though evidently no relation to John W. Dunbar Moodie.

When he heard the news of Colonel Moodie's assassination, Bond Head went into a panic, now exaggerating the danger as he had previously under-rated the threat. His folly in sending all the troops out of the province and in discouraging Fitzgibbon's efforts to defend the city now came home to him. Riders were immediately dispatched to all parts of the province calling on half-pay and militia officers to come and save the government and the Governor from the terrible onslaught that was soon to take place.

The real force of the rebellion was broken on Tuesday, 5 December in an after-dark skirmish during which the sheriff and a handful of men ambushed and routed the rebels, sending many of them home and the rest back in disarray to their rallying point at Montgomery's Tavern. The militia near Toronto started pouring in to the city and the final battle was fought on Thursday, 7 December, with the loyal forces under Fitzgibbon easily putting to rout the remnants of the rebels under Van Egmond. In all the war little over half a dozen men had been killed because the tendency was to run for the woods as soon as either side saw the other. Van Egmond was captured and died in disgrace a few days later in jail. Mackenzie fled.

While all this was going on the Governor's call to arms finally reached Douro. The news filtered its way up the Otonabee from Peterborough, through the Stewarts and Reids, to Samuel Strickland on the evening of 7 December, the same day that Mackenzie took flight.[7]

Samuel was still nominally a lieutenant of the Durham Militia which he had joined when he first came to Canada. Since it was much too far to attempt to join his regiment in Whitby Township, and urgency was obviously important, he decided to attach himself to the Peterborough group. Samuel waited only long enough to clean his double-barrelled gun and go over to the Traills with the news, before he set off. While Thomas was making ready, Catharine passed the word on to the Moodie house, although she knew that John and Susanna were away at the upper end of the lake having their grist ground.

Fear, excitement and rumour spread through Douro, but very little fact. The immediate effect of the news was illustrated by Catharine's diary entry for Thursday, December 7:[8]

> ... It seems we have been slumbering in fancied security on a fearful volcano, which has burst and may overwhelm us ... Surely ours is a holy warfare; the rebels fight in an unholy and unblessed cause. My dear brother has already left home for Peterborough, and my beloved husband goes at daybreak. It is now past midnight; the dear children are now sleeping in happy unconsciousness of the danger which their father and

relatives are about to expose themselves; they heard not the fervent prayer of their father as he kneeled beside their bed, and laid his hands in a parting blessing upon their head. O, my God, the Father of all mercies, hear that father's prayer, and grant he may return in safety to those dear babes and their anxious mother.

Thomas Traill left in the early morning of Friday, 8 December, joining Samuel and the Peterborough Volunteers; 400 left Peterborough twenty-four hours after they had received the call.[9]

Meanwhile, the Moodies had returned and were met at the landing by old Jenny with the news, "how some gentleman had called . . . and left a large paper, all about the Queen and the Yankees; that there was war between Canada and the States; that Toronto had been burnt, and the Governor killed . . ."[10]

The weary, crippled Moodie, who had fought the canoe all the way down the freezing lake with an ice-covered paddle, climbed the hill on his home-made crutches and settled down by the fire before turning to a copy of the Governor's Proclamation and Catharine's letter explaining that Samuel and Thomas had already gone to "march to the aid of Toronto".

The excitement caught them, and weary or not, John and Susanna went over to Catharine's for dinner and further news – of which there was very little – only that the Peterborough men were probably marching to Port Hope where a steamer was expected to meet them and take them to Toronto.

Catharine told Susanna not to let Moodie go, that his weakened condition made him unfit. But back home again, John convinced Susanna that he must go.

Little sleep visited our eyes that night. We talked over the strange news for hours; our coming separation, and the probability that, if things were as bad as they appeared to be, we might never meet again. Our affairs were in such a desperate condition that Moodie anticipated that any change must be for the better; it was impossible for them to be worse ... [11]

The next morning, Saturday, 9 December, after a breakfast which Moodie could not eat because of the cries of the children and old Jenny, he set off, accompanied by Susanna as far as the Traills.

The women were left then with nothing to do but wait and wonder. They watched the occasional groups of men filtering out of the woods on their way down-river to join the loyal forces. The lack of any real information made the field ripe for rumour. They heard that there had been a battle with the rebels and the loyalists had been defeated; that Toronto was besieged by 60,000 men; that 400 Indians had attacked Toronto and slaughtered the inhabitants. Catharine visited Mary Strickland and Susanna visited Catharine in a search for news and company.

Late Saturday night the first real news started to come through, although still with the status of rumour. One of Mary Strickland's brothers came up to tell her of Colonel Moodie's death (which had, in fact, occurred five days earlier), of the unexpected loyalty of the town of Cobourg, and of the military manoeuvres of the eastern districts which of course were not involved in the rebellion but had the advantage of being close enough to Douro to provide some fresh news.

On Sunday, Catharine was about to send someone to Peterborough to see if Moodie had stayed there to guard the "Government house" as she had wanted him to do; Catharine seemed more concerned than Susanna about Moodie's weakened condition. Before Catharine took any action, Susanna received a message from a friend in Peterborough that Moodie had borrowed a horse and led 200 Smithtown men towards Toronto.

Also on Sunday, although it had been snowing heavily for several days, one of Mary Strickland's sisters walked up from Peterborough (all the Reid boys, the usual messengers, had by now gone off to the wars). She brought the news that the rebels had all dispersed and twenty had been killed. This was an exaggeration, but she was right that the rebels had dispersed. Ironically, they had done so before the Douro men had set out. Mary Strickland sent the word on to Catharine, and Catharine sent it on to Susanna with an invitation to come and spend the next day with her in celebration of the end of the war.

The Volunteers, with Samuel and Thomas, had been joined by upwards of a thousand men by the time they reached their encampment a few miles outside Port Hope. There they waited for the steam-boat which unfortunately went right on by without stopping. On Saturday they had started to march to Toronto but they received a Proclamation from the Governor, in typical Bond Head style: "The party of rebels under their chief leader is dispersed and flying before the loyal militia – the only thing that remains to be done is to find them out and arrest them."[12]

The trouble was that so many volunteers had answered Bond Head's summons that Toronto was unable to feed and house them all; the rest of the volunteers were requested to go back home. The only enemy that they had seen were two unfortunate spies apprehended in Peterborough, surely an unlikely place for espionage. These were taken to jail in Amherst (outside Cobourg) by Moodie and his Smithtown troop.

Samuel and Thomas were home by 12 December, four days after they had left, and Moodie came back in another few days. All were very satisfied with their adventure, a little frustrated at missing the fight, but now in a patriotic fury at the rebels, many of whom, including Mackenzie, had not yet been captured. They still had little idea of what the fight had been about or what had actually happened in Toronto. But they were proud to be among the thousands of men who came out of the backwoods spontaneously to defend Queen and Country.

As Susanna put it, in retrospect, "The honest backwoodsmen, perfectly ignorant of the abuses that had led to the present position of things, regarded the rebels as a set of monsters, for whom no punishment was too severe, and obeyed the call to arms with enthusiasm."[13]

Susanna had done her bit for the war effort by writing a patriotic poem which implied that the fight had been to defend the British connection against the inroads of the Americans. The general feeling was that the rebels had been terribly ungrateful to the Mother Country which fed them and protected them and to whom they should always be loyal because Britain was so loyal to them.

The whole thing might well have ended there, with the previously amorphous colony now united by a common experience against a common enemy, and ready to go back to the battle with the bush. But Mackenzie was still at large, and his name had taken on all the attributes of Public Enemy Number One, the devil, Guy Fawkes, and American Revolutionary. His flight to the United States further confused the issue, for as soon as the Americans got wind of the rebellion a large number of them rallied to free the Canadians from the yoke of British imperialism, something they had wanted to do ever since the Revolutionary War.

The Douro men were called again in a few days to attend a meeting of the militia in Peterborough and to scour the rear townships of Ops and Mariposa looking unsuccessfully for rebels – and Douro had its first casualty. Mr. Traill feel off his horse and sprained an ankle on his way back from the meeting. Moodie, on Thomas' horse, brought the news that Thomas had gotten only as far as their friends the Stewarts, and Catharine had to send the horse back for him.

Christmas Day the Moodies spent with the Traills, a happy family group with four Moodie children and three young Traills, the recent excitement distracting them from thoughts of the poverty that was now so acute after two years of crop failure and depression. The Moodies returned the hospitality on New Year's Day 1838, a period of happy respite, of hunting and sleighing and playing games, although now both John and Thomas had great difficulty navigating on their wounded legs.

John Moodie, however, could not afford to ignore for long the brutal fact of his poverty and debt. He had volunteered enthusiastically in the hope that some of his own troubles might thereby be solved. Now, the men he owed for chopping two years earlier were pressing for their money; they too were badly off in the general depression. Susanna, in an attempt to raise some cash, had written several articles for the *North American Review* and was asked for contributions by editors of several other American periodicals. But she had to give it up; the Americans had paid her nothing and she could no longer afford the stationery and postage.

The rebellion gave Moodie the idea of returning to his old profession of soldiering. Sporadic attacks by the Americans and Mackenzie's last stand at Navy Island gave him the opportunity. He wangled a captain's commission in one of the full-time, fully-paid militia regiments formed to defend the colony. Moodie's object was not service to Queen and Country; it was openly the regular pay he would receive, a sign of his maturity and the death of the youthful idealism he had shown in the battles of Holland more than twenty years earlier.

On 20 January 1838, Moodie departed for his new duties in Toronto, leaving Susanna alone and pregnant again. Out of his pay, he liquidated many of his debts and still managed to send money home, much of which Susanna in her glorious stubbornness and pride paid out again to the choppers.

This was the ultimate challenge to Susanna, whose character had been growing and strengthening with each new misfortune. Now, she was alone on the farm in the backwoods, to look after herself and the children, to plant the crops in the spring, and to tend the stock, with only old Jenny to help her.

Eventually, the Moodies and Traills figured out that the rebellion had, in fact, something to do with their own fortunes, and their caustic comments toned down considerably. Moodie even became something of a reformer himself, in his political views if not in his actions.

Samuel, however, was not to be pacified. He never got over the Rebellion Losses Bill through which everyone, including the rebels, was reimbursed for losses sustained during the revolt.

The British Government regarded the rebellion and its aftermath very seriously. Bond Head, instead of being rewarded as a glorious leader, was replaced by Sir George Arthur who was to be the last Lieutenant Governor of Upper Canada. As Governor General, the Colonial Office sent out Lord Durham who was perhaps the most intelligent, sensitive and liberal gentleman ever to visit a colony.

From the brief but open-minded investigations of Durham, and events subsequent to Durham's Report, the most important of the rebels' grievances were eventually corrected and the foundations were laid for responsible government and a new type of empire.

Out of Durham's Report also came, more immediately, the establishment of municipal government and the end of the rule of "little local family compacts", as well as the end of Upper Canada. In a futile attempt to solve the problems of Lower Canada, the two colonies were joined together in 1840, and Upper Canada became known as Canada West – at least until 1867 when the colonies themselves broke up the spurious union and the Dominion of Canada was born.

The change in government administration and the change in thinking, however, came very slowly. The Rebellion itself would be interpreted, re-interpreted, and mis-interpreted for over a century. The facts of the specific events were perhaps less influential than what people rightly or wrongly thought had happened. It was clear that something had gone wrong, but what that something was, exactly, was not a subject of agreement even among the rebels. Only in more recent times has it become apparent that the Battle of Yonge Street had a great deal of farce about it. Equally farcical is the fact that Susanna Moodie first became truly famous as a poet with her patriotic poems about the war; her loyal poetry lasted only as long as Mackenzie's disgrace, but long enough for her to establish herself in other forms of writing.

Yet there was nothing farcical about it at the time. Nor is there anything unusual in the fact that the participants and the observers had immense difficulty in understanding what was happening to them; "twas ever thus" in any war, especially in civil war. And that it took years for the Douro backwoods to understand even the events, let alone the reasons for them, was still another castigation of one of the causes – the intolerably poor communications.

CHAPTER EIGHT

Aftermath of War—Back to the Bush

Captain J. W. D. Moodie spent part of the winter of 1837/38 in the provincial militia in Toronto, then was assigned to the Queen's Own Regiment stationed at Point Albino on Lake Erie. The organized defence of the border, of which Moodie was a part, was entirely justified. The rebel Mackenzie, piqued by his failure, had won a large following among the citizens of American border towns by loudly demanding the liberation of Canada and the establishment of a free and sovereign state.

The other rebels, pursued by the loyalists, rallied around Mackenzie on Navy Island above Niagara Falls. After the British sank his supply vessel, the *Caroline*, in U.S. territorial waters, little groups of Americans all along the border organized and armed themselves, openly preparing for attack. The Canadian militia, however, was successful in defending against the sporadic invasions and enjoyed dampening the enthusiasm of the American volunteers.

There was another call-up after the Navy Island episode, and Samuel Strickland, with his status now clarified as a Captain in the 4th Northumberland, led a group of forty-five Douro men to answer the call. They took six days to march to Toronto, but when they got there found little to do. Some of his men volunteered for the Queen's own, but Samuel preferred to go back to his farm when he saw that he was not really needed.

Samuel, as a gentleman, was automatically an officer from the time he first came to the colony, but he was also a yeoman, and like most pioneer farmers, preferred to go back to work his farm instead of fighting wars.[1] Most of his men felt the same way about it; only the few who were failures at farming or whose farms were not well enough advanced to need their personal attention, were willing to volunteer. But it was not the same for the settlers along the Front and near the American border, men who could shoulder a musket and be in action against the invaders in a matter of hours, and men who also had the most to lose from invaders.

Border incidents continued from the St. Lawrence to Lake Erie until 1839 when Mackenzie was belatedly jailed for offending against American neutrality laws. The incidents kept the colony in continual turmoil, searching out, imprisoning and hanging both rebels and innocent men, on grounds of high treason. The American involvement had solidified colonial hatred of the Republic and republicanism, and revived the fear of American aggression which had been dormant only since the War of 1812. The intensity of the feeling was in direct proportion to physical proximity to the border and emotional proximity to the Crown.

Lieutenant Governor Bond Head had encouraged the vindictive hunt for rebels. His successor, Sir George Arthur, had been advised by the Colonial Office to let the ill feelings die down, but he still found it necessary in the tide of Tory reaction to let the law take its course against suspected traitors.

Nevertheless, some of the reform attitudes had managed to filter through to the backwoods. Editorials in the *Backwoodsman*, a Peterborough newspaper, in May 1839[2] made vicious attacks on the appointment of officers in the 7th Provisional Battalion suggesting that some of the officers were not qualified to lead the men of the District. Egalitarianism, if not republicanism, had reached Douro.

Moodie, in the thick of things in the southern end of the province, saw the anguish caused when neighbour is turned against neighbour, and the disheartenment in the communities

153

which had supplied both rebels and loyal volunteers to the fight. His opinions of colonial government began to change. Yet, as a militia officer, grateful for and dependent on his pay, he had to support the Family Compact which was apparently more firmly entrenched then ever.

Whatever Moodie's thoughts on the subject, his two-week furlough in June 1838, after being away from home since January, brought him back to the realities of his personal problems. Susanna and their four children greeted him with love and enthusiasm and sad stories of their adventures during the intervening months.

They were terribly poor. The children had often been without shoes, for Susanna had been keeping only two dollars a month out of Moodie's salary for her own use, sending the rest off to their creditors. They had tapped the sugar bush in the spring, but had broken an iron kettle borrowed from a neighbour to boil down the sap, and Katie the eldest daughter had to give up the only piece of jewellery left in the house to pay for repairs. They had managed to get the crops planted. By loaning their oxen for two days to a friendly neighbour, the neighbour in turn harrowed the Moodies' land. Susanna and old Jenny then manured, planted and hoed the fields for oats, corn, potatoes and a vegetable garden.

Along with her work in the fields, Susanna was finding ways to earn some cash on her own. She painted pictures on tree fungus, which Samuel sold in quantity for her, mostly to his regimental brothers in Peterborough, and some of these quaint souvenirs found their way to England to decorate the mantels of wealthy homes.

Her writing was more rewarding. Although Jenny fussed about the fatigue that followed from working in the fields in the daytime and writing for long hours every night, she manufactured some candles out of rags dipped in pork fat and stuck in a bottle. Susanna had been writing off and on ever since she had arrived in Canada, but the troubles of the short-lived magazines combined with her own personal difficulties had prevented any consistent effort. Now the *Literary Garland* was being put together in Montreal, the most ambitious publishing project yet launched in the colony; it was able to pay Susanna for postage as well as for manuscripts, and her need for money as well as her need for some kind of cultural activity to counteract the effect of hard physical labour were all the stimuli she needed. "I actually shed tears of joy over the first twenty-dollar bill I received from Montreal. It was my own; I had earned it with my own hand; and it seemed to my delighted fancy to form the nucleus out of which a future independence for my family might arise."[5]

This was unjustifiably optimistic, as Susanna would admit, but she had no faith in the farm as a means of livelihood. She had an aggressive drive to find a way herself in a manner that would not damage her husband's reputation as a breadwinner. She loved and respected Moodie, but she was realistic enough to have learned something from their dismal experiences.

Only John's presence could give their farm the continued development it needed. Susanna and Jenny could keep going what had been cleared, but the success of a frontier farm depended still on more acres being cleared every year. Though John's income was desperately needed to pay off their debts, their farm could never amount to anything without the regular and continued effort of a man. Susanna knew this and therefore also knew that the farm was not going to provide the security she expected for her family. So she wrote and, because her patriotic verse had made her popular, she could also sell material she had written years earlier, in the more leisurely days of England.

In the meantime, Old Jenny Buchanan was the perfect foil for her efforts. Illiterate, dour, and very hard working, Jenny had a great respect for her mistress's talent. She stayed longer than any other servant with the Moodies, yet she did not have any of the subservience that Susanna had originally expected in her staff. The Susanna who first came to the colony would hardly have tolerated Old Jenny; the Susanna tempered by the bush was grateful for Jenny's help, company and loyalty.

The Moodie farm looked even worse in contrast with the successful farm of Samuel Strickland. Samuel had taken only enough time in the wars to retain his position of responsibility in the community. He was more willing to give his time to building roads, bridges and mills than to fighting wars. Nor was he yet willing to admit that he could not carve a whole settlement out of woods by his own labour, without any help from the government. Yet, his bridge fell down, his road was not maintained, and his mill was no good without an active, prosperous community to use it. And so far, the only prosperous farm in the area was his own.

Thomas Traill had lost heart for the settlement; John Moodie had been plagued by bad luck; but Samuel Strickland had enough heart to keep everybody going and he made his own luck. Disaster could strike him too, but somehow he always managed to come out of it better than he went in. For instance, in July 1838, the house that he had so lovingly built was struck by lightning; the damage was so severe that he found it easier to build another than to repair the remains.

The disaster which would have been enough to destroy most early settlers hardly troubled Samuel at all. His new house was bigger and better than the old, all frame on a stone foundation, with proper laths and plaster, a house to attract envy from everyone else in the community.[4]

John Moodie was just the opposite. His "several hundred pounds" of debt were still not all paid off when he had to write home to Susanna the disheartening news that his regiment was likely to be reduced. Once again, they were threatened with abject poverty.

Susanna and John both had felt that their only hope for paying their debts and accumulating the little capital necessary to a comfortable life lay with Moodie's continued employment by the government. She wrote the whole story down, therefore, in a letter to Sir George Arthur, beseeching him to keep Moodie on in the militia.

She was a little frightened at her own temerity in doing this, and resolved to keep it a secret from her husband. She thought that Moodie's pride would be compromised by beseeching favours from anyone. Yet Moodie himself had written just such a letter to Sir Francis Bond Head, in January 1837. But she could not keep it entirely to herself; she discussed it with the Traills, and Thomas looked over her letter, approved it, and took it to the post office for her. Catharine and Thomas obviously agreed that this was the best way out.

Nevertheless, Moodie came home in August, out of a job. Although their prospects were as bad as ever, his backwoods family were glad to have him back. He was pleased with Susanna's efforts in looking after the farm over the summer, and he was able to reap the first good harvest they had yet managed to grow.

Susanna too felt better about the farm, now that her husband was with them:[5]

> That harvest was the happiest we ever spent in the bush. We had enough of the common necessaries of life. A spirit of peace and harmony pervaded our little dwelling, for the most affectionate attachment existed among its members. We were not troubled with servants, for the good old Jenny we regarded as an humble friend, and were freed, by that circumstance, from many of the cares and vexations of a bush life.

Here again, Susanna was making a virtue out of necessity, and demonstrating the amazing extent to which the Moodies' standards and aspirations had changed since they first arrived in the bush. A good harvest with the head of the family at home was its own reward. Their only ambition now was to pay off the rest of their debt.

On the 16 October 1838, their fifth child, a son, was born, and a few days later, Moodie received word that he had been appointed as Paymaster to sixteen companies of militia along the shores of Lake Ontario and the Bay of Quinte in the Victoria District. Fortune finally seemed to be smiling on the Moodies.

Susanna interpreted the appointment as being the reply of Sir George Arthur to her letter. She had received no other reply, but she trusted in the generosity of the great. Moodie, on the other hand, assumed it was because of his temperate habits which had been a sharp contrast with the drunken misbehaviour shown by his fellow officers while he was stationed on the Niagara Peninsula. They were both right.

Moodie went off to his new duties immediately. Because they had no way of knowing how long the new appointment would last, and because they wanted to save the maximum amount of money, Susanna remained with old Jenny and the five children to face another winter in the bush.

She had just launched into a new novel for the *Literary Garland*, which was preparing for publication of its first issue, when, one after the other, the children were struck with scarlet fever, one of the most dangerous and contagious diseases known in the bush. The Peterborough doctor would not or could not come, and the neighbours were forced to quarantine the Moodie house to protect their own children.

Miraculously, none of the children died, but the weeks of round-the-clock nursing that were necessary to pull them through took its toll on Susanna's strength. Nervous exhaustion confined her to bed for ten weeks. During Susanna's illness, a neighbour took in her second daughter Agnes to relieve some of the burden. But to add to the difficulties, their infant son contracted another unspecified ailment that was almost fatal. Old Jenny herself was weakening under the strain of looking after the household, milking the cows, and cutting and hauling in firewood.

Isolated in the bush, struggling every day with the enormous labour needed just to keep warm and have enough to eat, when even minor illness or injury could become catastrophe, and without the comforting presence and strength of the father, the little family lived constantly with fear and fatigue.

Then, early in the next year, Catharine and Thomas Traill sold their farm and prepared to move away – not very far away, only to Ashburnham just outside Peterborough. But as far as Susanna was concerned it might as well have been the other side of the earth, for it effectively removed from her the daily support of Catharine's comfortable and steadying cheer.

The reason for this decision of the Traills is not clear, for Catharine had been silent about their affairs since the Rebellion. The probability was, however, that it was Thomas' wish and decision. Catharine appeared to enjoy the bush, but Thomas had advertized their farm for sale as early as 1835 in the Cobourg *Star*.

Thomas Traill was almost fifty years old, and his background made him even less suited, if possible, than his friend Moodie, for the gruelling labour of pioneering. The sophisticated, well-educated, cosmopolitan gentleman, who had socialized in all the capitals of Europe, could hardly have been pleased with his farm that was advanced from the bush by only six years. His farm could not have looked much more promising than the Moodies' place, and he too had had his share of poor crops, illness, even a broken leg, like Moodie. Catharine, like Susanna, was winning an important reputation in the colony as a writer and Thomas may have felt that he wanted more for her than the farm could give. A "town house" even in a tiny village must have had more attraction than the long years of work still required to bring the Traill farm up to a fully operating state.

There is a possibility, also, that Thomas inherited around this time, for he had spent a great deal on his farm, and yet the Traills lived comfortably in Ashburnham and Thomas became an active member and leader of the community.

With her sister gone, Susanna was now more alone than ever. Samuel was busy with his new house and schemes for his village, but in any case, he had always been more involved with and closer to his wife's family, the Reids, than with the Moodies. He had given the Moodies a great deal of help, and his nearness was of course comforting to Susanna; indeed, John Moodie would never have left his family alone if Samuel had not been there to keep an eye on them. But Samuel could never take the place of the Traills. Catharine and Susanna had been the closest of sisters, and John and Thomas had been friends since they were youths in the Orkneys.

In the spring, Susanna was still weak from her illness, John was still away, and she arranged with a neighbour to put in their crops in exchange for the use of their oxen. This deal turned out to be a reversion to the Moodies' old luck of Hamilton Township; their oxen were abused and almost worked to death logging up the neighbour's fallow while the Moodie's crop was put in too late.

But Susanna no longer cared. She had made up her mind that they were not going to continue on the farm, and she had lost interest in it. The neighbour's poor behaviour was only a minor annoyance. She was content just to look after the children, the garden, the cows and poultry, with Jenny's help.

Moodie's appointment as paymaster, however, was not permanent, and with the quietening of the border raids, the militia was reduced. Once again, he was home in time to take in what little harvest there was. Their main ambition had been met: their debts were now paid off and the pressure on their pride was relieved to that extent. But their strength and their hope had gone.

Sir George Arthur, however, had not forgotten Mrs. Moodie who was winning a considerable reputation for herself as a frequent contributor of poetry and fiction to the now very popular *Literary Garland*. Against the wishes of everyone in Belleville, the Governor appointed John W. Dunbar Moodie to the position of sheriff of the new District of Victoria, with headquarters in Belleville.

John chose to regard the shrievalty appointment as a reward for the excellence and honesty of his work as paymaster, when he had handled more than £30,000 of government money with no complaints from anyone.[6] Yet, Susanna pointed out that Moodie was "perfectly unacquainted with the difficulties and responsibilities of such an important office".[7]

Moodie's departure was delayed slightly over a bit of confusion concerning the bond he had to present before his appointment could be confirmed. But he left as quickly as he could to find a place for his family and to take up his new duties in Belleville, leaving instructions with Susanna to dispose of the crops, furniture, stock and farm implements in the best way she could and as soon as possible. His eagerness to be off showed just how much Moodie too had become disenchanted with the woods. Yet he could do little else, for he had many arrangements to make in Belleville before he could act as sheriff in the first Court of Quarter Sessions scheduled to be held within the month.

Moodie promised to send for his family on the first day of sleighing. Nor did he forget to send back clothing from Belleville so that his wild little family could make an entrance to the town befitting his position as sheriff. This was obviously necessary; all their respectable clothing had been sold. Besides, the boys, Dunbar, Donald and John, had all been born in Douro and had never seen a town before, not even Peterborough, and had had no need of city clothes.

Susanna was more than a little frightened at their change in prospects, though it was what she had wanted:[8]

For seven years I had lived out of the world entirely; my person had been rendered coarse by hard work and exposure to the weather. I looked double the age I really was, and my hair was already thickly sprinkled with grey. I clung to my solitude. I did not like to be dragged from it to mingle in gay scenes, in a busy town, and with gaily dressed people. I was no longer fit for the world; I had lost all relish for the pursuits and pleasures which are so essential to its votaries; I was content to live and die in obscurity.

Once again then, when it was time to leave Susanna was loath to

L

go, but this time with more mature reason than when she left England and later Hamilton Township.

Susanna had matured in more ways than years or grey hairs would signify, though she was still only thirty-six.

The snow came late that year, giving them plenty of time to think about and prepare for leaving. Not until 1 January 1840 did the two sleighs arrive to take them to Belleville. In great turmoil and last-minute confusion, they set about loading them. Unannounced, Samuel arrived in the Moodie clearing, supervized the loading, and told them that he would drive the family to Belleville, rather than have them go all the way perched on top of their possessions.

Their good friend Jenny Buchanan was coming with them of course and, if possible, was in a greater dither than Susanna. With dogs, children and Indians milling about, and Samuel issuing orders to everyone in sight, Jenny appeared, ready to go, with her most prized personal possessions, three hats, all perched on top of her head. The comic relief provided by Jenny, and the rest of the chaos, distracted Susanna from the fear and painfulness of leaving.

Samuel, laughing and indignant at the same time, flatly refused to drive Jenny unless she took off two of the hats. But Jenny refused to be intimidated or shamed into changing her mind or her hats. The problem was not solved until the next day when they overtook the sleighs of furniture and transferred Jenny to one of them, to everyone's satisfaction including Jenny's.

Susanna Moodie was on her way out of the bush that she had learned to accept and even to love a little, a bush that more surprisingly had accepted her – surely the strangest mouthful the frontier had ever swallowed. But the real greatness and freedom of the frontier was the way it accepted all idiosyncracies, even the pompous wilfulness of Susanna.

The trip took two days, down the ridiculous road by the roaring Otonabee, through Peterborough, where the cultured lady's five-year-old son asked:[9]

"Are the houses come to see one another? How did they all meet here?"

It was a bitterly cold ride out to the Front, to Amherst and Cobourg. The journey was filled with happy associations and old friends were greeted at every clearing, including a joyful encounter with the woman who had run the hotel in Cobourg where Susanna had unhappily stayed in 1832. The journey was a demonstration that Mrs. Moodie was no longer a stranger nor an emigrant; whether or not she had wanted to be, she had become an accepted veteran of the bush.

In fact, the bush itself was not the same any more. Samuel Strickland could see major improvements since the days when he first arrived – sawmills, grist mills, the beginnings of a lumber industry, and the greatest triumph – the village of Lakefield, still very small but able to supply the necessities to the growing population and carrying a promise of better things to come. In contrast, Peterborough was a metropolis, with churches, newspapers, and other signs of advancing culture. It was making plans for becoming the county seat of the new District of Colborne which would give the back townships their own government, separate from the old Newcastle District dominated by Cobourg.

In effect, the Moodies, Stricklands and Traills with their neighbours had succeeded in pushing back the frontier, infinitesimally perhaps, but enough that the total isolation implied in the invidious term "backwoods" no longer applied.

While it cannot be said that the Traills and Moodies were great successes at pioneering, neither can they be called total failures. They *survived* in the bush, through the most difficult phases of pioneering, the Moodies for six years, the Traills for seven. And they might well have gone on surviving, since the worst part was over – the first clearing and housebuilding phase.

Although the bush had changed their ambitions, they still wanted more than simple survival; they could have had that much had they stayed in England. They were not driven out of the bush; they chose to leave it, accepting that they were not really suited to this kind of life. Had they thought at all about going back to England (as many others did), they might well have been classified as failures, but they did not. Instead, they undertook to carve out a different sort of life within the colony, one more suitable to their background and education.

Ultimately, then, their contribution to their adopted homeland was not to be their cleared farms, but rather the contribution that they were more capable of making: the advancement of literature, public service and science. In these areas they were pioneering also, pushing back frontiers that were just as intractable as the bush itself, just as important to the growth of the nation, but frontiers which the Moodies and Traills were better equipped to battle.

The backwoods were never so totally isolated that the outside world was unfamiliar with its inhabitants. By 1840, both Mrs. Traill and Mrs. Moodie were well-known figures in the world of literature, in their own right and because of their sisters in England. The cumulative total of all the Strickland sisters' efforts was already impressive. Catharine Parr Traill was noted particularly for her *Backwoods of Canada*, but she also wrote essays and stories for magazines. Susanna Moodie had not yet started to write about the frontier to any extent, but her novels, magazine stories, and patriotic poetry were winning her reputation. In both cases, their work was as well or better known in England than in Canada.

The two eldest Strickland sisters, with home-base still in Reydon Hall where their mother lived, but more actively working in London, had undertaken some pioneering of their own. Elizabeth had been editing the *Court Journal,* a magazine of newsy notes on the aristocracy; this gave her the idea of a series of biographies of the Queens of England. She broached the subject to Agnes, who had already published two minor historical works,

Pilgrims of Walsingham in 1835 and *Tales and Stories from History* in 1836.

While Elizabeth was willing to do more than her share of the research and writing, she was pathologically shy of having her name in print and therefore was not well enough known to approach the notables with requests for their family documents. Agnes in contrast was highly ambitious socially and literarily; she became particularly adept at attacking closed doors, thereby making their research possible. At the same time, she moved up the social ladder to heights that she might otherwise never have dreamed of.

Agnes Strickland now became famous as an historian and as a socialite, when in 1840 the first volume of *The Lives of the Queens of England* appeared and created a considerable stir in the academic and literary worlds.

Volume II was well on its way and the series did not stop until, in 1849 with twelve volumes in print, the Stricklands ran out of Queens of England except for Victoria's own family which through delicacy (and words of warning from the Court), they decided not to touch. Nothing daunted, Agnes and Elizabeth started on the Queens of Scotland in eight volumes, the Bachelor Kings of England, Seven Bishops, and the last four Stuart princesses.

During this whole period, Agnes was also producing epic poetry and essays for a multiplicity of magazines throughout the English-speaking world, including several in the United States and a few in Canada. Agnes knew everyone worth knowing, including colonial notables; and those who were not well known sought her out to cultivate her acquaintance. Elizabeth remained happily anonymous.

Thus, through her publications and through her omnivorous social activity, Agnes Strickland was as well known in Canada as either Catharine Parr Traill or Susanna Moodie.

Yet even for Agnes, there were very few outlets for creative writing in Canada. Except for political newspapers, Canadian publishing was far more primitive than Canadian farming. The bulk of the population had neither the time nor the education to appreciate and support literary talent. What there was of culture was mainly centered in Montreal, the only city big enough as yet to have any pretensions about art. The few publishing firms that did manage to survive more than a few months (including those in Montreal) followed a slavish obedience to the standards set in England, unable to believe that a purely Canadian work could have any intrinsic value.

Not until the 1840s and 1850s, when Canada was beginning to find its own way politically and economically, did the notion arise that it also needed its own cultural expression. It was in this artistic pioneering that Catharine and Susanna were to make their greatest contribution to their adopted land. Their work had already been well received in Britain (thanks in part to Agnes), and when Canadian publishers still under colonial habits of thought became aware of this, the way was open for them to publish anything they cared to write as long as the publishers themselves managed to stay solvent. To their great credit, they used this acceptance to try to introduce the work of native Canadians whenever they found any that looked the slightest bit promising.

Critics have argued about the literary merit of their work, but, good or bad, it had the value of quantity, filling up the wide-open spaces left by an otherwise thin native productivity. Thus, as their first years in the colony had been devoted primarily to pushing back the physical frontier, their remaining years were spent in an all-out attack on the literary frontier. If their failure in the former was not pure, neither was their success in the latter. But unqualified failure and unqualified success were both rare on the frontier; again, *survival* becomes the significant measure.

CHAPTER NINE

The Sheriff of Hastings and Mrs. Moodie

The inefficiency of the public service and the patronage system of appointment played central roles in the grievances that led to the Rebellion of 1837. Patronage itself was not the issue; rather, it was the *control* of patronage, the question of who should exercise the power of appointment to the public service and who should direct the public officials once appointed.

That the public service was large enough to create such an issue at all was a sign of the colony's growing maturity.

Up to this point, the Governor, as the representative of the Crown and the Colonial Office, had the power of appointment entirely in his own hands. However, because Governors were always strangers to the colony, they could not be aware of the relative merits of candidates for office. They had to accept recommendations made by their colonial advisers who were in most instances the Family Compact members of the Executive Council.

The elected representatives in the Assembly wanted the power to advise because they thought they could make better appointments and because they wanted to ensure that their reform plans, once made law, would be enforced. If the Reformers in the Assembly were enabled to influence appointments, they would of course recommend Reformers, in the same way that Tories tended to appoint Tories, and for the same reasons. A politician could trust only those who demonstrated right thinking by open expressions of the same political views.

167

The Governor and his advisers were very touchy on the subject, for they did not take the responsibility for appointment lightly. On the one hand, there was an acute shortage of well-qualified, experienced and educated men in the colony; on the other hand, there was a surfeit of place-seekers who wanted the prestige and security of a public position and who believed that no government job was too complicated for any ordinary citizen.

The Governor wished to make the best possible appointments and naturally tended to favour recent British emigrants, for these were often better educated than the native-born and he was more familiar with their capabilities. But the native-born felt that they should have first preference, since it was their country; they had cleared it and fought for it and wanted it managed by people who understood its needs.

They had a telling point which even the leaders of the Compact respected. In fact, the drive for schools and universities was, in the beginning, an attempt to resolve the dilemma by providing the means for native sons to become qualified for the public service.

In the meantime, the conflict between the British emigrants and Loyalist descendants, which had started as an inevitable cultural clash between peoples of widely different backgrounds, became focused on the matter of public appointments.

Susanna and J. W. Dunbar Moodie, escaping from their chrysalis in the bush, fell right in the middle of this conflict. Moodie's appointment as the first sheriff of the new Victoria District, with headquarters in Belleville, was a classic example of the conflict between the good intentions of the Governor and the wishes of the community.

By colonial standards, Belleville[1] was a cohesive and mature community. It was populated almost entirely by old Loyalist families who had been there for generations, and it had its own accepted local leaders and social structure based on Loyalist traditions and a proud record of service in the various conflicts with the United States. As well, it had its "secret societies", the

Masons and the Orangemen, who were cutting a wide swath in the politics of the day. Unlike the backwoods, this community was progressive enough to have lines rigidly drawn on the basis of religion, politics and racial origin, distinctions so bitterly maintained that no one was allowed to be neutral.

It was the local leaders who had succeeded in having the Victoria District established, separate from the original Midland District. The petition of "Thomas Parker and 2165 others" in January 1836 was moved for adoption in the Legislative Assembly by Henry Yager, M.L.A. In 1837 construction of the new courthouse was started in Belleville, and in 1839 the new District came formally into being, but not without a great deal of turmoil over who should fill all the new civic offices.

The system used for filling an office was relatively straightforward. Whenever word got around that there was the slightest possibility of a vacancy or when there were signs that a new job was being set up, everyone who was remotely interested prepared a petition asking the Governor for the appointment. Each petitioner also asked as many important people as he could find to prepare testimonials supporting his request. Those who did not approve of him for the appointment prepared petitions against him.

On hand also were all the requests for unspecified offices, such as those received from Susanna and John Moodie. Many citizens, unwilling to pin their hopes on only one possibility, simply requested an appointment to any vacancy that might arise.

When a position was to be filled, the Governor's Provincial Secretary assembled all the petitions, memorials and letters of praise and condemnation. If there were any doubts, or gaps in the documentation of a specific applicant, the Governor's Secretary would make further inquiries which added still more to the file. All the material was then carefully screened and weighed. If there was no suitable person among the requests for the vacancy, then the requests for unspecified offices were screened.

Finally, an announcement was made, automatically pleasing

the winner and his supporters and disappointing all the other candidates. The losers often raised more petitions objecting to the appointment and reiterating their claims to superiority.

This was really a rather democratic system in that the views of every interested party were given a hearing. The only difficulty was that the ultimate appointment was at the sole discretion of the Governor, who was put into a position of final arbiter, a sort of umpire in the scramble, and like all umpires his decision and his judgement were often questioned by the losing side. A conscientious Governor preferred to select a candidate who was personally known to him. If he knew none of the candidates, as was most often the case especially in the "outside service", i.e. positions outside the provincial capital, he had to rely on references from those he trusted. Such references were for the most part given carefully, because the trusted adviser had no wish to jeopardize his own reputation.

The system may appear a little odd today, but it should be borne in mind that the population of the province was still very small, and everyone knew everyone else, or had connections with people who knew someone close to the seat of power. Moreover, the system was a natural outgrowth of the culture of the day, of a society which was still highly class-conscious even among the Reformers.

One of the most important customs of this society was the letter of introduction. Whenever anyone left his home area where his class position was unquestionable, he took with him letters of introduction to members of the equivalent class in the area to which he was going. For instance, Samuel Strickland had letters to Peter Robinson and T. A. Stewart when he first visited Peterborough.

The petition and its supporting letters of reference were simply a variation on this custom. While the system tended to solidify class distinctions, it encouraged responsibility on the part of those involved. As a result, appointments made in this way tended to be satisfactory, though they obviously did not attempt to select, or make claims to have appointed, the one best man for the job.

The appointment of the sheriff of the Victoria District followed the pattern closely and, as a result, Moodie was in trouble with the disappointed local aspirants to the shrievalty and their supporters, before he had even arrived in Belleville. There were many small part-time positions in the new District, but the plums were the permanent full-time jobs, one of which was the office of sheriff. The competition for this job had been keen for three to four years before Moodie was finally appointed.

As early as 1837, Henry Yager, M.L.A. and merchant of Belleville, had petitioned for the sheriff's appointment.[2] He would probably have won it too, since he had moved the establishment of the District in the Assembly, and his request for the position was supported by a petition from three of the local lawyers including Benjamin Dougall, and three justices of the peace including Billa Flint, Jr.; all big names in the community. Yager withdrew his application, however, to pursue other political objectives. Another Member of the Provincial Parliament, Anthony Manahan of Kingston, also wanted the job and also withdrew.[3]

The field was then open to Thomas Parker, the man who had originated the petition to establish the District. From 1837 to 1839, a series of petitions, recommendations and memorials on behalf of Parker for sheriff flooded the office of the Governor's Secretary.[4]

Parker was supported by M.L.A.s, lawyers, J.P.s, the Board of Education, and ordinary citizens. He was a long-time resident of Belleville; he had been postmaster there for many years and had a recommendation from the colonial headquarters of the General Post Office; as deputy sheriff in the old Midland District, he was familiar with the duties and procedures. Parker thought he had the job in his hands, for he had played the system exactly right. But perhaps he played it a little too thoroughly, with too many petitions and recommendations. For some reason, the Governor's Secretary made his own inquiries.

From the Toronto office of the Commercial Bank, for whom Parker had been an agent in Belleville, came word that Parker had been removed from that post because of a deficiency in his accounts. Although the Bank pointed out that Parker had subsequently made up the amount, they still had found it necessary to remove him from their service. This was enough from the Governor's office.

They were aware of the high feelings running in Belleville and of the splits and divisions in the community. Rejecting Parker in spite of his strong local support, they were forced to select an outsider. They looked through their file of requests for unspecified offices and found Mrs. Moodie's husband – a deserving person in dire straits in the backwoods, an educated man and a military hero, who had already been helped out by a temporary appointment and who had performed satisfactorily and who therefore still had a claim on the government's benevolence. In the government's view, Moodie could not be considered a foreigner to the District because he had been militia paymaster there for several months.

In the opinion of the Governor's office, Moodie was perfect. To assuage any possible local discontent over making the sheriff's appointment from outside the area, they would fill all the other positions with citizens of Belleville. For instance, as District Court Judge and Chairman of the Commission of the Peace, they would accept the petition of Benjamin Dougall, the dean of the local lawyers. The traditional British genius for compromise would be upheld, at least as far as the Governor's office was concerned.

Susanna had said that few of Moodie's problems were of his own making; whether this had been true before, it certainly applied in Belleville. Although he had asked for an appointment, he could not possibly have known the trap that had been set for him. To the Belleville citizens, and particularly to those with whom he was going to be in daily contact – the lawyers, the judge, and the J.P.s – he was an outsider, a Britisher, and the man who got the job that Parker should have had. As even Susanna admitted, Moodie had not the faintest idea of what the sheriff's office was about; his only concern had been to look after his family, preferably in a way that would not compromise his old-world ideals of honesty and integrity. This is not to suggest that Moodie would be derelict in his duties or that he would put his family first. He would, as he had before, conscientiously learn his job and do it well. And, as had happened before in every encounter with native-born Canadians, his sense of honour would be mistaken for weakness and stupidity; the "Yankee' standards of behaviour were more clever and realistic.

In due time, they would all learn that Moodie would bend over backwards in order not to compromise his integrity, but that in so doing he was neither weak nor stupid. He had matured in the backwoods and lost some of his romantic idealism but not his integrity.

For another quarter of a century he would stick it out with no further help from the Governor's Office, never being accepted as a native, winning many rounds over those who distrusted and challenged his honourable mannerisms, never compromising with what he thought was right, and being vindicated only after his forced retirement and death. He often asked for another job, preferably in a less hostile community, or one with duties that would not force him into confrontations on the field of honour, but his requests were ignored. Thus, he had to stay in order to feed his ever-increasing family.

John W. Dunbar Moodie's particular contribution to his adopted land was to be the standards he set in the behaviour of a public servant. His career was not entirely without blemish, but it sparkled in contrast with the usual standards of behaviour. And he did have some small influence in raising those standards.

Sheriff Moodie's career in the Victoria District (renamed

Hastings County soon after his appointment), also had an enormous influence on his wife's career as colonial writer. The details of the Moodies' life in Belleville were not given by Susanna in anything like the detail in which she talked about their farming adventures. Yet both *Roughing it in the Bush* and *Life in the Clearings,* her major autobiographical works, were mainly written in Belleville. Many of her caustic remarks, ostensibly made as an impartial observer of the Canadian scene, can be better understood in the context of her trials as the wife of the controversial sheriff. The ill-contained anger against Canada that Susanna expressed, even when she tried to soften the force of her words by vehemently affirming her faith in the country, can only be explained by her love for the man and her wholehearted respect for his integrity. This same anger, however, only compounded the difficulty of her husband's position.

The one Strickland work that was neither edited by nor dedicated to Agnes Strickland was Susanna's *Life in the Clearings,* her impressions of life in Belleville. This work was dedicated to:[5] "John Wedderburn Dunbar Moodie, Esq., Sheriff of the County of Hastings, Upper Canada, By His Attached Friend and Wife, Susanna Moodie." Yet, about the only direct reference to Sheriff Moodie in this work was a short sketch about a visit to the Penitentiary at Kingston when Susanna accompanied Moodie as he escorted some convicted criminals there.

The story of the Moodies in Belleville began in the backwoods of Douro.

Because a sheriff was a custodian of public funds, Moodie had to post a bond of £2000 before his appointment would take effect. The money did not have to be put up in cash, of course; otherwise Moodie and many others would never have been appointed. Rather, he had to commit £1000 of his own property, with the rest to be guaranteed by at least two other sureties whose cash and property would be liable to seizure by the government if there were any difficulties about the handling of public funds.[6]

In October 1839, while he was still in Douro, Moodie had a bond drawn up, with Thomas Traill and Samuel Strickland as sureties, signed and sealed in the presence of Catharine Parr Traill. This document was dispatched to the Lieutenant Governor who turned it over to Inspector General J. Macauley.

On 1 November, Macauley sent it back to Moodie in Douro.[7] There were two things wrong with it; Macauley had never heard of Thomas Traill or Samuel Strickland (though both were J.P.s), and could not accept them as sureties until Moodie provided letters from other gentlemen whom Macauley did know and who could confirm that Thomas and Samuel were adequate. And the document itself was not right:

> I do not like to have any but a *perfect* instrument in a case of this nature in my custody. You will perceive that this which I return is not so, for your own and Mr. Strickland's signatures are partly written upon the the bits of paper used for the seals.

It is not clear what Mr. Macauley meant by "a case of this nature"; perhaps he anticipated trouble over Moodie's appointment, or perhaps he simply meant sheriffs' appointments in general, all of which may have had to conform precisely to the letter of the law. In any case, he was certainly being extraordinarily nit-picking about it.

Samuel must have been as disappointed as John Moodie. He thought he was well-known in the colony, but the Inspector General had never heard of him.

Moodie quickly located two men who were better known, T. A. Stewart and the Reverend Mr. Armour of Cavan Township (next to Douro), and asked them to affirm the bona fides of Traill and Strickland in letters to Macauley. He re-made the Bond on 8 November, being careful not to sign on the "bits of paper", and sent it back.

Before he received acknowledgement of this, he had to leave

for Belleville. Time was running out and the first Court of Quarter Sessions which would take the oaths and documents of the new district officials was scheduled to meet in a few days. Judge Dougall was in no mood to accommodate the sheriff if he did not arrive on time.

In Belleville, Moodie was forced to have still another bond prepared with two local men as sureties, so that he could present it to the Court on 13 November.[8] All the documents taken that day were then sent on to the Inspector General, which must have confused him a bit, because he had already written to Moodie accepting the bond with Strickland and Traill as sureties, stating that he had now received the necessary letters from Messrs. Stewart and Armour.[9]

Despite the muddle, Moodie was now sworn in and documented as sheriff, and he had had his first encounter with his Belleville colleagues, all of which had gone off peacefully enough. Everyone was busy organizing the new district and arguing over other appointments yet to be made.

In all this, Moodie received a vivid impression of the arguments and divisions in the town: Tories *vs.* Reformers, Methodists *vs.* Anglicans, Orangemen *vs.* Catholics. But he had undertaken to be entirely neutral in the local politics and disputes, mainly because he considered that his position as sheriff required him to be neutral, and to a lesser extent, because his personal political and social views were still British-oriented rather than Canadian-oriented. The only other local appointment he was immediately willing to accept was secretary of the District Board of Education, a public service post which he incorrectly thought would not draw him into local politics.

Nevertheless, Moodie was labelled, rightly or wrongly, as a Reformer and a Presbyterian, thereby slotting him in the various battles. Though Moodie had fought on the side of the Tories in the Rebellion, he had given voice to his strong feelings about the behaviour of his fellow officers and about the extremes to which the Tories went in tracking and persecuting anyone suspected of being a rebel. (Though not all Reformers were rebels, all rebels were Reformers.) In addition, Moodie was the centre of a dispute over the sheriff's appointment; the disappointed candidate, Thomas Parker, was a Tory and Moodie's enemy; therefore Moodie had to be a Reformer.

Parker made it clear that he was going to use every means in his power to prove that Moodie was incompetent as a sheriff. And Parker had many allies in this, while Moodie as yet knew no one very well in Belleville.

By February, less than four months after he arrived, Moodie found it necessary to write to the Governor, ostensibly to thank him for his appointment but also to clear himself of any derogatory suggestions that Parker might have made against him.

Sir George Arthur replied, in a mildly patronizing but gentle tone: [10]

I beg to acknowledge your letter marked "Private" of the 22nd Inst. – written under the impression that Mr. Parker had made some representation to me to your prejudice.

In reply, I am happy it is in my power to undeceive you – Mr. Parker has not made any communication of the kind directly or indirectly, of which I am aware.

For the valuable information your letter conveys I am much obliged to you; and I am much pleased with your very sensible reflections. At your convenience, I shall be glad to hear from you upon the subject of immigration, and the means of facilitating the settlement of the Wild Lands – the most important and the most difficult problem we have to deal with in Upper Canada.

With respect to your office, I hope it is agreeable to you; and as to your loyalty and attachments to British Institutions, it was unnecessary for you to say one word – I took it for granted that you must possess both, or you would not have been the husband of Mrs. Moodie, for whose situation I felt so deeply interested that I was quite mortified it was not earlier in my power to confirm some appointment upon you.

Encouraged by Arthur's reply, Moodie prepared a twenty-page essay analyzing the problems of the settlement of the Wild Lands, the evils of land speculators, abuses in the land office, and the ill effects of all this on emigration. He enclosed it with the following covering letter: [11]

> May it please Your Excellency,
> I herewith beg leave to inclose a few observations on the subject of Emigration etc in the sincere hope that you may find some of the suggestions I have ventured to submit to your consideration, of some practical utility. Should they prove so, Your Excellency may believe me, that I shall feel much more satisfaction than I could derive from any emolument arising from the office Your Excellency has been pleased to confer on me. I have to thank Your Ex'cy for the kind feelings you have expressed to one so justly dear to myself and I hope there is no ego-tism in my saying that she is in every respect truly worthy of your good opinion.
> Though often brought to the verge of want, through unforeseen misfortunes, she has never ceased, even for a moment, to rely with confidence on a merciful Providence which has so wonderfully befriended us in our greatest need.
> Mrs. Moodie begs me to express her grateful sense of Your Excellency's kindness in having so generously placed us in a situation of so much respectability and comfort.
> I was very happy to learn from Your Excellency that I have been misinformed respecting Mr. Parker, who I believe has no unfriendly feeling towards me.

As a further expression of the Moodies' gratitude to the Lieutenant Governor, their fifth child, born in June, was named George Arthur Moodie.

All that year, the new officers, boards and commissions

devoted themselves to settling in to their new appointments, sizing up each other, and trying to clarify just what their duties and responsibilities were. By November, Moodie had a fair idea of his situation and tried to equalize his own position in the community hierarchy by preparing a memorial to the Governor's Secretary, recommending the appointment of a friend of his, William H. Ponton, to the vacant position of Registrar.

Moodie could not refrain from intruding his own problems with the community:[12]

> I trust that the terms I use in speaking of Mr. Ponton will not be attributed merely to the partiality of friendship; – for independently of the interest I must necessarily feel for a person of his character, in a place where, – I am sorry to say, – highmindedness and integrity, united with temperate habits are so seldom to be found; –
>
> I also deeply feel the powerful influence which the character and habits of such a man must have in raising the standards of morals amidst a vicious community.

And so the battle lines were drawn. Ponton won the appointment, but he was able to do little to raise the "standards of morals in the vicious community". This was within the aegis of the sheriff, not the registrar.

Susanna by this time had also sized up the community and had mixed feelings about it. She was entertained and puzzled by the volatility and strange customs of the colonial town, a society totally unlike anything she had expected when she fearfully left the backwoods. Not the least of her disappointments came from the physical appearance of the place.[13]

> The town of Belleville, in 1840, contained a population of 1500 souls, or thereabouts. The few streets it then possessed were chiefly composed of frame houses, put up in the most unartistic and irregular fashion, their gable ends or fronts turned to the street, as it suited the whim or convenience of

the owner, without the least regard to taste or neatness. At that period there were only two stone houses and two of brick in the place. One of these wonders of the village was the courthouse and gaol; the other three were stores. The dwellings of the wealthier portions of the community were distinguished by a coat of white or yellow paint, with green or brown doors and window blinds; while the houses of the poorer class retained the dull grey which the plain boards always assume after a short exposure to the weather.

In spite of the great beauty of the locality, it was but an insignificant, dirty-looking place.

Susanna was disappointed with almost everything in the town, because she had expected it to be so much better than the backwoods. Apparently, she had thought that the towns at the Front would have improved enough in the years since she had seen them, to resemble more closely the towns of England. Her fears on leaving the bush that her clothing would not be appropriate and that her person would show the ravages of years of manual labour suggested that she expected an important place in society befitting the exalted post granted to her husband by the grace of the most important gentleman in the colony.

Yet her disappointment with the physical appearance of Belleville was nothing compared to her astonishment over the ways of the people, especially the women:[14]

> The state of society when we first came to this district was everything but friendly or agreeable. The ferment occasioned by the impotent rebellion of W. L. Mackenzie had hardly subsided ... Men looked distrustfully upon each other, and the demon of party reigned pre-eminent, as much in the drawing-room as in the council chamber.

> The town was divided into two fierce political factions; and however moderate your views might be, to belong to the one was to incur the dislike and ill-will of the other. ... Even women entered deeply into this party hostility; and those who,

from their education and mental advantages, might have been friends and agreeable companions kept aloof, rarely taking notice of each other, when accidentally thrown together.

In other words, when Sheriff Moodie was branded a Reformer in spite of his moderate views, Tory ladies would not speak to Mrs. Moodie, although there were some among them with "mental advantages" whom Susanna would like to have known. Susanna considered that it was unladylike to enter into the political arguments of the men, but being forced into it, she became a strong Reformer herself.

She was astonished at the hypocrisy of the Belleville ladies, the way they put on airs, unsuccessfully pretending to be above the station in life of their forefathers, their affectation of delicate health, their sneers at farmers and "mechanics", and their diligent pursuit of ostentatious display.

Social status appeared to be based solely on the possession of money, a commodity in which the Moodies were conspicuously deficient. No respect was given to education, intellectual achievement, good manners, or personal honesty, with which the Moodies were well supplied. Susanna, on her part, had learned a healthy respect for "honest toil" from her experience in the backwoods, a respect second only to her convictions of the glory of education. She could not understand why those people who were only one step removed from labourers should deny the worth of labour.

Susanna Moodie was an equally fascinating and curious object of interest to the Belleville ladies. By the end of 1840, four of Susanna's serialized novels and fifteen of her poems had appeared in the *Literary Garland*. The response to this achievement was demonstrated by Susanna's son having to defend his mother's honour:[15]

> One of my boys was tauntingly told by another lad at school, "that his ma' said that Mrs. M — invented lies and got money for them".

Yet when the Moodies' house burned down in December 1840, Susanna was delighted at the way the volunteer firemen turned out and risked their lives to save the furniture. She had respect and admiration for the way the community rallied round in time of emergency; she had missed this part of colonial life in her first home in Hamilton Township, although it had surely been there; and in the backwoods of course there had been only her own family to give immediate help in such a disaster. She was deeply appreciative of offers of help, including one from the Catholic priest who offered both a house and money and who was not resentful when the Moodies refused his offer in favour of another.

Some of the effect was lost when many of their prized possessions were looted from their front lawn after the fire; evidently the local thieves were not impressed by the fact they were stealing from the sheriff. But Susanna by this time had matured enough not to castigate the whole community for the crimes of a few scavengers.

Perhaps the most curious of the Belleville customs in Susanna's eyes was the Orangemen's Parade on 12 July. She thought the parade "a useless aggravation of an old national grievance to perpetuate the memory of the battle of the Boyne". She asked, "What have we to do with the hatreds and animosities of a more barbarous age?" Her solution was, in effect, a plague on both their houses: [16]

If the Protestant would give up a little of his bigotry and the Catholic a part of his superstition, and they could consent to meet each other half way, as brothers of one common manhood, inspired by the same Christian hope and bound to the same heavenly country, we should no longer see the Orange banner flaunting our streets on the twelfth of July, and natives of the same island provoking each other to acts of violence and bloodshed.

This bit of sweet reasonableness would hardly endear Susanna to either side. Assuming the role of peacemaker in a dispute she cared little about, her facile solution endangered her and her family with the lively possibility of a joint attack by the Irish of both sides. She failed to recognize the need for ceremony and pageantry in an otherwise dull colonial landscape and the need of the boisterous society of labourers-cum-gentry to have an excuse for a fight.

Susanna was entirely unjustified in assuming her posture of impartial observer of the native customs. The sheriff was the one man in the district who had the responsibility for keeping the peace. Whether it was 12 July, 17 March, Election Day, or any of the other days appointed for a fight between the Irish Catholics and Protestants, Tories and Reformers, and any of the other social groupings in Hastings, Susanna's husband was in the thick of things, trying to force peace upon people who wanted and expected to fight. As a result, despite Susanna's highminded criticism of the Belleville antics, she and her family were intimately involved whenever Sheriff Moodie stood alone in the untenable position of peacemaker in all conflicts.

CHAPTER TEN

Conflict in the Clearings

The County of Hastings, District of Victoria, was the battle-ground for two different but inter-related conflicts. One of the quarrels surrounded the insistent attempts of Messrs. Dougall, Parker, Murney and others to have Sheriff Moodie relieved of his position. The other was the two elections for a seat in the Union Parliament contested in both cases by Robert Baldwin and Edmund Murney, with Sheriff Moodie as Returning Officer.

The attack on the sheriff began as soon as Moodie arrived in Belleville. The technique used centred on creating maximum financial embarrassment for him – supplemented by derogatory insinuations about Moodie's competence and honesty, in an attempt either to have Moodie removed or to force him to remove himself.

All sheriffs of the day were vulnerable to this form of attack. The office carried no salary with it, following the principle that government services should be self-supporting as far as possible. The sheriff earned his living from fees received for serving writs and subpoenas, for holding sheriff's sales of impounded property, for court appearances and similar duties. In the new and sparsely populated districts, there was not enough of this business to keep the sheriff in security, let alone affluence.

This difficulty was compounded in Hastings by deliberate delays in paying the sheriff what was owing to him, thereby keeping his accounts out of balance and embarrassing him before the civil servants at the capital who wanted his reports in on time.

To some extent, Moodie was able to defeat this tactic by hiring two bailiffs, one Tory and one Reformer. But there was little he could do about those who deliberately avoided the use of the sheriff's services. There were several types of writs and legal actions that by law did not require the sheriff to have anything to do with them, and the local lawyers took advantage of this. Not content with letting these devices take their toll, men like Parker started nuisance lawsuits against the sheriff, which never came to anything, but which cost Moodie money and kept him on the defensive.

Thus, by the end of their second year in Belleville, the Moodies were clearly aware that the sheriff's appointment was not going to solve their persistent problems about money.

Moodie wrote to the Governor to ask for an additional appointment, that of District Treasurer. He said:[1]

> ... At present I am hardly able to support my family with the most rigid economy ... After my long experience in the backwoods, you may readily suppose, my desires as to emoluments are of the most moderate description. I merely desire to enjoy that degree of independence which I think essential to the responsibility of my office ... I have ample leisure ... as my present duties seldom employ me more than two or three hours daily.

But the authorities felt that the offices of sheriff and treasurer were incompatible; at least, that was the reason they gave for not giving the appointment to Moodie.

In fact, few sheriffs in Upper Canada were free of financial difficulties. A petition to the Governor from a Committee representing all the sheriffs made the situation clear. One of the most important points outlined in the petition was that the sheriff's biggest responsibility, that of keeping the peace, was not compensated for at all, and the committee felt that they should not be expected to work in this way without remuneration:[2]

> . . . The Sheriff being the principal conservator of the peace within his District is as a matter of course called upon by the Government to investigate and report upon all matters in which the Queen's peace may be involved, and to suppress all riots and breaches of the peace . . . There can be no doubt but that in Canada West where no Police force exists, they will engross much of his time and attention . . .

Sheriff Moodie was a member of this Committee and undoubtedly had much to do with the composition of the petition. In Moodie's case, the normal difficulties of the sheriff were given extra keenness by the diligence of Moodie's tormentors.

The first critical attack on Moodie struck right at the heart of the problem; the sheriff's bond and sureties, his proof of financial responsibility without which he could not hold the office.

Moodie had been rushed in the preparation of his bond, because of the mix-up in Douro, and at the last minute had secured two local men to act as his sureties. Adam Henry Meyers and Sheldon Hawley were strangers to Moodie and he to them. Their readiness to serve him in this way was explained when one of them, Meyers, whose forefathers had been the original settlers of Belleville, became involved in a complex series of lawsuits. To win, Meyers needed and expected the sheriff's support.

As Moodie told the story, Meyers was fighting with a man named Reeves over a piece of property. Meyers had purchased the property from Reeves' mother and tried to evict the son. Reeves brought a counter-suit against Meyers for trespass and, because of an unclear title, the case was removed to Toronto courts.

In the meantime, Meyers bought up some outstanding notes against Reeves and foreclosed on them, getting an execution against Reeves' property. Moodie as sheriff was required to hold a public auction to sell Reeve's property. Reeves approached

Moodie asking him to postpone the sale for a few days until his suit against Meyers in the Toronto courts could be finalized; if he won it, he could easily pay off Meyers and keep his property. Moodie said:[3]

> Under these peculiar circumstances, I thought it was my duty, in common humanity, to accede to his request; though I well knew from the knowledge I had acquired of Mr. Meyers' character, – that I would become the object of his bitter animosity.

In caution, however, Moodie consulted Judge Dougall on the matter. Dougall advised him to postpone the sale though not longer than the current sitting of the Quarter Sessions. Reeves' lawyer, John Ross, also conferred with Dougall and secured the judge's opinion on the legality of the brief postponement.

Meyers considered Moodie derelict in his duty for not carrying out immediately the terms of the writ, but his biggest complaint was against Moodie's ingratitude: the sheriff had foiled the legal strategy of his own surety. Moodie had to find other sureties in a hurry. Rumours were allowed to reach him that his enemies intended to see that he found no other sureties.

In fact, Moodie had no difficulty in lining up a whole gaggle of new sureties, all of whom were rejected for one reason or another by Judge Dougall, although they included some of the most outstanding men in the District.

Starting on the first day of the next Quarter Sessions of the Peace, 12 April 1842, Moodie presesented a new bond with four sureties: John Gilbert, David Roblin, Nelson Gilbert Reynolds, and John Ross (the lawyer who had represented Reeves in the last case).

Judge Dougall rejected this bond on two grounds. He said he preferred only two sureties on a bond, and they would have to be Roblin and Gilbert. Reynolds and Ross would not do because the magistrates did not know their financial resources, "and from motives of delicacy did not wish to make inquiries respecting them."[4]

This was nonsense, of course, and Moodie knew it. Ross was one of the most active lawyers in the District, and Reynolds was a wealthy philanthropist, providing among other things much of the backing for Belleville's new Methodist Episcopal Church. When Moodie reported back to Reynolds and Ross, they were naturally insulted and did not wish to see the matter dropped there. They demanded that the sheriff go back and tell the judge that they were ready to be investigated.

Thus fortified, Moodie went back to Judge Dougall and promptly got into an argument with him. Dougall said he did not care if the feelings of Reynolds and Ross were hurt because they were only influenced by partisan motives. Startled by this, Moodie retorted that there was more reason to suppose that if anyone was being partisan it was more likely to be the magistrates.

Dougall still had not clarified the matter of the bond, and Ross himself went with Moodie to see the Judge in his courtroom, with the Clerk of the Peace, Edmund Murney, present as a witness. Ross offered to submit an affidavit respecting his property, and Moodie repeated Reynolds' willingness to do likewise. Nevertheless, some time later, Murney returned the bond to Moodie as unsatisfactory; no inquiries had been made and no affidavits asked for.

In despair, Moodie prepared still another bond, leaving out John Ross and Nelson Gilbert Reynolds. The new sureties were John Reynolds, Caleb Gilbert, David Roblin, and B. F. Davy, a really sterling line-up. They were all important names among the founding fathers of Belleville, founders of the Masonic Lodge to which most of the magistrates including Dougall belonged, founders of churches, cricket club, etc. Moreover, B. F. Davy would eventually become the first Mayor of Belleville and David Roblin's family was to include two premiers of Manitoba.

Judge Dougall was not to be outdone so easily. He objected to this bond on the grounds that the name "Davy" had been omitted from one of the copies. Nor would he allow Moodie to correct it on the spot; changes to the bond could only be made in the presence of all the sureties and the witnesses.

Moodie was angry and confused. He insisted on a commitment that these sureties would be accepted before he went to the trouble of re-making the bond, and he brought up the matter of Dougall's refusal to let his earlier sureties prove themselves.

Dougall was offended by this complaint, and in front of the whole court he denied Moodie's statement about Reynolds' and Ross' offers of affidavits. In effect, he called the sheriff a liar. Moodie said he had witnesses to confirm the truth of his statement. Dougall took a different tack; he said:

> "That a very improper use had been made of the facts already stated out of doors, which he had heard from a person in whom he had confidence. As these observations were evidently pointed at me [Moodie], I told him whatever others might have done, I had made no improper use of them ... and insisted that he would state what improper use I had made of the facts. Mr. Dougall then said that I had accused the Magistrates to him of being influenced by party feeling. To this accusation I made no reply, not knowing what use might be made of my admission."

Dougall then adjourned the Sessions, leaving the sheriff without a bond and without an opportunity to present a revised one. The baiting had worked very effectively; the sheriff felt that he had been publicly insulted without any means of redress and that the whole affair had been a "deep laid scheme" to injure or ruin him. He felt sure that Judge Dougall had no intentions of accepting any bond because the judge was motivated solely by "violent party hostility".

On 18 April, Moodie made a deposition to the Governor, telling the whole story and, in effect, asking for protection against the local magistracy.[5]

On 13 May, he had yet another bond prepared, this time with Gideon Turner replacing B. F. Davy as one of the sureties. (Davy had evidently decided to have nothing more to do with it), and on 24 May, Moodie was again writing to the Governor asking for more time to register his sureties.

Dougall then decided to put Moodie out of his misery and accept the latest bond.[6] It was registered on 26 May; however, when it was forwarded to the capital, it was enclosed with a certificate from Dougall stating that the court had unanimously accepted it on 14 May, ten days *before* Moodie asked the Governor for more time. Possibly the Clerk, Mr. Murney, neglected to tell Moodie that the bond had been accepted. In any case, still another bond was registered, on 4 June 1842. It was Moodie's original bond with Thomas Traill and Samuel Strickland as sureties, the same one that had been signed on 8 November 1839 and accepted at that time by the Inspector General. Moodie had been keeping this one up his sleeve all the time and in desperation finally produced it. Even when he did learn that it was no longer needed, he preferred to stick with it anyway, no longer relying on financial support from the local people.

Moodie came out of this round of the sheriff *vs.* the judge looking rather silly, as a person does who has been pushing against a resistant door and the door suddenly opens. The next round, however, was clearly won by the sheriff one year later, though the list of his "enemies" was growing ever larger. It had started with Parker, then Meyers was added, then Dougall and Murney. It was obviously extremely embarrassing for the sheriff, an officer of the court, to be in conflict with the judge and the clerk of the court. The situation was untenable and had to be resolved.

Moodie was again a defendant in a nuisance suit, and Dougall was acting for the other side as a private lawyer. The coroner, Mr. P. O'Reilly, summoned the jury after consulting with Dougall on who the jury members should be. This was obviously illegal. Moodie brought charges against both the judge and the coroner for attempting to pack a jury. On the basis of his charges, a committee of the Executive Council recommended that the Solicitor General, T. C. Aylwin, should go to Belleville and conduct a full inquiry. Aylwin did so, and prepared a report to the Government. The judge was fired.

The report of the Executive Council Committee was written in very strong terms:[7]

> ... From Mr. Aylwin's Report founded on evidence taken in Mr. Dougall's presence at Belleville, and giving all due weight to his character and standing in society, the Committee feel forced to form an unfavourable opinion respecting Mr. Dougall's conduct, and even if he be in reality free from the motives imputed to him, the Committee think that he had placed himself in a position so questionable, that a due regard to the Administration of Justice, and to the public confidence in the integrity of Judicial Functionaries, make it unadvisable to continue him in office as Judge of the District Court.

> The Committee regret therefore that they have no alternative, but respectfully to recommend Mr. Dougall's removal.

The Committee Report also censured Mr. O'Reilly, the coroner, for "a degree of disingenuousness which cannot be passed over without reprehension". Moodie was disappointed that O'Reilly had not been fired too, since he regarded the coroner as having been guilty of "double treachery".

Dougall, seeing the handwriting on the wall, tried to resign but was not allowed to do so; indeed, he was put in a position of having to apologize for trying it. Dougall was thoroughly disgraced before his court and before the entire country. The mild-mannered sheriff thus had shown his claws.

Even if he had not been embroiled in the earlier disputes, Moodie would have brought the action against the judge; his views about the integrity of the law and of public servants were stronger even than his need for personal revenge. It is doubtful, however, that the situation would have arisen or that Dougall would have been caught in such a trap, had he and his fellows not been so absorbed in their campaign to rid Belleville of John Moodie.

Conspicuous by its absence in this fracas was the name of one of Moodie's early enemies, Edmund Murney, who had been Clerk of the Peace and Dougall's right-hand man in badgering the sheriff on the subject of the bonds. Murney too had been fired from his post as a result of the other of the two concurrent fights in Belleville, the elections.

If there was anything the Tories of Hastings hated more than Sheriff Moodie, it was the Reform Party and its plea for Responsible Government.

After the Rebellion, the Reform Party had had to re-group, and they chose as their leader a man who had taken no part in the Rebellion, Mr. Robert Baldwin. Baldwin's one political aim was to achieve responsible government for Canada. The idea had been accepted in principle in the Durham Report, but there was a long way to go before the dream could be realized. Baldwin accepted an executive post under the new Governor General, Lord Sydenham, in the hope that he could expedite responsible government.

Thus, in the first elections after the Act of Union (of Upper and Lower Canada), as leader of the Reform Party and new Solicitor General for Canada West, Baldwin sought a seat in the Assembly. He decided to run in two ridings, one in York which would assure him a seat for he was unopposed there, and the other in Hastings because he wanted to bring this uncertain seat into the Reform fold.

Edmund Murney, who had represented Belleville once before and was a confirmed opponent both of the Union and of responsible government, decided to run against him. Sheriff Moodie would be Returning Officer. There were two elections, in fact, one in 1841 and another in 1842 with the same cast of characters and the same issue.

The first election was not regarded as unusual by anyone except perhaps the very green returning officer. There were riots all over the province, including Belleville, as the opposing sides gave vent to their animosities. Ever since the Rebellion in 1837, anger, recrimination and heart-break had been building up over the matter of politics. They knew they were building a new nation; some of the farmers and shopkeepers thought differently than others about what sort of nation it should be; therefore, they knocked each other's heads in.

The Orangemen played an active part in this. Though some politicians thought Orange support was more embarrassing than useful, they represented very strong political support in both voting and fighting strength. Orangemen, of course, were originally all Tories, "true-blue", loyal to Queen and Empire. In Hastings in 1841, the Orangemen supported Edmund Murney, Tory candidate.

Not all Belleville Orangemen were club-swinging ruffians. Their membership included such personages as Thomas Parker whom we have met; George Benjamin, editor and publisher of the *Intelligencer*, founder of St. Thomas' Anglican church, and later M.P. and railroad builder; A. D. Dougall, nephew of Judge Dougall, lawyer and churchman; and Mackenzie Bowell, a printer's apprentice in 1841 but later Grand Master of the Orange Order, publisher of the *Intelligencer* (after Benjamin), M.P. and cabinet minister under John A. Macdonald, and in 1894-6, Prime Minister of Canada.

Orangemen or not, everyone in Belleville took their politics very seriously. That the sheriff failed to keep the peace can hardly be held against him. None of his colleagues in the other districts was any more successful.

The physical arrangements for the voting added to the returning officer's difficulties. The secret ballot was not yet in use, and in 1841 there was only one poll for the whole district which stood open for six consecutive days to allow everyone to get in from the back country.

These were the days of the open poll, when each vote was a blow which was known and cheered; and when the electors on both sides marched to the hustings like men-at-arms of two medieval private armies.[8]

It was a close race throughout the polling with continuous rioting and each side blaming the other for the disorder. Murney supporters insisted that, despite Baldwin's denials, he had been a leader in the rebellion and, moreover, that he attended mass "twice every Sunday".[9] This was an appeal to the Orangemen and a reference to Baldwin's alliance with Lafontaine and the Lower Canadian reformers.

After the first day of polling, Baldwin wrote a hurried note to his cabinet colleague, S. B. Harrison:[10]

We stand even tonight 35 each – My friends however seem to think we shall beat them. We took the votes by telling which of course tends to keep us even – The show of hands was greatly in our favour . . .

The procedure Baldwin was referring to went like this – on the appointed day, the sheriff publicly read the writ of election and asked for nominations. He then called for a show of hands among the freeholders (property owners entitled to vote) present at the meeting, and declared which candidate had the most supporters. The other side challenged, and asked for a poll of all freeholders. Then the voting, as such, commenced and continued for the next six days.

Baldwin's report reached Lord Sydenham, a very anxious Governor, who felt that his administration depended upon his ministers being returned. Sydenham's advisers were unable to enlighten him, because of the general mayhem, but they took some heart from Baldwin's rather premature note.[11]

Sheriff Moodie eventually decided that Baldwin had won the

election by a margin of thirty-six votes, and he was immediately attacked for showing political favouritism and for undue manipulation of the poll.

In a petition to the Legislative Assembly, presented on the second day of sitting in the new House, 15 June 1841,[12] Thomas Parker and others of Belleville complained that the election of Robert Baldwin was illegal because : first, Baldwin already had a seat in the House, as member from the fourth riding of York; second, Baldwin's election committee had hired "a large body of armed shanty-men, bullies and ruffians, armed with bludgeons, clubs, and sticks and other offensive weapons", who were placed near the hustings to prevent Murney supporters from approaching, "behaving in a noisy, riotous and brutal manner, using threatening language and gestures"; third, Baldwin votes were accepted from people who did not live in Hastings, while Murney voters were turned away by the returning officer "illegally and without reason"; fourth, the general conduct of the returning officer.

With reference to the last point, the petitioners accused Moodie of "wilful and unwarrantable partiality", and of being "grossly biassed in favour of the said Robert Baldwin"; that he had turned down the magistrates' request to have the bullies disarmed, because Baldwin was against it; that he had refused to stop the ruffians from abusing Murney voters; and that he had refused Murney's demand for a review and scrutiny of the poll books."

On the face of it, this was a rather routine sort of complaint, standard procedure in the days of more enthusiastic elections, notable only in that it was the first major item of business in the Legislature of the United Canada. Despite many witnesses brought up to prove these allegations, the special committee of the House decided that the petition had not been supported by adequate evidence and it was therefore "frivolous and vexatious".[13]

As an indication of how the returning officer felt about the election riots, Moodie himself prepared a petition to Parliament asking for a law to make all secret societies and secret meetings illegal.[14] He seemed to feel that it was not Baldwin's election committee that was responsible for the trouble but rather that it was the Orangemen.

Although Moodie still had ambitions to be above politics, this was becoming increasingly difficult. The Tories had attacked him personally from the day he came to Belleville, and their supporters caused riots which he as sheriff was supposed to control although he received no emolument for keeping the peace. And now, he had met one of the most cultured, gentle and honourable men in Canada West, Robert Baldwin. Despite his claim to political neutrality, Moodie became a personal friend of the leader of the Reform Party, entertained him in his home, and named his next son Robert Baldwin Moodie.

The next round followed quickly. Baldwin went off to Kingston where the first sitting of the new Union Parliament was held on 14 June 1841. The same day he resigned from the Executive Council over a dispute with Sydenham on the definition of responsible government. Sydenham had a fatal illness and was replaced by Sir Charles Bagot, and Bagot formed a new Council with Baldwin as Attorney General. The members of the new Executive were required to face the voters again, and Baldwin chose to run once more in Hastings.

The poll was supposed to be open from the 3-8 October 1842, Baldwin *vs.* Murney, with Moodie as returning officer. The 1841 fracas had simply been a preliminary to this, the main bout.

The opening of the poll was delayed several hours by impassioned speeches from Baldwin and Murney and demonstrations by their supporters. When the poll finally did open, riots started immediately among citizens armed with clubs, sticks, swords and firearms. Fearing for the safety of the town, Moodie called up the militia and swore in special constables, to no avail. By the end of the third day (Wednesday), he asked the Governor for two companies of troops to help him keep the peace, in the meantime adjourning the poll.

The troops did not arrive from Kingston until five o'clock on Thursday. While Moodie was watching them disembark at the wharf, Murney men in anticipation of the re-opening of the poll completely inundated the approaches to the hustings and the enclosure around the entrance. Moodie hurried back and tried to remove them and then tried to compromise by dividing up this space equally between the two parties, but the Murney men refused to move even though the troops had now drawn up in battle formation within sight of the poll. The obstructionists then started threatening Baldwin supporters and prevented them from voting.

That evening, Moodie wrote to the Governor asking for an indefinite extension of the time allowed for polling:[15]

> In consequence of the dangerous riots . . . I feel it my duty as Returning Officer to state that I do not think it possible to poll more than one half the votes within the time allowed by the Writ of Election. *Four* days of the six are now passed and only 410 votes have been polled, not quite one third of the number polled at the last election.
>
> It is therefore obvious that the state of the country cannot be fairly taken by the end of the week . . . particularly as it is the obvious intention of one of the parties to create all the delay in their power by riotous manifestations and acts of violence . . .

In case the government did not believe that the situation was worse than usual, Moodie enclosed a statement from John Turnbull, J.P., describing the riots and verifying that Moodie had unsuccessfully tried to arrange protection for the voters attempting to get to the poll. Rather than use the troops against the 200 to 300 Murney men, Turnbull said, Moodie had postponed the poll until six o'clock the next morning. Turnbull supported Moodie completely in his request for an extension of voting days. Their idea apparently was to out-sit the obstructionists rather than meeting them head-on with violence.

In a reply by special messenger the next day, the Governor

stated that special legislation would be required to extend the voting time, and it was too late for that: [16]

His Excellency therefore expects that under these circumstances you will act according to the writ and at the same time to the best of your prudence and judgement, leaving it to the proper authorities to consider the matter more fully hereafter.

This was little help to the frantic returning officer; all the prudence and judgement in the world were not going to get all the voters in, in the time remaining. But he abided by the instructions, assuming the Governor wanted a full investigation after the election.

There were further attempts at riot on Friday. Again, Moodie closed the poll. On Saturday, the last day, he closed the poll at noon and returned a report to the effect that Murney had won a majority of the votes actually polled, 482 to 433, but that as returning officer, he could not certify that the writ had been carried out because not enough people had been able to vote. [17]

His report was presented to the 1843 session of the Assembly. On the strength of it and and an accompanying statement from Robert Baldwin, *et al.*, a new writ of election was ordered and Murney was not allowed to take his seat.

There was some confusion about who should be returning officer in the new election. It had started out to be Moodie, but serious allegations had been made against him and a full investigation into his conduct had been requested. Therefore, the government thought it better to appoint someone else.

Both sides seemed glad to blame the whole chaotic situation on the returning officer – the Murney supporters because Moodie had refused to finalize Murney's victory, and the Baldwin supporters because Baldwin had lost and the name of the Attorney General had been dragged through the mud. Even those M.P.s who were not directly involved were embarrassed and angry, for Moodie's report and his flat refusal to certify the election one way or the other pointed up a situation which was general throughout the province. An honest returning officer could invalidate most of the elections by which the M.P.s had won their seats.

A particularly vicious petition from Charles O. Benson and William Robertson, freeholders of the County of Hastings,[18] seems to have decided the issue. Benson and Robertson attacked Moodie in much the same words as Parker had used after the 1841 election, that Moodie had shown partiality to the government candidate, adding that Moodie tried to force Murney supporters to make way at the poll in favour of Baldwin supporters. (This referred to Moodie's attempt to divide up the space in front of the hustings between the two sides which required that half the Murney men should get out of the way.) Although Parker's petition had been rejected, the allegations of Benson and Robertson were enough to dissuade the government from allowing Moodie to act in the next election.

Many people, including the Governor, thought that Moodie's persistent closing of the poll had been illegal, though admitting that Moodie had only been trying to prevent bloodshed.

In due time, another election was held. The new returning officer, William Hutton, was more effective if not more honest, and Murney's victory was confirmed. Baldwin had to seek a safer seat in Lower Canada.

In the meantime, Murney had been fired from his position as Clerk of the Peace in Belleville. Sir Charles Bagot, the Governor, was livid about the whole affair. He felt that an important principle of administration had been violated by a public servant openly campaigning against the government. But more than that, he felt that his personally-selected Attorney General should not have been opposed by anyone. In effect, opposition to the Governor's man meant opposition to the Governor, practically the same thing as disloyalty to the Crown.

Murney screamed and lashed out in all directions, not

forgetting to make a few vicious swipes at Moodie. He resented the implication that he was disloyal, and he pointed out with some justification that the same principles should have applied in the 1841 election when despite his opposition to Baldwin he had not been fired. Parenthetically, he added that he would have won the 1841 election also had it not been for the violence and intimidation imposed by Baldwin men. He offered to resign his commission in the militia because this too implied service to the Governor. Bagot accepted Major Murney's resignation by return mail.

The dispute over the Clerk of the Peace appointment continued on into late 1843, when Murney went over the head of Bagot's successor, Governor Metcalfe, and petitioned the Queen through Lord Stanley, the Colonial Secretary.[19]

Bagot had appointed Murney's successor in December 1842. He was Mr. W. Fitzgibbon, son of Colonel Fitzgibbon whom Bagot credited with saving Toronto in the Rebellion of 1837. The new Clerk of the Peace was a Torontonian and therefore an outsider. This gave Moodie a friend at court, and the Fitzgibbons and Moodies became great friends.

As Bagot said in a letter to the Colonial Secretary:[20]

It is my intention in appointing Mr. Murney's successor, to mark, as strongly as I am able, by the selection of the individual, that my object in dismissing Mr. Murney has been the Establishment of the principle of the Government being entitled to the support of its officers, and not a desire to punish him personally for his opposition to Mr. Baldwin, or to avail myself of the opportunity of providing for a partizan.

Although the Governor was supporting Baldwin in this affair, there were many principles behind the Governor's statements which offended Baldwin's principles of responsible government. It was a dispute over patronage appointments that brought about the resignation of Baldwin and Lafontaine in November 1843.

Both Governors Bagot and Metcalfe regarded all offices from

Attorney General to Clerk of the Peace as being within the personal prerogatives of the Governor. They had conceded that the Executive Council should be composed of members of the majority party in the legislature, and that Governors should consult with their Council on major matters. In making these concessions they thought they had granted responsible government, as recommended by Lord Durham. They did not concede that the Executive Council's advice must always be acted upon or that the Council should take over all the Governor's powers, especially not the power of appointment. The Council resigned, then, when the Governor refused to grant Baldwin and Lafontaine complete power over patronage.[21]

In the resulting election in 1844, Baldwin stayed away from Hastings, Moodie was no longer returning officer, and Murney won handily.

Thus, by 1844 Moodie was free to settle down again to his routine of being sheriff of Hastings: arguing with the school board; preparing requests for more lucrative appointments to the Governor and now also to Baldwin, arresting and jailing citizens on charges of drunkenness, assault, lunacy, rape, murder, and the sale of spirits without a licence; and of course his routine of lawsuits with Thomas Parker.

Parker was now Inspector of Potashes for the District, an office of greater prestige and money than that of sheriff. Yet Parker never stopped hating Moodie for beating him out of the shrievalty, and never stopped pulling tricks on the poor sheriff.

One of these will serve to illustrate the technique of sheriff-baiting. But it is necessary to give a little background first. When a person wished to collect a debt from another person who refused to pay, he took out a writ of *capias ad satisfaciendum*, which required the sheriff to arrest the debtor and hold him until he paid up. If this action failed to produce the money, the unsatisfied creditor as often as not blamed the sheriff and tried to get restitution from him, on the assumption that it was the sheriff's fault that the court action had failed.

Parker had taken out such a writ against Walter Todd but Moodie had not been able to apply it (for unknown reasons; possibly Todd had no money or possibly Moodie had been unable to find Todd). Parker then prepared a court action against Moodie. Moodie had to hire a lawyer and prepare a defence, but Parker never took the case to court so that he did not have to pay Moodie's expenses, as he would have had to do if he had lost the case.

Moodie thought he should be reimbursed by Parker anyway, and took out an execution against Parker's goods and chattels. The coroner returned the execution – "no goods". Parker had turned over everything he owned to another person, the Honourable Peter McGill, President of the Bank of Montreal, Member of the Legislative Council, and one-time business partner of the Montreal branch of the Parker family.

Moodie interpreted this as a deliberate trick, and so did Susanna. As she expressed it in one of her abstract generalities: [22]

A man loses very little in the public estimation by making over all his property to some convenient friend, in order to defraud his creditors, while he retains a competency for himself.

Moodie considered using a writ of *capias ad satisfaciendum* against Parker, as Parker had used it against Todd, but suspecting that he would not be able to catch Parker to make the arrest, he decided instead to write to the Governor using the fact that Parker, as Inspector of Potashes, was a fellow public servant.

In fairness, or just to threaten, Moodie sent his bailiff to inform Parker of his intentions. Parker sent back word that Moodie could do as he liked. With his bluff called, the sheriff then had to write to the Governor, asking redress for his legal expenses in preparing his defence and for the abortive execution against Parker, a total amount of twenty-seven pounds, three shillings, ten pence.[23] '(This amount, incidentally, was roughly ten per cent of Moodie's total income for a year, and it all went to another of the local lawyers, John Ross, who was a sometime friend, sometime enemy, depending on who was paying his fee at the time.)

The Governor's Secretary in reply stated that the issue had nothing to do with the Potash department and Moodie should seek redress through the normal provisions of the law. This infuriated Moodie, for it was his attempts to take advantage of the legal means for redress that had cost him so much money. He firmly believed that whatever type of skullduggery a private citizen might be involved in, a public servant such as Parker should be held to the highest possible standards of behaviour. But he was no longer surprised that the Tory Government would refuse to back him up.

It really made little difference to Moodie's career what government was in office, other than that the Reformers treated him with a greater deference. The same situation continued for another fifteen years. The nuisance suits went on, costing him money every time. He kept asking for other appointments, either a less controversial job in Hastings or any job somewhere else, but even his now-powerful friend Robert Baldwin could not or would not help him. Thus, he was never clear of financial difficulties, never able to relax in his job, and never accepted by the Belleville Tories.

In the meantime, Susanna Moodie had been soaking all this up, getting ready to launch her own counter-attack. She had been writing large quantities of material for the *Literary Garland*, appearing in every issue for years, with novels, poems, historical sketches, and essays. The bulk of her prose material was still being written in her old-country style, taking settings and subjects chiefly from continental Europe and Britain. Much of it she had written, or at least planned, many years earlier but by 1846 she was coming to the bottom of her trunkful of manuscripts. At the same time, a new personal philosophy was beginning to emerge.

She had been deeply impressed by Robert Baldwin as a gentleman, although she found it difficult to assimilate all the Reformers' views on popular government. She was vaguely aware of the movement in Britain, centering around the Reform Bills, to extend the franchise to almost everyone who owned property. In Canada, however, the possession of property bore little relationship to class, and the responsible government drive meant in effect the control of government by representatives of the electoral mob. Class was necessary to Susanna's view of society, but a class system based on property would automatically put the Moodies at the bottom of the heap.

She rationalized the matter this way: the true worth of any man and the sign of the gentleman was mental accomplishment. Education, therefore, was the only really precious possession a man could have. If the country had to be ruled by the mob, it would be necessary to convert that mob into an educated thinking group of men. Businessmen and persons in public office would necessarily be more honourable if they followed the pursuits of the intellect. A new and valid aristocracy should be based on the principle that the men with the most education and philosophic competence should be the leaders, and would be, if the followers were also a little familiar with books and the arts.

Thus equipped with a point of view she was ready to use the flail on Upper Canada.

She started first with the *Literary Garland*. The editors had been expecting something more from her, for her work in recent months had been thinning out; in the last half of 1846 she had produced only two poems. From January through October 1847, she published a series of stunning sketches on her early life in Upper Canada – mostly about Hamilton Township, with some Douro adventures – sketches which would eventually be the basis for *Roughing it in the Bush*.

At the same time, she launched a more direct campaign to raise the cultural taste of the people of Belleville and vicinity through the new *Victoria Magazine*.

Mr. and Mrs. Moodie were to be the new magazine's editors, but they did not have enough money to support the project in its first stages. Whether they approached Joseph Wilson or Wilson approached them is not known. In either case, Wilson was an experienced literary publisher – this was not his first nor would it be his last such venture – and he undoubtedly hoped to capitalize on Mrs. Moodie's popularity and through her that of the *Literary Garland*, which up to this point had been very successful with Mrs. Moodie as its major contributor.

Why John Moodie also had to be an editor is not clear. We can speculate that Mrs. Moodie insisted upon it, or even that Wilson thought the controversial sheriff might have some selling power of his own. While Moodie had written for publication, he was not a professional author. In England, he had written military articles and two books. In Canada, the several poems written for the *Garland* were good but whimsical, suggesting not so much serious claims to authorship as pressure from his wife to contribute.

For example, Susanna had written a poem for the *Garland* called "To Adelaide", all about the charms of mind being more lasting than the charms of youth or beauty. It was accompanied by this whimsical bit by J. W. D. Moodie: [24]

TO THE SAME

While others seek thy gentle hand,
　　And waste their nights in sighs,
Thy ripening charms I can withstand—
　　I'm bound by other ties.
It is not that my heart is cold,
　　That I so stubborn prove;
I am not cold—nor yet too old
　　To feel the power of love.

205

You'll think perchance that I'm a priest
  Of orders white or grey;
Bound to say grace at every feast,
  While I must fast and pray.
Oh, No! fair maid—though cold to thee,
  Less holy is my life;
To other shrine I bend my knee,
  For I have got a—wife!

The purposes of Sheriff and Mrs. Moodie's new magazine were to raise the cultural sights of the rural community including Belleville by offering a cheap but good journal, and to provide space for native-born authors. These purposes were explained in detail in the opening issue of September 1847, in Susanna's rather pompous and vaguely insulting style.

The *Victoria Magazine* failed. The peasants were not interested in cheap culture and the native-born Canadians could not produce the quality of work that would satisfy the editors (or would not, since the editors could not pay for it). Susanna suggested that the failure of the *Magazine* was really Wilson's fault,[25] but there seems little justification for this. The magazine had been filled up mostly with Susanna's and John's works, with some things from Susanna's sister and brother, and someone called "Anon" who probably was Susanna. Canadian literature was perhaps not yet ready for mass production, or perhaps had advanced beyond the Strickland style.

Few magazines lasted very long in the early days of Canadian literature (nor has it changed much since). The *Victoria Magazine* did better than most, and the best of them all, the *Literary Garland*, was on its last legs, dragging out to a miserable conclusion in 1851. With it went the end of the magazine market for Susanna's work, and, almost, the end of her hopes for making a living for her family through writing and for raising the cultural tone of Canada.

But she had not given up. With her favourite magazines gone, she followed the lead of her sisters and went into books. *Roughing it in the Bush* was first published as a book, in 1852; *Life in the Clearings* and *Mark Hurdlestone* followed in 1853; *Flora Lindsay* in 1854; *Geoffrey Moncton* in 1856. There was a good deal of work involved in putting all these together from her previously published sketches and serials, and preparing introductions and connecting material, but the fact remains that most of it had been seen before. Susanna was most at home with the short sharp sketch or episodic novel. Like a good professional, she made the most of what she wrote, publishing the same works in as many different places as possible.

Around Belleville, her work met with some admiration, but mainly she was regarded as a curiosity or a trouble-maker. Her character sketches of Canadian types were not taken kindly, and the fact that they were mainly intended for a British audience did not help the situation. In any case, Susanna was quickly taught that one does not toss off a funny story about a Canadian who also happens to be an Irishman without arousing the ire of every Irish-Canadian, something like half the population of Canada. But she never changed what she wrote, though she did defend it, re-interpret it and, by implication, apologize for it.

In *Life in the Clearings*, Susanna described with some amusement the way the local ladies approached with curiosity the "woman that writes". They were amazed to find that she looked very much like everyone else. One of them, obviously disappointed after waiting a long time to see Mrs. Moodie, asked all sorts of intimate questions about Susanna's age, teeth, susceptibility to headaches, and so on, and finally concluded that the authoress was "but a humly body after all".[26]

There can be no doubt that Susanna's activities and fame as a writer of commentary and criticism of the colonial scene had an important impact on Sheriff Moodie's status and career in Belleville. But there is also little doubt that John approved of everything Susanna wrote. Their writing styles were very similar, so much so that there is reason to suspect that they helped each other in their compositions. Sheriff Moodie's briefs to the government took on a more querulous, complaining tone, while Susanna's style was more aggressive, but the philosophy they expressed was identical.

It does not necessarily follow that a man and his wife should think the same about social and political matters, especially not when the two have such independent habits of mind as John and Susanna. But the Moodies shared not only the same trials and environment but also the same intellectual influences, from the day they first met Thomas Pringle of the Anti-Slavery Society of Britain. Similarly, Robert Baldwin spent many long evenings in the Moodies' home in Belleville, and Baldwin could talk about little else than his crusade for Responsible Government. At first glance, Pringle and Baldwin appear to have little in common, but they were both men who would give up, and often did give up, opportunities for personal security or power in the interests of a principle. The Moodies had no such pretensions but they respected those who did. Moodie's highest goal was to provide a decent livelihood for his wife and family without having to compromise his integrity as a public servant. And for Moodie, the achievement of this goal was just as difficult as Baldwin's fight for Responsible Government.

Nevertheless, the Moodies might as easily have been Tory as Reform when they first arrived in Belleville. Although they had a rather vague philosophic humanitarianism left over from Pringle, and although they were anything but uncritical of their surroundings, their political and social attitudes were still rigidly authoritarian and traditionalist. They were profoundly committed to the Crown and the British connection, to the concept of Empire, to class distinctions and to the British way of life – concepts that were all characteristic of the Tory. These views would not have prevented them from being Whig in Britain, where democracy was still an evil word for both parties, but the colonial politics had quite a different structure than the British.

In short, the Moodies were not committed to either side.

Although they had fought against the Rebels in 1837, the Reform Party had rid itself of rebels and Robert Baldwin was quite a different sort of man than W. L. Mackenzie. Life in the backwoods of Douro had not given the Moodies any strong views either way, nor much information on the issues dividing the two parties.

There is reason to suppose, therefore, that had the Moodies not been so intimately involved in the day-to-day life of the typical Upper Canadian community that Belleville represented (where, typically, no one could be neutral), they might never have developed any strongly partisan opinions. Even in Belleville, Moodie for a short time made an effort to be neutral; he could see that his job really required neutrality, but in this he was generations ahead of his time. The Belleville Tories chose to be their enemies while Robert Baldwin, the Great Reformer, was every inch the epitome of their ideals of the gentleman.

Offering kindness and good manners, Baldwin was easily able to convince the Moodies of the rightness of his cause of Responsible Government, showing them that it was not the same thing at all as popular government or colonial independence. Thus, the Moodies became Reformers.

o

CHAPTER ELEVEN

Triumph and Tragedy in the Backwoods
Samuel Strickland and Catharine Traill

While the Moodies were roughing it at the Front, the Traills and
Stricklands in their own ways had been doing their best to open
up the backwoods of the Peterborough area by providing active
and real assistance to new immigrants and through this activity to
improve their own positions. They were also increasing the
population in a more direct way. By the 1850s, Samuel and Mary
Strickland had twelve children and Thomas and Catharine Traill
had nine.

Samuel was agent for the Canada Company again, selling land
throughout the district to new immigrants. In partnership with
the Reids, the Stricklands had built a dam across the river at
Lakefield in 1844, and erected a sawmill. Despite the end of the
"little local family compacts", Samuel retained his position of
leadership in the community, serving as justice of the peace and
county councillor, and by 1850, he had achieved the rank of
major in the militia.

Their most critical problem, however, was still unsolved, the
transport facilities. The stretch of the Otonabee from Peterborough to Lakefield was proving to be the most intractable of
the inland waterway system. Samuel regularly petitioned the
government and the county council for a new road or a canal to
Lakefield and was regularly turned down.

Hope was dawning in the late 1840s and early '50s when a
railroad was built from Cobourg to Peterborough, running across
Rice Lake over a specially constructed bridge. A great celebration

was held in Peterborough in 1854 when the first train arrived; many hopeful and proud speeches were delivered, including one by Samuel Strickland. Unfortunately, the Rice Lake bridge fell in six years later and the back townships were again incommunicado.[1] For many years yet, the steam-boat was to be the main means of transport, and eventually the Kawarthas and the Trent-Rice Lake system would be improved enough to enable a surge of steam-boat activity – everywhere except on the Otonabee between Lakefield and Peterborough.

Despite Samuel's procreative and pro-migration efforts, his village of Lakefield had achieved a population of only seventy-five by 1857, though it did boast a postmaster to look after its bi-weekly mail deliveries, Robert Casement, J.P., township clerk, township treasurer, and general merchant.[2] It was a fairly important harbour, at the south end of the navigable Kawarthas, a centre for the growing lumbering business in which one of Samuel's sons participated.

In 1850, Samuel's disappointment over the slow growth of his community faded before the shock of a series of personal tragedies. His eldest daughter Maria, who as a curly-headed baby had brightened Samuel's Huron Tract days, had married well, a fine young man named Beresford of whom Samuel thoroughly approved. The young couple were expecting their first baby at the same time as Samuel and Mary Strickland were expecting their thirteenth child. Then Maria's husband contracted cholera and died while he was away on a business trip. The shock was too much and despite Mary Strickland's careful nursing, Maria lost her baby. Then Mary Strickland's strength gave way and she died in childbirth.

Samuel had not known such tragedy for twenty-three years.[3] His wife Mary had been the perfect companion for the successful pioneer and indeed had contributed in many ways to his success. Together they had conquered the bush that had destroyed so many others; their combined strength had made it seem effortless as they met and overcame the daily trials of the bush settler; it was their personal strength that created not only a prosperous homestead but also a whole community. Yet Samuel was not to have the luxury of grieving for his wife. His daughter Maria was completely broken by the loss of her husband, her child, and her mother, in quick succession. In July 1851, Samuel and his daughter left Douro and headed for England.

Their arrival in England was awaited with mixed feelings. Samuel's mother, an old lady still living at Reydon Hall, was anxious to see him and to hear at first hand about her daughters Catharine and Susanna. Samuel's famous sister Agnes, however, had struggled for her social and literary reputation. It was with some trepidation that she waited for a brother she had not seen in over a quarter of a century, a brother who had spent all those years hunting and farming deep in the colonial backwoods. But Samuel did not appear in buckskins.

Major Strickland, J.P., turned out to be very presentable, a tall, strong and handsome gentleman who had lost nothing of his education, his British mannerisms, or his taste for literature. With his intimate knowledge and authority on the subject of emigration, a very popular subject in England, and his willingness to discourse on his successful adventures in the colony, he became a social asset at Reydon Hall.

After a few months of showing Samuel off and listening to his stories, Agnes persuaded him to venture into print himself. He had written a few pieces for magazines, including Susanna's *Victoria Magazine*, but Agnes had a more ambitious project in mind. She would help him, edit his work, and with her name connected to it, the success of the book would be assured. Thus, Samuel spent much of the next year writing his autobiography. *Twenty-Seven Years in Canada West* was published in 1853 in two volumes, a work which was to be one of the most authoritative documents on pioneering yet written.

Samuel had also met a girl. Katharine Rackham lived in the neighbourhood of Reydon, spending most of her time looking after her aged mother. Samuel wanted to get married immediately and take his new wife back to Douro with him. Miss Rackham's mother, however, could not be left alone and was much too old to take with them. Samuel therefore had to return to Canada alone, wait until the old lady died, then return to England to claim his third bride, in April 1855.

In the meantime, during his wait, being J.P., councillor, farmer, Canada Company agent, etc., did not use up all his energies. To keep occupied, Samuel established a school for farmers.

The idea of the agricultural school was simple, and went back to his days in the Huron Tract and the theories of John Galt. The colony needed immigrants, but either many of the most likely immigrants knew nothing at all about farming, or what they did know was entirely inappropriate for the frontier. If the new settlers were to stay and be successful, they must be taught how. The best way to learn was by doing. Thus, Samuel took in young gentlemen as resident scholars and for a small tuition fee let them practice on his land. Everyone had a grand time, especially the gregarious Samuel who enjoyed the company. They learned to hunt, fish, clear land and build houses. If they liked the life, they would then buy some land of their own with Samuel's help to pick it out, and very often from Samuel, as Canada Company agent. If, on the other hand, they found they had no aptitude or liking for backwoods life, they had lost only their tuition and had gained at least a good holiday.

This was the scene in 1854 when Charles Richard Weld, a gentleman tourist of the day, made his way over the still terrible Smith-town road to visit the brother of Agnes Strickland. His buggy took five hours to cover the twelve miles between Peterborough and Lakefield, but this most persistently bad of all backwoods roads at least gave Mr. Weld a real satisfaction about getting into the heart of the bush.[4]

Presently we came to small houses and log-huts sown broadcast on the land: the commencement of a town to which the name Lakefield had been given. . . Fortunately, the Major was at home. . . . Dinner was immediately ordered, and as *impromptu* repasts are of constant occurrence in the bush, where even stage-coaches are unknown, we were soon seated before fare which, if a little rough, had the advantage of being highly appreciated by the zest of keen hunger. But it would have ill accorded with my expectation to have found luxuries in the bush, for I had come to see the life led by the bold settler who makes his home in the wilderness.

This reaction was not unlike Catharine's when she first came to stay with Samuel in the bush twenty-two years earlier. Samuel must have been getting a little bored with it by this time; however, "the Major" was hospitable:

> As we sat down, the major's son stepped out into the verandah, and blew a loud and long blast upon a horn, which was answered by the arrival of half-a-dozen fine young men wearing loose trousers and red flannel hunting-shirts secured round the waist by a leather belt, from which formidable weapons depended. In a few minutes, another party of young men made their appearance similarly attired. I was somewhat puzzled; for although I knew the Major had more than one son, I had not heard that his children were as numerous as those vouchsafed to the patriarchs of old.

The young men of course were Samuel's students, obviously enjoying themselves tremendously. And Samuel welcomed the opportunity to tell Weld all about the school.

The next day, Samuel took Mr. Weld on a tour of the settlement of Upper Douro, showing him clearings and explaining how to clear land, the value of land, the cost of log houses, comparing prices proudly to what they were when Samuel first came to Douro. During this tour, Weld reported Samuel's observation, "It frequently happens that the numerous wants of recent arrivals press heavily on the generosity of old settlers." In short, Samuel was getting tired of going to bees. Even though more settlers meant a more prosperous community, the exchange of labour implied in the bee system, was all one-sided for the old established settler.

Yet wherever Samuel went, he received a welcome that startled Mr. Weld; they walked in and out of houses without so much as a knock on the door and no one seemed to mind. The tourist was delighted at this strange "freedom of bush-life", but he found the inside of the houses very comfortable; "were it not that the bush shuts out the distant view, it would require no great effort to imagine the scenery English."

On our return we found the young gentlemen putting their rifles in order, and eagerly planning for a deer hunt the following morning. . . . We sat down to supper, after which songs were sung with *fortissimo* choruses; for, at the time of my visit, Major Strickland's domestic establishment had not the advantage of a lady at its head. At the same time, I must say, social conviviality never degenerates to coarseness; and though the red hunting-shirts, looming through tobacco-smoke, gave the company a brigandish appearance, gentlemanly conduct was as strongly maintained as if the scene of our merriment had been a London drawing room.

But after all, most of these gentlemen, including Samuel, had just come from English drawing rooms. Evidently some of Mr. Weld's priggishness got through to Samuel, for the next day's outing was far rougher than the first had been. Deer-hunting, fishing, and a visit to the Indian encampment were planned.

Major Strickland paddled me in his log canoe, giving me, before starting, strict injunctions to maintain as perfect an equilibrium as possible, as the slightest swerve would in all probability result in precipitating us into the lake; a difficulty which promised to be increased, as part of our plan was to troll for maskinonge ... matters were so arranged that, while I half-reclined at one end, the Major, squatted on his hams, paddled at the other; and a stout trolling-line was towed astern, one extremity of which was secured to my right arm. ...

Samuel was a proper guide, and Mr. Weld caught a fish. Then they went ashore to visit the Indians.

A wild whoop from my companion was answered by an Indian, who burst through the bush and motioned us to a little creek where we disembarked ...

We returned to Lakefield in the evening, and the following day my kind host drove me to Peterborough. On our way, he frequently expatiated on the state of the road, which I thought wretched, but which he contrasted with the condition of things when it took him an entire day to journey from Peterborough to his home in the bush.

Many visitors came to Lakefield to see the gallant Major in his wilderness home[5] but none provided such a vivid picture of the fifty-year-old Samuel as Charles Richard Weld. The rather prissy gentleman found what he wanted to find, while the swash-buckling pioneer spent most of his time trying to describe what the frontier had been like back in the old days. To Weld's eye, Upper Douro was rugged enough in 1854; for Samuel Strickland, nothing could compare with the unbroken bush that he had faced and conquered as a young man in 1831. Perhaps Samuel lingered on the early days because he wanted to make it clear that his settlement had made such progress – progress that could only be appreciated if one knew what it had been like originally. Or perhaps he was expressing nostalgia for his more vigorous youth; he was still impatiently energetic but he had now to search harder to find new worlds to conquer.

Ironically, when Catharine and Thomas Traill had first visited Samuel he had encouraged them to look forward to the days when they would have cleared farms. But the Traills were gone from Lakefield now. They had sold their farm and moved first to Ashburnham, nearer Peterborough, and from there they had gone to the Rice Lake area, to a part of the country that Catharine had always found especially attractive. They lived in three different places on the shores of the Lake: "Wolf Tower", Mount Ararat, and finally "Oaklands" which they bought in 1846.

As Catharine described their moves:

> . . . When I came to reside at the "Wolf Tower", in the spring of 1846, I was in weak health, scarcely recovered from the effects of a dangerous fit of illness, but so renovating did I find the free healthy air of the hills about the Tower, that in a very short space of time, I was strong and able to ramble about with the children among the wild ravines . . .[6]
> . . . For years that lovely lake haunted my memory and I longed to return to it; and fondly cherished the hope that one day I might find a home among its hills and vales. The daydream has been realized; and from the "Oaklands", I now look toward the distant bay beyond the hills where I spent my first night on the Rice Lake Plains and can say as I then said, "truly it is a fair and lovely spot".[7]

Catharine had never stopped writing since her first book of children's stories. All through her pioneering days in Douro, through the hard physical labour of establishing a home, and raising her large family, she continued her nature study and her writing. Around Rice Lake, however, she became more productive than ever. Like Susanna, Catharine wrote a number of poems, sketches and fables in the English style with English or European settings, for magazines of the day, including the *Literary Garland* and the *Anglo-American Magazine*. But her serious work was becoming more and more Canadian in content.

Catharine had identified two specific problems which she was

capable of doing something about, using her talent for writing:
first, the need for guidance and information to help the wives of
new emigrants during the first critical years of settlement, and
secondly, the need for conservation of the wildlife and flowers of
the backwoods against the destructive onslaught of civilization.
She was much before her time with both these subjects, and for
many years Catharine Parr Traill's books were the only attempts
being made in the colony to meet either of the needs.

While she was still in Douro, and more actively around Rice
Lake, Catharine was busy collecting and recording every piece of
information she could find which would be of use to the
emigrant's wife. She talked to old settlers and to Indians,
gathering recipes and hints on household practices which could
be used in an isolated frontier home. She tested these herself and
at the same time experimented with and invented new cooking
and housekeeping techniques. The results she carefully recorded,
along with moral hints on the need for and techniques of keeping
a cheerful and happy spirit despite the inevitable adversities.

Information on farming as such she left to her brother Samuel
and men like Dr. Dunlop; her concern was informing not the
emigrant but the emigrant's wife, who was as important to the
success of the pioneer farm as the farmer himself. Yet she did not
entirely ignore the problems of agriculture, because, of course,
the wife needed to understand these matters also. In the same
way, she included data on migration, the value and exchange of
money, the location of government agents, and hints about the
ocean passage.

The results were recorded in *Backwoods of Canada*[8] and in
The Female Emigrant's Guide[9] both of which went through
many reprints, new editions, and changes of title. Unfortunately,
because of the lack of copyright protection, Catharine received
little financial reward for her efforts. She would not have minded
this too much, had her desire to be of service been satisfied. In
this also she was disappointed, for although her works had a wide
distribution and popularity, she felt that they had not reached the

people for whom they were intended – the women who would benefit most from them.

In the Rice Lake area, Catharine also found time to take up her stories for children again. *Canadian Crusoes*[10] combined her interest in nature study and folklore, household hints, hints on survival in the bush, and faith in God – all through the vehicle of an exciting fictional story of Canadian children lost in the bush around Rice Lake. *Lady Mary and her Nurse*[11] was also a vehicle for Catharine's story-telling ability, this time with an upper class theme but still containing her nature study and folklore anecdotes.

Literary critics had a difficult time assimilating and evaluating these works, but the children loved them and both books reached a wide and appreciative audience. The New York edition of *Lady Mary*, however, had to be re-named *Little Mary* to avoid offending American democratic sensibilities.

At the same time, Catharine was diligently pursuing her nature studies, roaming the woods and plains with her children, gathering atmosphere and information for her books, and collecting specimens of plant life. She became more and more scientific in her studies, developing a wide correspondence with naturalists in Canada, Britain and the U.S.

For instance, Catharine became friends with John Macoun, a young Irishman who had migrated to Canada with his family in 1850, settling in the Belleville and Seymour Township areas. Macoun would eventually become the Dominion Botanist in the Department of Agriculture, and known as "Canada's greatest exploring botanist".[12]

But Catharine's concern was less with science than with conservation. Though much of Canada was still uncleared bush, she had the foresight to realize that the axemen diligently chopping down one tree at a time were the vanguard of a civilization which could change the face of nature and eventually destroy much of the beauty of the virgin forests and fields. When the railroad came to Rice Lake, Catharine was profoundly distressed by a dilemma which only she could create: her backwoods emigrants were in dire need of communication with the outside world and the future prosperity of her adopted country depended on the railroad. But the train was an ugly blot on the Rice Lake Plains, defacing the landscape, frightening the animals away and killing vegetation.[13]

Yet, as Samuel's concern over the development of his community faded before more immediate personal tragedy, so the academic and literary pursuits of the Traill household were sharply interrupted by calamity.

In August 1857, "Oaklands" burned to the ground and with it went all the Traills' possessions, their keepsakes from the old country, their large collection of books and maps, and Catharine's manuscripts and botanical collections.

Fire was a tragically common occurrence and, for the isolated frame or log house, it usually meant total destruction. As we have seen, the Moodies were hit twice by this catastrophe, and Samuel's house was so badly damaged by lightning that he had had to rebuild. But Samuel Strickland and John Moodie were still fairly young when their houses were lost. For Thomas Traill in his late sixties, the loss of "Oaklands" meant the irreparable loss of a lifetime's accumulation of property and possessions. The following year, in June 1858, Thomas died, leaving Catharine and the younger children alone and virtually penniless.

Much less is known about Thomas Traill than about the Stricklands or the Moodies. Thomas appeared in Catharine's autobiographical sketches mainly as an ever-present and comfortable shoulder to put her head on when she was weary or frightened. That he was a sensitive, intelligent, and much-loved man is clear. That he enjoyed the bush and adapted well to it is less obvious.

There is reason to suppose that Thomas Traill was the epitome of the gentleman-settler, the type often discussed by Catharine and Susanna as the least adaptable to the frontier life. He was more highly educated and came from a wealthier family than either the Stricklands or the Moodies. His Orkney Island family contained some outstanding academicians, including another Thomas Traill (a contemporary of Catharine's husband) who won high academic honours, was professor of medical jurisprudence at Edinburgh University, founder of literary societies, and editor of the eighth edition of *Encyclopaedia Britannica*.[14]

Assuming that Thomas Traill, the emigrant, had similar inclinations, it should not seem strange that he did not respond to the woods. He was intensely interested in Catharine's research and writing, and his influence helped to raise the quality of her studies from the mere poetic-emotional to a more scholarly plane. But being relatively poor for his class, Thomas had followed the pattern of the soldier-emigrant, and when he died he left his family little but memories.

Catharine, of course, was not alone. She had her large family, the eldest of whom were now adults. And she had her brother Samuel who asked her to move back to Lakefield with him and his new wife. But the loss of her home and possessions left her in a tight financial situation. Word of her trouble reached her friends and admirers in England; they took the story all the way to the Prime Minister, Lord Palmerston, who arranged a grant of £100 for Mrs. Traill as an acknowledgement of her botanical and literary contributions.

With the grant, Catharine bought a house in Lakefield, named it "Westove" after her husband's Orkney home, and lived there for the rest of her very long life, with as many of her children, grandchildren, nieces and nephews as she could gather about her.

She continued her studies and her writing. Her best botanical works were yet to come: *Canadian Wildflowers*[15] in 1868, *Studies of Plant Life in Canada*[16] in 1885, and *Pearls and Pebbles*[17] in 1895. Susanna's second daughter Agnes, now Mrs. Fitzgibbon, had inherited her mother's talent for sketching and her aunt's interest in botany; she collaborated with Catharine in the production of *Canadian Wildflowers* by painting and lithographing the plates, "the first illustrated book of its kind published in Canada".[18]

Mrs. Traill was well known and respected in literary and government circles, in fact, everywhere that her favourite topics of botany and emigration were discussed. Yet she was never satisfied that enough had been done to help emigrants or to ensure conservation and appreciation of Canadian natural resources. There was a large amount of religious and maternal fervour involved in her concern for all God's creatures, especially the weak ones, whether they were wildflowers, birds, or young immigrants.

The one man at Ottawa who seemed to listen most attentively to her pleas was also a profoundly religious man, Sir Sandford Fleming.[19] But Fleming was best known as a builder of those enemies of nature, railroads.

As with the botanist Macoun, Catharine had first met Fleming when, as a young emigrant, he arrived in Peterborough in 1845. As draughtsman, surveyor and civil engineer, working in and around the Newcastle District, Fleming had visited the Traills, Stricklands and Moodies in their respective homes from Belleville to Lakefield, before he set off to the Pacific Coast with John Macoun and others to plan the route for the C.P.R. Fleming was a phenomenally talented man, one of the greatest achievers in the history of the Dominion, with an encyclopedic range of interests. Those he shared with Catharine included migration, religion, education and settlement.

Catharine formed a life-long friendship with Fleming, they corresponded regularly and, when he became an influential man in Ottawa, he was able to do many services for his old friend. For instance, Catharine became concerned for the preservation of Polly Cow's Island in Stoney Lake, a piece of land that had significance only because of an Indian legend that the daughter of a chief had been buried there. Through Fleming's influence, the Dominion Government ceded the island to Catharine. Polly Cow's Island then became important to Catharine not only as an

Indian shrine but also as a place where she could continue her search for botanical specimens without interference from advancing civilization.

To take a giant's step forward in time to the year 1882, Catharine, like everyone else, was looking West. The Province of Manitoba was well established; the C.P.R. was not yet completed but had found its way to the Pacific Coast, with the help of magnificent land grants; and the new Districts of Assiniboia, Saskatchewan, Athabaska and Alberta were being established. The way was open to the settlement of the prairies. One of Catharine's sons was already there, working for the Hudson Bay Company.

Sir Sandford Fleming, now retired as engineer-in-chief of the C.P.R. had sent a book of his prayers to his friend, the aged authoress in Lakefield (the rugged engineer-explorer, besides building railroads, inventing the universal time system still in use today, designing postage stamps, and founding scientific and literary societies, loved to compose prayers in his spare time). Catharine was appreciative of the gift, but she was still more interested in settlement problems:[20]

... I wish I could send it [the book of prayers] forth into many lonely far off homes where is a scant supply of the bread of life for hungry and thirsty souls – I am thinking now of my own far away Norwesters located on the lonely shores of Lesser Slave Lake.

. . . I think L.S. Lake is in the Peace River Dist. Mr. E. Traill is now a junior trader in the H.B. Service. He entered the service as a junior clerk, when he was only nineteen, not quite. He is now thirty-seven and has been married for many years to the eldest daughter of Factor W. Mackay and has a young family to cheer the life in that lonely far away place. You will know the situation. Do you think it lies near the track of the NPR . . .?

This was the Northern Pacific Railway, an American competitor for a transcontinental route with the C.P.R., which was forging ahead so quickly it was causing a great deal of embarrassment to Sir John A. Macdonald.

There was a frantic excitement in the air, with this competitive rush across the prairies. Catharine wanted to get into it somehow:

And now dear Mr. Fleming, I am going to ask your advice about a matter you may be able to help me in.

Many years ago – it was in the year 1854, I wrote a small work for the information and instruction of the wives and daughters of the Canadian Emigrant . . . I think from looking over an old copy now before me that it embodies much useful matter and that revised and with some addenda to suit the change of time that it might again be made available as emigration has taken a fresh start to the Dom'n. What I want is a little reliable information, such as the route of travel, the probable outlay on the road, and the best and most reliable persons or government agents to apply to. Also the amount of women's wages in Winnipeg or other towns, and also some hints to working men and men of small capital who desire to obtain land for settlement. . . .

I am now old, I am four score years of age. I believe that I have not been altogether a useless member of the community though I have reaped little pecuniary benefit from my literary labours, my yearly income being very small but I would like to do something more for Canada, my adopted country, before I am called to my rest.

The eighty-year-old lady worked hard to re-draft her *Female Emigrant's Guide*, but it was never re-published. She simply did not have the personal knowledge to be of assistance to the new pioneer of the West, and no amount of official information could take the place of the personal experience which made her original works so valuable. Dismayed but undaunted she continued her nature-study works and stories for children, but there is a suggestion in her letter to Fleming that she might have preferred to be on the shores of Lesser Slave Lake with her son.

CHAPTER TWELVE

Tired Pioneers

By the 1860s, the pioneer adventurers who crossed the ocean in 1832 on the *Laurel* and the *Anne*, seeking in the new world redress for the social misfortunes of England, were getting old and rather mellow. Their children were grown up, and several of these native-born Canadians had moved on to the West and to the United States. Though Thomas Traill and Mary Strickland were dead, Catharine and Samuel were still enthusiastically following their favourite vocations in Douro Township. They were highly respected members of the now-prosperous Peterborough community, though they were no longer active leaders of it. This they left to those of their children who were still around.

John and Susanna were showing the effects of age much more than Catharine and Samuel. The Moodies had suffered more trials and continuous stress over the whole period of their lives in Canada than either Catharine or Samuel, and the stress was beginning to take its toll. None of them, except possibly Samuel, had been able to accumulate any significant fortune, though this had been one of the objects of their migration. Their troubles in Britain, however, had long since faded into the background and their aspirations had become entirely Canadian.

Sheriff Moodie was still trying to make a success of himself as a public servant, but the succession of wounds he had collected over his lifetime were bothering him more and more. His body carried a graphic record of his life-story: his left wrist smashed by a bullet at Bergen-op-Zoom, his scars received from the enraged elephant in Africa, his left leg broken by the pioneer harrow in the Douro backwoods, and finally, his left knee-cap broken in a fall during the sittings of the Court of Quarter Sessions in Belleville in 1845.

With his flowing white beard and distinguished limp not obscuring his military bearing, Sheriff Moodie was a familiar part of the Belleville landscape after twenty years of service and controversy. His wife, the famous and equally controversial author of *Roughing it in the Bush*, was pointed out as she went shopping in the streets of Belleville.[1] She was a spokesman for the old days of Canada, the backwoods days that none of the newer emigrants or the younger generations had experienced.

Samuel Strickland's home was still regarded by British tourists as an interesting place to visit, but his school for settlers had become more an object of amusement, an anachronism in a Canada no longer primitive agriculturally, a school where young men received "a thorough training in manly sports and a fine discrimination in the selection of liquors".[2] As tall, physically active men are prone to do, Samuel had developed a magnificent paunch along with a terrifyingly dignified demeanour as he handed out diplomas to his graduates or presided as Colonel and Commanding Officer over the Peterborough Battalion of the militia. He had wanted to be the patriarch of Lakefield, but while he was there he overshadowed his dream until it faded into insignificance beside him.

In effect, Samuel, Catharine, Susanna and John had become celebrities in their respective communities. Though they felt an intimate part of the world around them, they were still regarded by others as being rather special people, different in undefined ways from other citizens. The only one to receive whole-hearted love and respect from all Canadians was Catharine; the personality that had made her the favourite of the family as a child was still with her. For the others, there was still much suspicion, some envy, and perhaps a little hatred: total acceptance was withheld.

227

Sheriff Moodie and Susanna had one more battle to fight before they could call it quits in Belleville, for the local Tories had a score left unsettled with the sheriff. Most of Moodie's victories had had their share of defeat also, as in the election of 1842 when Moodie stood firm before Murney and won his point but still had to take most of the blame for the riots that Murney had caused. The one exception, the unresolved grievance, was the sheriff's unseating of Judge Dougall. Even after twenty years, the Dougall family were not prepared to let that one go as a clear victory for Moodie. They found the way for revenge when Moodie, tired of running into the back country of Hastings with writs and summonses, hired a deputy to take over the "outdoor work" for him.

In the spring of 1856, Dunham Ockerman approached Moodie with the suggestion that the sheriff needed help. Ockerman had been the district court bailiff and was familiar with the routine. Moodie knew him well and trusted him. It was agreed that Ockerman should take over part of the sheriff's duties in return for half the fees he collected, the customary financial arrangement. Moodie's income, never very great, would be reduced by that amount, but he felt it would be worth it to be relieved of the more active parts of the job. At sixty, the battle-scarred Moodie felt he deserved to relax a little.

There was nothing unusual about a sheriff hiring a deputy; in fact, it was common practice when the population of a district grew too big for one man to handle. The cautious and punctilious Moodie took Ockerman to a lawyer to have the legality of the arrangement checked and a formal agreement drawn up.

Allan Ramsay Dougall, a prominent Belleville attorney and nephew of the former Judge Dougall, watched this arrangement for over two years. He saw the deputy dealing directly with the lawyers and the courts, evidently acting entirely on his own rather than under the immediate direction of the sheriff. Moodie had insisted on this method of operation. Though he trusted Ockerman, he was still liable to nuisance suits and he had too often seen other deputies being less conscientious about finances when they were not allowed to deal directly with the parties involved in writs and other legal proceedings. Unfortunately, the extent of responsibility shown by Ockerman suggested the "farming of offices" to the suspicious Dougall.

"Farming of offices" was one of the cardinal sins of the old system of patronage, the natural result of the principle of self-sustaining government services. In essence, it implied an influential gentleman securing one or more offices under the Crown, and selling the office to another at a profit. This sort of thing had been fairly common in England a hundred years earlier, and had led to gross injustices and irresponsibility. It had never been quite so prevalent in the colonies, and by 1856 was outlawed everywhere.

Moodie had not farmed out his office to Ockerman, but the freedom of the deputy in carrying out his share of the duties and collecting fees for them gave enough of the appearance of office-farming to provide A. R. Dougall with enough justification for him to commence investigation and attack. He thought he had enough evidence or could get enough to bring a formal court action against Moodie – not just a nuisance suit this time, but one which would force Moodie out of his job in disgrace as Moodie had forced out Judge Dougall.

In October 1859, Dougall received rather grudging permission from the government to proceed against the sheriff in the name of the Queen, "for the purpose of bringing before the Court of Queen's Bench the legality or otherwise of the proceedings of Mr. Sheriff Moodie in reference to his office."[3]

The Government was accustomed to these periodic attacks on Moodie, for Moodie had always reported them meticulously; it had never been possible to start even a whispering campaign against the sheriff without the intended victim making the whole thing public. This time, the accusations against Moodie had been serious enough and sufficiently well founded that the Government wanted Dougall to prove them in open court if he could – but not well enough founded for the government itself to take action. Dougall then was allowed to make the charges in the name of the Queen, but he must do so at his own expense and must give security for any costs or indemnities that the Crown might be liable to as a result of the action.

Dougall had not yet seen the Moodie/Ockerman agreement; he was basing his charges only on appearances. But with his bluff called by the government, he now had to get a copy of the agreement and he had the full force of the law to help him search for it. Dougall was again frustrated by the Government's unwillingness to help in the attack on Moodie. In answer to his letters, demands and subpoenas, Dougall was told that if a copy of the document had been on file in the capital it was not there any more.[4] That official documents could be lost in this way was not too surprising. Until Ottawa was finally selected as the capital of Canada, the Union government took regular trips with all its civil servants, furniture and records up and down the St. Lawrence between Canada East and Canada West. Many records were more or less conveniently lost in the shuffle.[5] For Dougall, however, the difficulty in locating an ordinary piece of paper confirmed in his already suspicious mind that there was something wrong with it.

He eventually found a copy of the agreement and studied it carefully until he found a legal flaw in the wording. With this one substantiation of what had been only opinion and innuendo, Dougall was ready to proceed.

Moodie was brought before the Assizes in Belleville in December, before a jury which ironically he had summoned as sheriff, and he was found guilty. The presiding magistrate, Mr. Justice Burns, instructed the jury to find against Moodie, and had reserved his own judgement subject to the opinion of the Court of Queen's Bench. The latter Court, held in the spring in Toronto, unanimously agreed that the Moodie/Ockerman document was not legal and that Moodie was technically guilty of infringing the statute regarding the farming of offices. The document as drawn up by Moodie's lawyer had omitted to mention how Ockerman was to be paid: the critical words "out of the fees" had been left out, words which would have made the arrangement perfectly legal and in accord with custom. The fact that this was the way that the deputy was paid was beside the point; by the omission the document was illegal.

The resulting situation was acutely embarrassing for everyone. The government had no wish to discharge Sheriff Moodie, because he had been guilty only of a technical error made by his lawyer. Dougall was frustrated because he was unable to prove any of his other allegations of misconduct and because Moodie continued to function as Sheriff of Hastings and would do so until the government decided to move.

Sheriff Moodie, in a panic of his own, had found himself another lawyer – a good one this time, the Honourable Lewis Wallbridge, Q.C., Member of Parliament for Hastings (and later, Solicitor General, Speaker of the House of Assembly, and Chief Justice of Manitoba). Although Wallbridge was a Belleville Tory, he fought with both law and politics in the interests of his client.

Moodie's case was taken to the Court of Appeals before Chief Justice John Beverly Robinson. Everyone realized that the judgement could not be reversed because the illegal agreement was an unalterable fact, but the Court of Appeals put off its judgement for almost two years, unwilling to force the discharge of Moodie.

Wallbridge had also helped Moodie prepare an appeal to the Governor, to the Legislative Council and to the House of Assembly, setting out the facts, admitting the error, showing that no corruption had ever been associated with Sheriff Moodie, and asking that the action on the case be indefinitely postponed so that Moodie would be relieved of the prosecution.[6] Both the Appeal Court and the government, by their lack of action, acceded to this request.

In March 1861, Dougall petitioned the Governor demanding

that Moodie be fired. In July, he wrote again, reiterating his demands that justice be done despite the deliberate delay of the appeal. He received a non-committal reply that his petition was "still under the consideration of the government".[7]

The strain of the delay and Dougall's unceasing and increasingly hostile attacks were too much for the old sheriff. His anxiety was heightened by another contested election for which he was returning officer having been reinstated in this function, and he had to spend several anxious and difficult days laboriously copying the Poll Books.[8]

On 28 July 1861, Moodie had a stroke which paralyzed his left side. The invalid sheriff was then even more of an embarrassment to the government. Despite only partial recovery, Moodie tried to solve the difficult situation himself, by petitioning for some other government appointment, to give him an income. However, it was difficult to find such a position under the circumstances. Government jobs were still as eagerly sought as ever, and putting Moodie in over someone else who had a claim to the position would cause a great deal of resentment, especially since Moodie was still under a cloud.

Adam Wilson, the Solicitor General, and Lewis Wallbridge, now Speaker of the House of Assembly, approached Moodie with the suggestion that he resign *before* the Appeal Court had to accede to Dougall's pressure and bring down a final judgement against him. They said that this would free the hands of the government to give Moodie another post.

On 15 January 1863, J. W. Dunbar Moodie resigned as the sheriff of the County of Hastings, after twenty-three years of service.[9] His resignation was accepted with no comment other than a request that he stay on until a replacement could be selected.

Because Moodie had resigned voluntarily, total victory was withheld from Dougall; his Uncle Benjamin had not been allowed to resign. But while Moodie had won the battle he had lost the war. He was old, penniless, and ill. His expectation of another government post was never fulfilled and he could not help but regard this as a betrayal. The government had simply used Moodie's resignation as a way out of their dilemma. Though Wilson and Wallbridge had probably been sincere in their advice about Moodie's resignation, the rest of the government had no wish to raise the matter again. They assumed no further responsibility for their former servant.

With poetic justice, only the people of Belleville seemed to feel any concern or regret. In March 1863, as Moodie was about to be replaced by a new sheriff, the Grand Jury gave him a vote of thanks, confirmed by the presiding judge and by the editor of the *Hastings Chronicle*:[10]

We have great pleasure in publishing the following Presentment of the Grand Jury, in reference to the retirement of Sheriff Moodie. The document is alike creditable to those who originated it, and to the man to whom it refers. It would be impossible to find another man who had for the same length of time discharged the arduous duties of a public office, who retires with the same universal esteem and respect that Sheriff Moodie does. This reflection will serve in a great measure to compensate him for the distress of mind occasioned by the cruel and vindictive prosecution which occasioned his retirement from office. It must be gratifying for him to know that his memory will be fragrant in the minds of the public when they have forgotten, even to depise, the authors of his misfortune.

The following is the

PRESENTMENT

The Grand Jurors for Our Lady the Queen, Present:

That J. W. Dunbar Moodie, Esqr., was the first Sheriff of this County, and has held that honorable position for the long term of twenty-three years. Now that he is about to retire from the discharge of the duties of that office, we have pleasure in being able to state that it is our belief that he does so with few enemies, and the warm sympathy of many friends. We also believe that he unwittingly transgressed the law in the transaction that has caused his retirement from the position he so long occupied, and being innocent of intentional wrong, we think this should not militate against his appointment to the discharge of the duties of any other office in the gift of the Crown, and we have reason to believe that his appointment to some other office would give general satisfaction to the inhabitants of the County.

For Self and Fellows,
Geo. Neilson,
Foreman.

In replying to the above. His Lordship, Mr. Justice Hagarty, expressed his great satisfaction that the Grand Jury of the County had not allowed the late sheriff to retire from the position he had occupied for so many years without this kind expression of their sympathy and regard.

He would add, on his own behalf, his strong conviction that he to whom this honorable tribute was paid, was emphatically an honest man – that the name of his friends was "Legion", and his enemies a very small fraction.

He would direct their Presentment to the Provincial Secretary where, no doubt, the recommendation it contained would meet with every consideration.

John Moodie was deeply moved by this and gratified that at least some of the people of Belleville believed that he had been an honest sheriff. But presentments, votes of thanks or testimonials do not provide an income.

Realizing the government was not trying very hard to find him another appointment, John and Susanna put their heads together to try to work out a solution to the problem of living.

As always, Susanna knew only one way to make money – by writing a book. As the literary expert in the family, she advised

John to make a collection of all his past writings, and add an autobiographical note as an introduction. John had to accept his wife's greater experience in the matter, though he was hesitant about the approach. It was, however, the only approach that Susanna knew. All her books had been collections of other shorter works which she had published earlier.

John's book was to be published "By Subscription" – that is, the costs of printing were covered by contributions from friends who agreed to pay for the book before it had been produced, an open form of charity which many in the government and in Belleville were happy to use to assuage their consciences.

Thus, in 1866, J. W. Dunbar Moodie's *Scenes and Adventures as a Soldier and Settler during Half a Century* appeared, a plaintive, tragic document with an introduction containing all the disappointment of the old man, his need to vindicate his honour and the honour of his family, and his protestations that he was still sensible and able to work if only someone would give him a job. His dry sense of humour which had brightened so many of Susanna's books in the past was completely gone from his autobiography as he listed all the aches and pains and hardships of his lifetime, and went into infinite detail on the court case which led to his disgrace and was obviously still preoccupying his mind.

This introduction was followed by two poems and seven essays and sketches, all of which had been in print before, some of them many times and many years before: his description of the campaign in Holland in 1814; his impressions of South Africa in the 1820s; "The Ould Dhragoon" from the *Literary Garland* of 1844 and *Roughing it in the Bush* of 1852; "The Advantages of Being Ugly" from the *Victoria Magazine* of 1847; and so on.

Since some of these sketches had been autobiographical when they were written, and little if any editing had been done, the contrast with the Introduction accentuated the plaintive story. The troubles of the old sheriff appear side by side with the adventures of the sixteen-year-old Lieutenant in Holland, drinking Dutch gin, making love to Dutch girls, and losing his place in the line of battle when the attack finally got under way.

Yet, for all its incongruousness, it is a delightful and attractive work, because Moodie had the ability to bring alive for the reader everything he had experienced; the forthright Moodie, incapable of dissimulation in his life or in his writing, comes through as a total person with strengths and weaknesses, hopes and disappointments, in a way that the more talented but more devious Susanna could never achieve.

Susanna was working on another novel, the first she had done in ten years, and as it turned out, *The World before Them*, published in 1868, was to be her last, for John Moodie died the following year. While she wrote a few more items for magazines and brought out more editions of *Roughing it in the Bush*, Moodie's death was the effective end of Susanna's career as an author.

She buried him in Belleville, and moved immediately to Toronto to live with one of her married daughters and preside in gracious widowhood over ladies' learned societies for another fifteen years. In 1885, she was taken back to Belleville to be buried beside John.

Samuel Strickland too had died, two years before John Moodie, in January 1867, six months too soon to see the coming of age of the country he had spent a lifetime pioneering. The elder Strickland sisters in England, Elizabeth and Agnes, had died within a year of each other, in 1874 and 1875, leaving the copyright of *The Lives of the Queens of England* to Catharine Parr Traill, more of a sentimental than a valuable inheritance.

Catharine was the last of her generation of Stricklands, but she was not alone. Two new generations of lady writers had risen: Susanna's daughter Agnes who collaborated with her Aunt Catharine in botanical work, and Agnes' daughter (Susanna's granddaughter), Mary Agnes Fitzgibbon who wrote *A Trip to Manitoba*, or *Roughing it on the Line*,[11] emulating Susanna's work, and *A Veteran of 1812*,[12] a biography of her other grandparent, Colonel Fitzgibbon.

Catharine Parr Traill lived on in Lakefield until 1899. She was honoured by everyone as a living symbol of the pioneer days of the nation. She had been entertained at Government House in Ottawa, she had been the guest of honour at the opening of the museum in Peterborough on the occasion of Queen Victoria's Diamond Jubilee; a new variety of plant which she had discovered was named after her; and her stories of the old days were always eagerly listened to by the children.

Then on 29 August 1899, after a Sunday with her family on the island in Stoney Lake, she took a weak spell; the doctor came the next morning and ordered the family to take her home; an American gentleman offered his steam yacht for the trip to Lakefield; and she died there on Tuesday, "with all her dear ones about her".

Perhaps the most appropriate epitaph for Mrs. Traill was written by her granddaughter, Katherine P. Traill, in a letter to Sir Sandford Fleming:[13]

> It is so comforting to think that she never lacked love. Her own sweet loving nature called it forth from all with whom she came in contact, and her old age was brightened by many thoughtful loving attentions from friends, far and near.
>
> We love to think that she was valued not so much for her talents as for her beautiful personality . . .

"The Katie" had had her share of troubles, hardships and adventures, but her happy spirit and gentle sense of humour had rarely deserted her. "Her beautiful personality" is still evident in every word she ever wrote and makes them all worth reading even though the subject matter now is mainly of historical or literary interest. Throughout her life, even when she was a small child, she gave the impression to those around her of being even-tempered, cheerful and ingenuous, always gentle with all things and all people, perpetually amazed and delighted by the beauties of the world around her, perpetually ignoring that which was not so beautiful. In fact, Catharine's personality was almost too good to be true, had she not maintained it so consistently in all her dealings with people and in all her writings. And Catharine's life and literature also reflected the hard core of toughness that all the Stricklands had, a toughness that just saves Catharine's "beautiful personality" from giving the appearance of childish naïveté. The sweetness of her soul would have made her writings excessively sweet, almost cute, had those same writings not also been laced with high and exacting standards of craftsmanship. For Catharine was above all a Strickland and as such was born to discipline, high standards of integrity, and hard work. Catharine's spirit then is best understood in the context in which she lived – in the family.

Four books, autobiographies of Canadian pioneers, shed much light on the way all our forefathers lived, and as such are grist for the historians' mill. But for those who feel that people are more important than environment, these same four books tell a different story, a story of four people with essentially the same background, who migrated to Canada together or within a short space of time, settled in the same place, were all related to each other, but for whom the new environment meant a different response, illuminating distinctiveness of personality. Despite similarities in class, origin, morality, and ancestry, and despite the similarity implicit in being disrupted and transplanted to a new but shared environment, each of these people had a totally different response, the difference being emphasized by the commonality of background and environment. The four major works, Catharine's *Backwoods of Canada*, Susanna's *Roughing it in the Bush*, Samuel's *Twenty-Seven Years in Canada West*, and John's *Scenes and Adventures as a Soldier and Settler*, are each quite, quite different, given that they were all talking about the same subject. Oddly, the differences become clearer and the enlightenment of the environment greater, when they are read in conjunction. The true value of our ancestors was in their joint efforts, each having full meaning only in the context of the others.

The story of the Moodies, Traills and Stricklands brings home the fact that generalizations about "the pioneer" have little meaning. Simply, they used the same tools, but in different ways. And it was these different ways that shaped the nation.

NOTES

CHAPTER ONE

Several studies describe the early life of the Strickland family. See especially:

Catharine Parr Traill, *Pearls and Pebbles*, William Briggs, Toronto, 1894. (Including biographical sketch by Mary Agnes Fitzgibbon.)

Una Pope-Hennessy, *Agnes Strickland, Biographer of the Queens of England*, Chatto and Windus, London, 1940.

Jane Margaret Strickland, *Life of Agnes Strickland*, William Blackwood and Sons, Edinburgh and London, 1887.

1. Harris, London, 1818.
2. Samuel Strickland, *Twenty-Seven Years in Canada West*, Richard Bentley, London, 1853.
3. See "Thomas Pringle" in *Dictionary of National Biography*, London, 1894; and in *Appleton's Cyclopaedia of Biography*, New York, 1856. See also Helen Cowan, *British Migration to British North America*, University of Toronto Press, Toronto, 1961: on p. 47 (footnote) is a letter describing Pringle's migration to South Africa in most unflattering terms.
4. See note to "The Apostate" by Susanna Moodie, in *Literary Garland*, Vol. IV (Old Series), April 1842.
5. J. W. D. Moodie, *Scenes and Adventures as a Soldier and Settler During Half a Century*, John Lovell, Montreal, 1866.
6. See "Dor d Moodie" in *Dictionary of National Biography*, London, 1894; and J. W. D. Moodie, *Scenes and Adventures*, op. cit.
7. J. W. D. Moodie, "Narratives of the Campaigns in Holland in 1814", in John Henry Cooke (ed.), *Memoirs of the Late War*, Henry Colburn and Richard Bentley, London, 1831. Also in an early edition of the *United Service Journal*.
8. Richard Bentley, 1835.
9. P. xvi, "Introduction to the Third Edition", Susanna Modie, *Roughing it in the Bush*, McClelland and Stewart, Toronto, 1923.
10. P. 39. ibid.

CHAPTER TWO

1. P. 28, C. P. Traill, *Backwoods of Canada*, McClelland and Stewart, Toronto, 1929.
2. See E. C. Guillet, *The Great Migration, The Atlantic Crossing by Sailing Ship Since 1770*, Thomas Nelson and Sons, Toronto, London, New York, 1937.

3. Some authorities quote 66,000, based on departures from U.K. Statistics were unreliable, but all agree that 1932 was a peak year.

4. P. 34, Traill, op. cit.

5. Pp. 11 and 12, Vol. I, Samuel Strickland, *Twenty-seven Years in Canada West*, Richard Bentley, London, 1853.

6. E. C. Guillet, *Cobourg*, 1798–1948, Goodfellow Printing Co., Ltd., Oshawa, 1948.

7. Lloyds of London show the *Horsley Hill* tonnage as 239; Susanna reported that *Anne*'s tonnage as 192 — not quite as big a difference as Susanna implied in her account of the accident. The accident was not reported to Lloyds; the account given here is a re-interpretation of Susanna's description, by Lt. Commander J. W. Buckingham, R.C.N. (Ret'd.).

8. P. 105, Traill, op. cit.

9. In G. H. Needler, *Otonabee Pioneers*, Burns and MacEachern, Toronto, 1953, the author suggests with good reason that this was the vessel built by Peter Robinson to transport the hundreds of Irish emigrants across Rice Lake in 1825. If so, the scow had seen better days, as well as better crews.

10. Thomas W. Poole, *A Sketch of the Early Settlement and Subsequent Progress of the Town of Peterborough*. The Peterborough Review, Peterborough, C. W., 1867, reprinted 1941.

11. P. ix. J. W. D. Moodie, *Scenes and Adventures as a Soldier and Settler*, John Lovell, Montreal, 1866.

12. Public Archives of Canada, R.G.5, C.1, Vol. 1, #138, 1 January 1837.

13. Ibid.

14. Gurnett's *Canadian Literary Magazine*, April 1833.

CHAPTER THREE

Much of the material in this chapter is taken from *Roughing it in the Bush*, chapters V through XII, and *Life in the Clearings*, chapters XI, XII and XIII, which describe in detail Susanna Moodie's impressions of Hamilton Township.

1. P. 101, Susanna Moodie, *Roughing it in the Bush*, McClelland and Stewart, Toronto, 1923.

2. Susanna had an annoying habit of showing only initials and dashes when identifying people. The reason was evidently to provide anonymity for her characters drawn from real life; however, they were easily identified by her contemporaries. It is not so clear why she would even go so far as to abbreviate her own and John's names in this fashion, since they hardly needed anonymity.

3. P. 188, ibid.

4. Pp. 188–189, ibid.

5. P. 203, ibid.

6. P. 219, ibid.

7. P. 73, E. C. Guillet (ed.), *Valley of the Trent*, The Champlain Society, Toronto, 1957. Guillet reprints a letter located in the British Museum of which the authorship is unknown. He adds the note, "Numerous references suggest that it was written by J. W. Dunbar Moodie". The references and the timing in fact leave only an academic doubt that anyone else could have written it. We have therefore used it, assuming Moodie as the author.

8. There are several sources on colonial money and land policies. We have used here:

    C. P. Traill, *Backwoods of Canada*, McClelland and Stewart, Toronto, 1929.

    C. P. Traill, *The Canadian Settler's Guide*, Fifth edition, Old Countryman's Office, Toronto, 1855.

    R. Craig McIvor, *Canadian Monetary, Banking and Fiscal Development*, Macmillan, Toronto, 1958.

    Chapter XIII, Easterbrook and Aitken, *Canadian Economic History*, Macmillan, Toronto, 1956.

9. Traill, *Backwoods of Canada*, op. cit.

10. Guillet, *Valley of the Trent*, op. cit.

11. Pp. 239–240, Moodie, *Roughing it in the Bush*, op. cit.

12. P. 33, Thomas Poole, *A Sketch of the Early Settlement and Subsequent Progress of the Town of Peterborough*, The Peterborough Review, Peterborough, 1867.

13. P. 22, T. Radcliff (ed.), *Authentic Letters From Upper Canada*, Pioneer Books, Macmillan, Toronto, 1953.

14. P. 25, ibid.

CHAPTER FOUR

Much of the material in this chapter is taken from Samuel Strickland's autobiography, *Twenty-seven Years in Canada West*, Richard Bentley, London, 1853. The description of the Traills' arrival is taken from this and from two descriptions by Catharine, in *Pearls and Pebbles* and in *Backwoods of Canada*.

1. P. 81, Vol. I, Strickland.

2. P. 147, Poole, *A Sketch of the . . . Town of Peterborough*, The Peterborough Review, 1867.

3. See Robina and Kathleen Lizars, *In the Days of the Canada Company* William Briggs, Toronto, 1896.

4. John Galt, *Autobiography*, Cochrane and McCrone, London, 1833, 2 vols.

5. W. H. Graham, *The Tiger of Canada West*, Clarke, Irwin and Co., Toronto and Vancouver, 1962.
6. P. 204, Vol. I, Strickland.
7. P. 266, ibid.
8. P. 241, ibid.
9. P. 150, Vol. II, ibid.
10. P. 198, ibid.
11. P. 154, Poole, op. cit.
12. P. 131, Traill, *Backwoods of Canada*.
13. P. 132, ibid.

CHAPTER FIVE

The majority of this chapter follows closely the description of the first days of the settlement given by Catharine Parr Traill in *Backwoods of Canada*, McClelland and Stewart, Toronto, 1929.

1. P. 138, Traill, *Backwoods of Canada*.
2. P. 139, ibid.
3. Traill, "Rambling By The River", Forest Gleanings No. VI, *Anglo-American Magazine*, Vol. II, No. 2, February 1853, Thomas Maclear, Toronto.
4. P. 146, *Backwoods of Canada*.
5. P. 153, ibid.
6. P. 156, ibid.
7. P. 65, Thomas Need, *Six Years In The Bush*, London, 1838.
8. P. 198, Traill, *Backwoods of Canada*.
9. P. 272, ibid.
10. P. 270, ibid.
11. P. xv, Traill, *Studies of Plant Life in Canada*, William Briggs, Toronto, 1906.
12. Pp. 37–39, F. M. Delafosse (ed.), *Centenary History, St. John's Church, Peterborough*, 1827–1927, the Review Press, Peterborough, 1927.
13. P. 258, S. Moodie, *Roughing it in the Bush*.
14. P. 216, Traill, *Backwoods of Canada*.
15. P. 260–1, Moodie, op. cit.
16. P. 261, ibid.
17. P. 261–2, ibid.
18. P. 263, ibid.

CHAPTER SIX

Most of this chapter is taken from Susanna Moodie's *Roughing it in the*

Bush, McClelland and Stewart, Toronto, 1923, read in conjunction with Samuel Strickland's *Twenty-seven Years in Canada West*, Richard Bentley, London, 1853, and Catharine Parr Traill's *Backwoods of Canada*, McClelland and Stewart, Toronto, 1929.

1. P. 311, S. Moodie, op. cit.
2. Pp. 315, 407, ibid.
3. Pp. 145–6, S. Moodie, op. cit.
4. P. 311, ibid.
5. Pp. 141 and 58, S. Strickland, op. cit.
6. P. 360, S. Moodie, op. cit.
7. P. 316, C. P. Traill, op. cit.
8. P. 322, ibid.
9. P. 323, ibid.
10. P. 324, ibid.
11. P. 349, S. Moodie, op. cit.
12. P. 350, ibid.
13. P. 361, ibid.
14. P. 370, ibid.
15. P. 386, ibid.
16. Public Archives of Canada, Record Group 5, C.1, Vol. 1, No. 178.
17. P. 396, S. Moodie, op. cit.
18. P. 417, ibid.

CHAPTER SEVEN

1. William Kilbourn, *The Firebrand, William Lyon Mackenzie and the Rebellion in Upper Canada*, Clark, Irwin and Co., Toronto, and Vancouver, 1956.
2. P. 234. D. G. Creighton, *Dominion of the North*, Houghton, Mifflin, Boston, 1944.
3. P. 322, Traill, *Backwoods of Canada*.
4. P. 91, Susanna Moodie, *Roughing it in the Bush*.
5. P. 206, Vol. II, Samuel Strickland, *Twenty-seven Years in Canada West*.
6. Mary Agnes Fitzgibbon, *A Veteran of 1812, The Life of James Fitzgibbon*, William Briggs, Toronto, 1894.
7. Susanna Moodie, Catharine Parr Traill and Samuel Strickland each discuss the events described in this chapter in slightly different ways with widely different timing. The timing followed herein is based on consideration of the distances involved, the chronicle of Toronto events given by Kilbourn (op. cit.) and the dates shown by Traill. C. P. Traill's dates seem more consistent with the other known events and were apparently recorded at the time in her journal, while Samuel

Strickland and Susanna Moodie were writing from recollection several years after.

8. P. 325, Traill, *Backwoods of Canada*.
9. See E. C. Guillet, *The Lives and Times of the Patriots*, The Ontario Publishing Company, Ltd., distributed by the University of Toronto Press, 1963.
10. P. 419, Moodie, *Roughing it in the Bush*.
11. P. 420, ibid.
12. P. 329, Traill, *Backwoods of Canada*.
13. P. 422, Moodie, *Roughing it in the Bush*.

CHAPTER EIGHT

1. Pp. 264–5, Vol. II, Strickland, *Twenty-seven Years in Canada West*.
2. For details of this dispute, see Public Archives of Canada, R.G. 5, C. 1, Vol. 18.
3. P. 426, S. Moodie, *Roughing it in the Bush*.
4. P. 213, Vol. II, Strickland, op. cit.
5. P. 436, S. Moodie, op. cit.
6. P. x, J. W. D. Moodie, *Scenes and Adventures as a Soldier and Settler*.
7. P. 487, S. Moodie, op. cit.
8. Pp. 487–8, ibid.
9. P. 496, ibid.

CHAPTER NINE

1. W. C. Mikel, *City of Belleville History*, Picton Gazette, Picton, 1943.
2. Public Archives of Canada, R.G. 5, C. 1, Vol. 7, #839, 11 August 1837.
3. Manahan should have accepted the post in Belleville, for his political career was to come to an abrupt end in 1844 when he faced the young John A. Macdonald on the hustings in Kingston. P. 99, Vol. I, Creighton, *John A. Macdonald*, Macmillan, Toronto, 1952.
4. Public Archives of Canada, R.G. 5, C. 1, Vol. 18, #2175, 11 June 1839.
5. Susanna Moodie, *Life In The Clearings*, Macmillan, Toronto, 1959. (First published 1853.)
6. For legislation, see 4 and 5 Victoria, ch. 91; and 3 William IV, ch. 9.
7. Public Archives of Canada, M.G. 24, I 73. Macauley to Moodie, 1 November 1839.
8. For the bonds themselves and related documents, see Public Archives of Canada, R.G. 5, B. 9, Vol. 71.
9. Public Archives of Canada, M.G. 24, I 73, Macauley to Moodie, 14 November 1839.

10. P. 437, Vol. 2, Charles A. Sanderson (ed.) *The Arthur Papers*, University of Toronto Press, Toronto, 1957.
11. Public Archives of Canada, R.G. 5, C. 1, Vol. 31, #1261, Moodie to Arthur, 28 May 1840.
12. Ibid., Vol. 44, #2484, Moodie to S. B. Harrison, 23 November 1840.
13. P. 29, S. Moodie, *Life in the Clearings*.
14. P. 35, ibid.
15. P. 42, ibid.
16. P. 9, ibid.

CHAPTER TEN

1. Public Archives of Canada, R.G. 5, C. 1, Vol. 75, #2175, 25 October 1841.
2. Ibid., Vol. 94, #4359, 15 September 1842.
3. Ibid., Vol. 87, #3394, 18 April 1842.
4. Ibid.
5. Ibid.
6. Ibid., R.G. 5, B. 9, Vol. 71, 12 November 1839; 13 May 1842; 4 June 1842.
7. Ibid., R.G. 5, C. 1, Vol. III, #6072, 21 September 1843.
8. P. 98, Vol. I, Creighton, *John A. Macdonald*, Macmillan, Toronto, 1952.
9. P. 101, G. E. Wilson, *The Life of Robert Baldwin*, Ryerson, Toronto, 1933.
10. Public Archives of Canada, R.G. 5, B. 25, Vol. 3, Election Papers, Canada West.
11. Ibid. Hopkirk to Murdock for Governor General, 25 March 1841.
12. Pp. 3–6, Vol. I, *Legislative Assembly of the Province of Canada, Journals*, 1841.
13. P. 278, ibid., 3 August 1841.
14. Pp. 578–9, ibid., 13 September 1841.
15. Public Archives of Canada, R.G. 5, C. 1, Vol. 96, #4515, 6 October 1842.
16. Ibid.
17. P. 3, Vol. 3, *Legislative Assembly Journals*, 28 September 1843.
18. P. 119, ibid., and Public Archives of Canada, R.G. 5, C. 1, Vol. 118, #6493, 4 October 1843.
19. Public Archives of Canada, R.G. 7, G. 12, Vols. 63 and 64, despatches from Bagot and Metcalfe, respectively, to Lord Stanley.
20. Ibid., Vol. 63, 11 November 1842.
21. Ibid., Vol. 64, 26 November 1843.
22. P. 42, Moodie, *Life in the Clearings*.
23. Public Archives of Canada, R.G. 5, C. 1, Vol. 162, #11489, 21 Augus 1845.

24. *Literary Garland*, New Series, Vol. 1, August 1843.
25. See introduction to *Mark Hurdlestone*, 1853; reprinted as Appendix to 1959 edition of *Life in the Clearings*.
26. P. 43, *Life in the Clearings*.

CHAPTER ELEVEN

1. P. 73, E. C. Guillet, *Coburg, 1798–1948*, Goodfellow Printing Company, Oshawa, 1948. See also John Craig, *By The Sound of Her Whistle*, Peter Martin Associates Ltd., Toronto, 1966.
2. P. 253, *The Canada Directory For 1857–58*, John Lovell, Montreal, 1857.
3. Pp. 333–335, Vol. II, Samuel Strickland, *Twenty-Seven Years in Canada West*.
4. Pp. 98–118, Charles Richard Weld, *A Vacation Tour in the United States and Canada*, Longman, Brown, Green and Longman, London, 1855.
5. For other visitors and sketches of Strickland's agricultural school, see E. C. Guillet, *Valley of the Trent*, pp. 412 and 416–423, op. cit.
6. "Forest Gleanings No. 3", *The Anglo-American Magazine*, November 1852.
7. "Forest Gleanings No. 2", ibid., October 1852.
8. C. P. Traill, *Backwoods of Canada*, Nattali and Bond, London (no date, probably 1835 or '36); also in *Canada and the Oregon*, M. A. Nattali, London, 1849; also *Backwoods of Canada*, in "Library of Entertaining Knowledge", Charles Knight, London, 1836. (Latest edition: McClelland and Stewart, Toronto, 1966.)
9. C. P. Traill, *The Female Emigrant's Guide*, Maclear and Co., Toronto, 1854; *The Canadian Settler's Guide*, Old Countryman Office, Toronto, 1855; *The Canadian Emigrant Housekeeper's Guide*, Lovell and Sons, Montreal, 1862, etc.
10. C. P. Traill, *Canadian Crusoes, A Tale of the Rice Lake Plains*, Arthur Hall, Virtue and Co., London, 1852. (Latest edition: McClelland and Stewart, Toronto, 1923.)
11. C. P. Traill, *Lady Mary and her Nurse*, or *A Peep into the Canadian Forest*, Arthur Hall, Virtue and Co., London, 1856, *Stories of the Canadian Forest*, or *Little Mary and Her Nurse*, C. S. Francis and Son, New York, 1857, etc.
    For a full bibliography, see J. L. McNeill, *Mrs. Traill in Canada*, M.A. thesis, Queen's University, Kingston, 1948.
12. "Botany", Vol. 2, *Encyclopedia Canadiana*. See also, John Macoun, *Autobiography—Canadian Explorer and Naturalist*, a Memorial Volume published by the Ottawa Field Naturalists' Club, Ottawa, 1922.

13. "Forest Gleanings, No. 12 — A Walk to Railway Point", *The Anglo-American Magazine*, Vol. III, No. 4, October, 1853. See also in *Pearls and Pebbles*, op. cit.

14. "Traill, Thomas Steward", *Dictionary of National Biography*, 1909 edition.

15. C. P. Traill, *Canadian Wildflowers*, John Lovell, Montreal, 1868, fourth edition by William Briggs, Toronto, 1895.

16. C. P. Traill, *Studies of Plant Life in Canada*, A. S. Woodburn, Ottawa, 1885, and William Briggs, Toronto, 1906.

17. C. P. Traill, *Pearls and Pebbles*; or *Notes of an Old Naturalist*, William Briggs, Toronto, 1894.

18. "Chamberlin, Agnes Dunbar (Moodie)", Vol. 2, *Encyclopedia Canadiana*.

19. L. Burpee, *Sandford Fleming — Empire Builder*, Oxford University Press, London, 1915.

20. Public Archives of Canada, "Fleming Papers", M.G. 29, A 8, Vol. 50, Traill to Fleming, 28 January 1882.

CHAPTER TWELVE

1. See Emma Jeffers Graham, "Three Years Among the Ojibways", *Transactions of the Women's Canadian Historical Society*, 1916–17. Reprinted in E. C. Guillet (ed.), *The Valley of the Trent*, Champlain Society, Toronto, 1957.

2. P. 412 (footnote), Guillet, ibid.

3. Public Archives of Canada, R.G. 5, C. 1, #1363, Attorney General for Upper Canada to A. R. Dougall, 24 October 1859.

4. Ibid., Dougall to Provincial Secretary, 3 November 1860.

5. Pp. 58–62, J. E. Hodgetts, *Pioneer Public Service*, University of Toronto Press, Toronto, 1955.

6. Public Archives of Canada, R.G. 5, C. 1, Vol. 677, #359, Wallbridge to Alleyn, 1 April 1861.

7. Ibid., #358 and #864, Dougall to Alleyn, 30 March 1861; 18 July 1861.

8. P. xi. Moodie, *Scenes and Adventures*.

9. Public Archives of Canada, R.G. 5, C. 1, #95 of 1863, Moodie to Provincial Secretary, 15 January 1863.

10. P. xvi, Moodie, *Scenes and Adventures*.

11. Mary Agnes Fitzgibbon, *A Trip to Manitoba*, or *Roughing it on the Line*, Rose-Belford Publishing Co., Toronto, 1880.

12. Mary Agnes Fitzgibbon, *A Veteran of 1812, The Life of James Fitzgibbon*, William Briggs, Toronto, 1894.

13. Public Archives of Canada, M.G. 29, A. 8, Vol. 50, Katharine P. Traill to Sir Sandford Fleming, 13 September 1899.

INDEX

PaperJacks

SAVE TAX IN CANADA AND RETIRE AT 45

Albert Volker

Have you been getting ulcers from the nine-to-five routine? Do you hate turning over thirty percent or more of your pay cheque to the government each year? Do you want to quit the rat race but think you can't afford to? Then read *Save Tax in Canada and Retire at 45.* It tells you how to get money back from the government, and how to use that money to build up a fortune large enough to retire on.

This book gives you not just one but ten early retirement plans to choose from. One of them is just right for you. $1.95

HOW YOU CAN MAKE A FORTUNE IN CANADA

Albert Volker

You can make a fortune... And you don't have to leave home to do it! Fortunes are now made more easily by Canadians than Americans! In *How You Can Make a Fortune in Canada,* Albert Volker tells you how to do it. He guides you through the maze of insurance gymnastics, and demonstrates the magic of compounding. He suggests ways to keep your dollars out of the government's grasp, and stashed away safely in mutual funds, mortgages, blue-chip stocks. He tells you how to live with inflation and still save money. Mr. Volker tells you how to plan your life style as well as your finances, so that you and your money can live happily ever after. $1.95

PaperJacks

DRUGS, SOCIETY AND PERSONAL CHOICE
Harold Kalant and Oriana Josseau Kalant

In recent years, there has been a great public demand for knowledge about drugs. However, the conflicting information which has inundated Canadians has only added to the confusion. *Drugs, Society and Personal Choice* provides data which will enable responsible citizens to form a perspective in order to intelligently evaluate the evidence and form their own balanced decisions about government policy. $1.95

THE FORGOTTEN CHILDREN
R. Margaret Cork

One of the greatest tragedies of our time is the disastrous effect of alcoholism on children of drinking parents. This research study examines in plain language the breakdown of family life and its consequences for the "forgotten children". *R. Margaret Cork* discusses treatment for the individual alcoholic and for the family as a group, and shows the future prospects for "forgotten children" when they reach maturity. $.95

THE PURSUIT OF INTOXICATION
Andrew I. Malcolm, M.D.

The effects of such controversial drugs as marijuana, LSD, mescaline and speed are discussed by Dr. Andrew Malcolm, a Toronto psychiatrist, who was formerly with the Ontario Addiction Research Foundation. He examines the use of psychoactive substances in many societies throughout history and considers their application under five broad categories: Religion, Medicine, Endurance, Extinction and Recreation. $1.25

TO UNDERSTAND JEWS
Stuart E. Rosenberg

Superbly enlightening, this book clarifies Jewish views on immortality, sex, sin, marriage, the "closeness" of the Jewish people, the Messiah and other significant points. It describes the evolution of Jewish culture and religion from biblical times to the present. Simple eloquence and lucidity rip through the veils of ignorance and misunderstanding to open the way towards one of man's noblest goals: the recognition of human brotherhood. $1.25

PaperJacks

THE SACRED MUSHROOM AND THE CROSS
John M. Allegro

After a thorough study of the etymology of the Sumerian and Middle Eastern Languages, *John Allegro* has formed a startling theory about the origin of Christianity. He has traced the existence of a mushroom cult which, because of its drug-taking practices, was cloaked in a respectable myth about an historical Jesus. This is fascinating and thought-provoking reading. $1.50

HOCKEY:
Tips on Playing Better Hockey
Tips on Understanding Hockey
Scott Meyers

Which plays keep defencemen awake at night? Give goalies nightmares? Are you confused by referees' signals? How does a coach use a "short-fused" player on the opposing team to his advantage? Do your drop passes embarrass your team? And you? Why do goalies slide back and forth across the goal mouth at the beginning of each period? How do the super-stars relax in the dressing room? These questions and hundreds more are answered by syndicated columnist *Scott Meyers* with clear explanations of the game and illustrated tips for minor league players anxious to improve their skill. $.95

FRED DALE'S GARDEN BOOK
H. Fred Dale

Canada's newest gardening guide with easy, step-by-step instructions that make it possible for home owners to grasp instantly the techniques that will result in beautiful lawns and gardens. Five sections cover lawns, the summer garden, woody plants, hardy bulbs, and a wide range of growing problems – growing in shade, preparing for vacation, pruning, making compost and dealing with plant pests." . . . a boon to all amateur gardeners." – *The Toronto Star.* $1.95

More titles in preparation

PaperJacks